D1631127

DEPLOYMENT

PSYCHOANALYTIC THERAPY SERIES

A SERIES OF BOOKS EDITED BY
SHELDON ROTH

Psychotherapy: The Art of Wooing Nature
  Sheldon Roth

Working with Resistance
  Martha Stark

Deployment: Hiding Behind Power Struggles as a Character Defense
  Rena Moses-Hrushovski

Psychoanalytic Reflections: Explorations through Dialogue
  Susan Rosbrow-Reich and Laurie Raymond

A Curious Calling: Unconscious Motivations for Practicing
Psychotherapy
  Michael B. Sussman

Losing and Fusing: Borderline Transitional Object and Self Relations
  Roger A. Lewin and Clarence Schulz

DEPLOYMENT: HIDING BEHIND POWER STRUGGLES AS A CHARACTER DEFENSE

RENA MOSES-HRUSHOVSKI, PH.D.

Jason Aronson Inc.
Northvale, New Jersey
London

This book was set in 11 point Bem by Lind Graphics of Upper Saddle River, New Jersey, and printed and bound by Haddon Craftsmen of Scranton, Pennsylvania.

Library of Congress Cataloging-in-Publication Data

Moses-Hrushovski, Rena.
    Deployment : hiding behind power struggles as a character defense / Rena Moses-Hrushovski.
        p.   cm.
    Includes bibliographical references and index.
    ISBN 1-56821-042-6
    1. Narcissistic injuries.   2. Defense mechanisms (Psychology)
3. Shame.   4. Humiliation.   5. Psychotherapy.   I. Title.
RC455.4.N3M67   1994
616.89—dc20   94-98

Manufactured in the United States of America. Jason Aronson Inc. offers books and cassettes. For information and catalog write to Jason Aronson Inc., 230 Livingston Street, Northvale, New Jersey 07647.

To the memory of my father and brother—

with love and gratitude

Contents

Contents

Foreword

This significant book is about patients who have been in prolonged analysis or psychoanalytically oriented therapy, and who
have felt that their essential problems had neither been changed
nor even touched. Such patients, who are essentially narcissistic,
have often been described in the literature as "difficult" patients,
and the argument is put forward in the chapters that follow that
they have a specific form of self-organization that has been
conceptualized as *deployment*. This can be regarded as a mode of
functioning designed to ward off unbearable tension arising from
feelings of envy, depression, shame, guilt, and humiliation.

Deployment seems to be a way of life. It does not in itself
arouse conflict, and as a consequence results in considerable
resistance to change in spite of its markedly self-defeating nature.
It fulfils a variety of defensive functions, but also leads to a
heightened sense of entitlement on the part of the patient, who
has become engaged in a lifelong battle for his "rights." This
battle is against felt injustice, abuse, and oppression, and for the
right to be emotionally understood, accepted, and held, especially when an error or failure has been experienced. The sense of
entitlement also leads to the demand to be legitimized, to be com-

pensated and repaired in a variety of ways. Above all, there is an expectation that others should take responsibility for their part in having caused the patient's suffering.

Throughout this fascinating book a different and distinct approach to the disorder is presented, both in terms of its understanding and its treatment. While from one point of view the use of deployment in the therapeutic situation can be viewed as resistance, it can also be regarded as a composite of specific personality characteristics that can be dealt with operationally. These can be taken up systematically by the therapist in active, detailed, empathic analytic work. By constantly examining the patient's motivations, and examining what is being avoided at any moment, it is possible to do therapeutic work on the forces driving the recurrent patterns of behavior subsumed under the heading of deployment.

The author sees shame as having a predominant role in the lives of patients of the sort described. Considerable clinical emphasis is placed on the feeling of shame—no less than on anxiety. What is examined is a way of life essentially determined by feelings of shame and potential humiliation, leading to modes of functioning based on concealing much of what is being subjectively experienced or enacted. The constant fear of shame restricts the inner space of deployed persons and prevents them from enjoying what they have. Much of their mental energy has to be invested in strategies aimed at avoiding shame, and this results in the taking up of rigid positions and attitudes to avoid humiliation and embarrassment. The therapist who is aware of the mechanisms involved can analyze the vicissitudes of shame as they interfere with the capacity to live emotionally in the present. The patients described are constantly anticipating unknown stresses and catastrophes and need to be constantly watchful for what they see as their predetermined future. They need to cleanse what they see as a stain of shame before they can begin their "real" present life.

The use of power is central to deployment. It is used to make others comply with the patient's needs, to make them apologetic and not to have to be apologetic oneself. The use of power shows itself through contempt, functioning both as a

defensive and an offensive weapon. It reflects a refusal to feel
guilty as part of the deployer's battle against injustice.

The understanding of the dynamics of deployment creates a
very different atmosphere in the treatment situation from that
which develops when emphasis is placed on sexual and aggressive drives as major motivating forces. The economics and dynamics of power, the ploys and measures developed in its service,
are useful sources for the reconstruction in therapy of narcissistic
traumata and unconscious conflicts from the past. The transformation of attitudes, roles, or positions back into the feeling states
and fantasies from which they were derived becomes a useful
analytic tool and can lead to a heightened inner sense of well-
being and competence in the patient.

Throughout the book the emphasis is focused on affects.
Chapters dealing with cognitive concepts relating to deployment
alternate with the presentation of clinical material. This permits
the reader to think about and to be empathic with what the
patient brings and the details of the therapeutic interaction. A
special and extremely useful chapter deals with the specific countertransference reactions often evoked in those working with
such patients. An analysis of the therapeutic approach that focuses on affects is given in the chapter "The Analysis Attitudes in
Treating Deployed Patients." Here there is an attempt to delineate the underlying assumptions that preconsciously guide the
listening, observing, and understanding of the analytic data.
Feelings are taken as basic units around which the patient's
experiences, thoughts, fantasies, and behavior are organized. The
multitude of discrete attitudes of the analyst, often enacted on the
nonverbal level, are stressed. These are regarded as contributing
substantially to the therapeutic ambience, to the working alliance
between therapist and patient, to the mental landscapes con-
structed and reconstructed in the treatment. They are central to
the special quality of the entire therapeutic process.

The consideration by the author of deployment leads to an
understanding that this specific configuration exists in everyone.
An awareness of where our power is unconsciously invested, our
alertness to the ways in which we counteract shame, guilt, and

humiliation, and the way we pay attention to the hindrance to our development because we refuse to abandon the settling of past accounts, help us to be open to the present and to its complexity. This allows us to deal with it flexibly and permits adaptive change, for example, to look at ways in which we console ourselves by correcting self-injuries through reparative operations of one sort or another. Awareness of the deployment configuration allows us to pay attention to authenticity, which can be viewed as a continuum in which attention can be given to different states of the self in various situations. Dichotomies such as false and true self are replaced by the awareness of where we are on the continuum between these two extremes. We can ask such questions as: When is the person emotionally present in the situation being considered? When does he disappear emotionally, play a role, assume a pose, and why? When is the person tense, when more relaxed, and why? When is he free and fluent, and when frozen and constricted? From the point of view described in this valuable book one can examine how the person conducts himself in the face of tensions, pressure, disappointments, and the whole range of affect-laden problems. Power conflicts can be seen as they work to interfere with listening to the various voices within oneself and in others. As a result one can give space to parts that are otherwise disavowed. From the beginning of treatment, the author's perspective is focused on obstacles to change.

The final chapter summarizes processes of psychic change that come about as a consequence of dealing therapeutically with the specific aspects and facets of deployment. The change from the unconscious motivations that operate in the service of self-survival to the achievement of the goals of self-development and growth after therapy is clearly conceptualized and described.

This book is a fascinating contribution to the theory of psychoanalytic technique, but it is more than theory. The clinical illustrations bring life to the approach described and analytic therapy will certainly be richer as a consequence of the work described in the chapters that follow.

Joseph Sandler

Acknowledgments

I began to write about deployment several years ago when my husband, Rafael, and I were working at the Austen Riggs Center, where he was the Erikson Scholar in Residence and I was a visiting scholar. It was a highly instructive and enjoyable experience for me to work in the center's stimulating and supportive community, and I want to thank Dan Schwartz, who was the Director, as well as my other friends there. It was at Riggs that I wrote what is now the first chapter of this book together with Rafael, who also accompanied me in many helpful ways while I wrote the rest of this book. I enjoyed his feel for the English language. The book would not have been written without his encouragement. My family and friends helped in many indirect ways. I feel warm thanks for their interest and support.

First of all, I wish to thank Sheldon Roth, who initiated the writing of this book. He accompanied me all the way through with his productive and helpful comments. It was also through his encouragement to be creative that my literary deployment gradually began to unfreeze.

The term *deployment* as well as other ideas conceived were

influenced through a productive ongoing dialogue relationship with Anne-Marie and Joe Sandler that I much treasured. Judy and Bob Wallerstein happened to pass by, took interest in the topic of this book and gave stimulating comments. I am grateful to them too.

My thanks to Norma Schneider for editing the book. I appreciated her thorough work and her stimulating remarks. For Sarah Leman's typing and her kind and flexible way of being available whenever I needed her, many thanks too. It was a pleasure to work with Judy Cohen, the production editor, whom I thank for her comments and help.

Last but not least, I wish to thank all those with whom I worked. The patients who are cited in this book all gave their permission to publish illustrations of what I mean by the phenomenon of deployment. Of course, the details of these patients' lives have been changed to protect their privacy.

Jerusalem, January 1994

Introduction: Remaining in Noah's Ark Long after the Flood Has Subsided

This book describes the clinical manifestations of deployment and the ways in which I have learned to work with deployed patients as part of the therapeutic process.

Many years ago I was struck by patients who presented themselves to me belligerently with an ongoing list of complaints of their suffering. Their grievances seemed to be primarily related to a strong need to find words for the unfair behavior they had been subjected to, and to their wish for acknowledgment or affirmation of their suffering and a correction of the injustices inflicted on them. They showed a stubbornness and a resolute determination to hold on to their misery. They seemed programmed to behave in set ways that were rigidly patterned, for instance, toward refusals—that is to feel guilty or to say whatever comes to their mind. They invested much power in disconnecting themselves as much as possible from emotional experiencing whenever they were facing discomfort. It is as if they built into their perceptual and motor apparatuses a structure that automatically triggers a mechanism for deploying a battery of functions against unbearable feelings, especially humiliation, guilt, and shame.

Their attitudes, the positions they held onto, and the actions they took were designed to increase their self-esteem and their sense of being in control. They had a need to convince themselves and others of the justice of their case and to counteract humiliation, oppression, and abuse. They tended to invest a great deal of power in avoiding the catastrophe of flooding, like the boy who put his finger in the Dutch dike. Power was also invested in repeating and reenacting childhood situations: this came instead of remembering such situations and working them through as we are wont to do in treatment. It was the emphasis on the different elements of power that led me to call this specific configuration *deployment*. Such persons deploy their psychic energies the way a general deploys his armies, with overt and covert power struggles and an insistent wielding of power at the core of the configuration.

An important part of understanding these ways of deployment is to see that such enactments are universal, utilized by us all. The use of deployment becomes pathological when excessive energy is invested in overly restricted ways of perceiving, feeling, and acting; the different quantity of such a reaction then becomes a different quality. The whole being of the person is suffused by these attitudes. While acting like adults in certain functions of their behavior, sometimes with clearly geniuslike aspects, they are often stuck in their more personal and therefore more affect-laden interactions, in their thinking and their feelings, at a level of childhood—usually from a specific crisis situation in which they seem to have become fixated.

Many of the patients I came to call deployed suffered from a disturbance of the self, a predominantly narcissistic pathology. They have been described in the literature as difficult patients. They are tense individuals who find it very hard to relax. They are constantly on guard lest any weakness of theirs be exposed and in order not to be unexpectedly shamed or humiliated.

Unbearable feelings, chief among them shame and humiliation, are constantly warded off.

Most excessively deployed persons lead a double life: they usually function well professionally; many are married and have children. But concurrently they seem to be living elsewhere; a part of themselves is immersed in their fantasy world. They seem still to be held over in a situation of unfinished business, a state that causes them a haunting restlessness. But the unfinished business is as it is perceived and wrestled with in the present, and not what painfully lingers from the past and continues to affect them.

When they differ with others about an interest of theirs, an opinion, or a wish, they find it hard, if not impossible, to negotiate an agreement. They either quit, remaining in the role of someone who has been hurt and offended, or they become extremely domineering, trying to bring about their victory over the other by any means. They react as if they are still in a stressful situation from the past in which powerful persons had dominated or abused them and nothing they could say or do would change the situation in any way. In the present they automatically use all their power to have as strong an impact as possible, or they become stuck in a position where they despair of fighting their battle, or of trying to resolve their problem; they just give up. It is as if they have chosen to remain in Noah's Ark when the flood is long over, without checking to see whether it is still continuing. They are determined not to let a childhood rival "get away with it," a rival who had unfairly triumphed over them in the fights of their childhood, a rival whom they easily manage to find in their present settings.

They all feel they have a mission never to forgive or forget, never to agree to a reconciliation before the others admit their share of the responsibility for having wronged them. They hold everything until the others feel "real regret."

I think it is appropriate here to delineate the following etiological factors that deployed patients have in common, since they shed light on the dynamics I have described. These factors at the same time have much relevance for their treatment. Over the last twenty years I have treated thirty-two such patients. They all suffered a significant failure of empathy on the part of the caregivers of their early years. At least one of the parents was a narcissistic personality. As a result the patients often felt exploited; they were expected to gratify the parent's need rather than be related to as separate autonomous persons.

Another major etiological factor was excessive shaming on the part of the parents. This caused the patients to become shame-prone. In addition, the enormous glory attributed to many of these deployed patients—who indeed did have many special talents—only increased their feelings of shame when they saw they could not live up to the high expectations of their parents. This expected glory increased their grandiosity and their dictatorial tendencies. This in turn led the parents to exert yet more pressure on them to be practically infallible.

All of these patients also suffered a traumatic event in their preoedipal or postoedipal phases. Sometimes this was a serious personal illness or that of a family member, sometimes a move from one city or country to another. Especially severe was a trauma due to a death in the family of a sibling, a parent, or a grandparent. Such deaths included losses resulting from the Holocaust. After the traumatic event, their parents typically became so absorbed in it that the patients experienced a loss of security in their everyday life and a strong sense of loneliness. This break in the continuity of their lives caused them either to become fixated on the state of stress (their own and that of the family) or led them to have the fantasy of regressing to the more harmonious state that had existed before the crisis/trauma. At least one parent—usually the mother—lived partially in a bunker, emotionally disconnected from the others. Since it was impossible to reach the mother emotionally, they felt that whatever they tried to do was not good enough. This then made them feel desperate, and they felt a strong sense of injustice; it was as if the mother alone had legitimation for her suffering and there was no space for their own feelings, their suffering, or their emotional needs. Another difficulty was related to their need to grow up too fast and too abruptly. As a result they had to make unusual efforts at a time when they did not feel up to it. This created in them a feeling of exhaustion that they carried with them into the present and that made them feel overloaded. As adults they often felt entitled to be compensated in the present. They were driven to demand the rights from the past in the present, now, as if this was still absolutely relevant and timely. Through their enactments many thus demanded legitimacy for their being depressed and desperate—as if to be granted the privileges they had not been given then. Others strove to be "reborn," to be brought up anew in a nonfailing environment and to be weaned, this time more gradually and more flexibly.

A different kind of trauma that many of them experienced as children consisted of power abuse and cumulative sadistic acts by the impulsive and abusive parent. This created an atmosphere of great fear. The other parent, most often the mother, tended to compound the abuse by ignoring its painful and detrimental effect on the child or by being a helpless victim herself, unable to change the situation. Thus the child not only felt helpless and lonely, constantly in danger of being abused and humiliated once more, but often, in addition, felt torn between the need to support the mother and the anger mixed with contempt and shame about her weakness and her misery.

We can never be certain what the objective reality of the parents of our patients was or what role fantasy and the child's perception played. I nevertheless felt from their reenactments in the treatment situation and from their narratives that there was some form of negligence or dereliction in these homes.

Sexual abuse suffered in the latency period or the pre-adolescent phase is often present in the history of deployed patients. The typical feelings and feeling states that keep harassing them in the present included their being shamefully different from others, a concern that they were guilty for not having objected to the abuse—feeling strongly that others would never have allowed such events to take place.

No matter how attractive and successful they were in the present, they all felt that their dignity had been stripped away, never to return until the stain of their shame could be erased. No matter what tough pose they presented to the world, they secretly worried that their shame, which they were trying so hard to conceal, is imprinted on their forehead as a mark of disgrace. They continue to live in a state of abuse that they powerfully try to disavow by leaving it encapsulated. Yet, encapsulated as it is, it does affect their feelings and their behavior into the present. No matter how much they try to prove their worth, they still feel worthless and fear being exposed for what they are so sure that they are. Much of their psychic energy is invested in switching on automatically a form of corrective programming aimed at fighting the abuse that, to them, is omnipresent.

What different types of deployment can be differentiated? Suffering from emotional unavailability and from traumatic events, these patients created different kinds of strategies to prevent their disintegration. One group developed a kind of "muscular skin" to immunize themselves against their tendency toward overwhelming vulnerability. This self-hardening was a way to escape their feeling of being constantly driven to be prepared to escape the trauma of being suddenly shamed, blamed, and hurt, as they had been in the past. Behind their self-hardening there was also the fear that if they would come in touch with their complexity and inner contradiction, they would be immobilized and paralyzed. Later on, when both they and circumstances changed, they found it difficult or impossible to relinquish this self-hardening because it had become their second nature, a fixed part of their self-image.

A second group resorted to roles that enabled them to regain a sense of equilibrium, thus providing a framework in which they felt contained. Assuming different kinds of roles helped them to overcome the frightening, chaotic, and overwhelming states caused by the traumas I have described. The roles thus adopted varied from that of a consoler or savior to the parent, thus often serving as a mother-to-one's-mother, to becoming the black sheep of the family. These roles provided security, self-esteem, control, or sweet revenge. However comfortable these roles were, they significantly restricted the ability of these individuals to react flexibly to current situations. They found it difficult to move into these roles and out of them according to what changing circumstances would dictate. Thus they were kept from being more themselves. It was not easy to give up designs that had helped to maintain their equilibrium for so long. It became even harder when the parents tried to achieve what they themselves could not attain by exerting pressures on the child, without either admitting it or even being conscious of it.

A third group showed a terroristic type of deployment. These individuals acted in a violent manner both in life and in treatment. Sometimes they acted this way because of accumulated aggression for which they could not find constructive channels of expression; at other times it seemed to derive from intensive disavowed feelings of shame and rejection, which were dealt with by aggressive acting out. For others, it seemed to result from a severe pathology of the superego. Persons with this type of deployment would immediately attack fiercely whenever they felt offended by what they saw as abuse, disrespect, or insult, while immediately disconnecting themselves emotionally. Their violence was usually verbal—loud continued abusive harassing, shouting, and cursing; at times this included a vigorous tendency to kill their "enemy" in fantasy. Their transference was often extremely intense, resembling a psychotic transference; whenever they experienced themselves as being forced into doing something against their will—free association or letting go of their control—they would cut themselves off emotionally or attack fiercely. At such a point, everything that had been slowly, painfully built up in the analytic work collapsed like a house of cards. At such moments, it was extremely difficult to rebuild the bridge between the patient and me. Often, they identified ideologically with terrorists. It was especially while working with these patients that I began to pay more attention to the political aspects interwoven in the clinical work, and to use deployment as signs to reach the personal Noah's Ark in which they had helplessly and stubbornly entrenched themselves. It was as if in their present reality the flood had not yet passed. They still were on their mission to fight abuse, which they saw everywhere.

Working with these kinds of deployment is extremely difficult and frustrating. However, when one succeeds in establishing an emotional connection with these patients and survives all the tests they require us to stand up to, it is a great relief to realize that what had been taken to be psychopathic or psychotic behavior was in fact a deploymental device in the lifelong battle that they were enacting.

An interesting question is whether my patients were affected similarly or differently from their siblings. From the accounts of my patients, it would appear that most of the siblings did suffer from some limiting effect on their functioning. However, it seemed that the specific form taken by the sibling's pathology differed from that of the deployed patient. Thus, when the patient had been the tough guy, the sibling or siblings would be more conforming or self-effacing, and the other way around: when the patient was the passive one, the one who was being forced, it was the sibling who was in the powerful position. This is one area that still needs more thorough study to examine what contributed to specific ways of developing. Clearly one can expect that the birth order, and the relation of each parent to the specific birth order—particularly in relation to the place he or she had in the family of origin—played a considerable role.

Affect is central in my work with deployed patients. One way of keeping the therapeutic work alive and meaningful, even with the constant attempt to reach the situations of the past, comes from living through the life of the hour together with the patient. I do this through identifying the network of the feelings and feeling states by attending to bodily expressions and other feeling signs. The patient or I reverberate to them, thus making possible reconnections to what has been split off. According to my experience with deployed patients, it is of paramount importance to constantly use the "zigzag approach"—from the present to the past and back to the present—time and again. This is so because of the particular structure of the self-organization of these patients. They experience their isolated feelings and feeling states from the past in the present; they partly remain in the corners of unbearably stressful events—lonely, frozen, frightened, and reluctant to open their eyes.

Determined as they may be not to be discovered in their hiding place, vigorously as they may kick when we come near their wounds, they still seem to wait for us not to be unduly frightened by them when they are in what amounts to a temper tantrum. They expect us to hold them firmly and caringly, thereby gradually enabling them to open their eyes, while at the same time they deploy all the forces at their disposal to dissociate themselves from the conflict and from the hurts they still feel.

When I speak of reaching the past, I do not only mean the reconstruction of memories of traumatic events. I do not only mean reaching the situation from which they have fled to Noah's Ark to find refuge and consolation. What I also, and particularly, mean is the importance of giving attention to the following multiple aspects: deciphering feelings and feeling states, the unfolding of unconscious fantasies, the reconstruction of the situation in which the person froze—in other words to identify all the various factors that cause the deployed person to remain stuck in the Ark and not venture out.

One such fixating factor is the tendency to sexualize disturbing affects; their addiction to deployment is similar to self-consoling masturbatory fantasies enacted compulsively in life and in the treatment situation. Thus I try not only to help them bring out repressed material, but no less to help them move away from their ruminative preoccupation with abusive and humiliating fantasies and experiences. One extremely important aspect in the process of treatment is to help the patients create dialogue relationships with their child parts. It is important that this

gradually take the place of becoming the child and acting in
childlike ways. Such an empathic acquaintance—not a mocking
one—with one's child parts is helped also through being encouraged to open oneself up to previously denied and concealed
shame events. My detailed interest in these events tends to
alleviate the patients' shame anxiety and allow them not to feel
humiliated when meeting their child's ways of thinking, their
child's perception of injustices and of entitlement. Thus they
become more willing to see, feel, and own what they secretly
experienced as hurtful and intolerable and can gradually give up
being totally oriented toward the other who should feel guilty
and ashamed.

It has been helpful to me to assess time and again during
treatment what was the conscious or unconscious intention; for
example, when was I facing a counteranalytic acting out, an orgy
of blaming and aggression—also projected into me with a feeling
that they are persecuted by it—and when was it more their need
to complain in order to correct the emotional experience of too
much restraint in the past on their part, I found it important to
distinguish when their motive was to figure out which insult or
pain kept them grieving—while endlessly blaming the other—
and when they were more expressing their resentment, retalia-
tion, and destructiveness, which then needed to be addressed and
analyzed.

I thought of the impasse in treatment and in life that these
patients present and represent in terms of remaining in Noah's
Ark long after the flood had ceased. A Jewish joke told to me by
the late Uriel Weinreich reflects this phenomenon. A group of
people were leisurely traveling on a ship when suddenly a terrible
storm broke out. Soon the ship began to sink. While all hurried to
the life boats, two of the passengers were busily engaged in
talking with each other and did not move. They were totally
absorbed in a talmudic debate. Another passenger passed by and
shouted at them that the ship was sinking and that they must
hurry to the lifeboats. They stopped the debate for a moment,
looked at him, totally surprised, and with contempt asked:

"How is this relevant to the debate?" and continued their argument.

My involvement with the phenomenon of deployment began a long time ago, even before I became a psychoanalyst. Perhaps it was when I became interested in the attitudes of the authoritarian person who avoided contact with his feelings and emotional needs as well as those of others. I left Germany as a child just before World War II broke out. Like so many others, I suffered the inconsolable loss of members of my extended family. Perhaps one corner of the bunker in which I am sitting is right there. I always carry with me the words written by the German commander of a concentration camp in France who had gassed inmates as part of large-scale medical experiments. On one of the walls was a photocopy of his confession: "I have had no emotional reactions to carrying out these acts. My upbringing prepared me for it."

Thus I was grasped and held by an interest in how we can raise children to avoid this kind of dissociation. Such a result is not necessarily based on personal pathology alone. Rather, it depends to quite an extent on the emotional climate and the existing cultural values—on failing environments and on circumstances. I chose Nevitt Sanford, one of the authors of *The Authoritarian Personality*, as a tutor for my dissertation because I wanted to study some of the roots behind the phenomenon of being blocked to the world of feelings. Following an evolving interest in education, I was busy for many years trying to change the authoritarian attitudes of teachers in a variety of settings. I worked with them on being too narrowly interested in the cognitive achievements of their students while ignoring their inner world of feelings and conflicts. Toward this end, I attempted to enable them to have more contact with their own subjective state so that a climate could be created in which the cognitive, the emotional, and the imaginative could take their places in a world of creative thinking and learning. I found it very satisfying to participate in a process of development with adults who had been rigid and insensitive to feelings and who then began to change gradually to become more flexible, open, and pluralistically minded educators. I was disappointed and I despaired when I met those who had no ear for the emotional qualities in themselves and in others, those whose power motives had interfered in learning, teaching, and attaining broader self-actualization.

Having realized in the process of trying to change attitudes in the adult how deeply the barriers to openness to feelings were buried and how hard it was to try to change them, I moved further into the clinical field until I became a psychoanalyst. Parallel to many of the patients who sought psychotherapy or psychoanalysis to find relief from their emotional problems, there was a group of patients who acted very differently. While those in the first group were quite pleased to talk about what they felt with somebody who listened, while they profited from deeper explorations, sharing their feelings and gaining insight, the second group came in order to become stronger and more successful in their personal and professional relationships. But their deeper and often unconscious motivation was to be recognized, consoled, and compensated for all the wrongs they had experienced in the past.

There was considerable difficulty in encountering in these patients a strong refusal to feel in any way responsible. Their reluctance to renounce their powerful control about what they allowed themselves to feel, say, or think in spontaneous ways presented another daunting difficulty. With this problem I consulted colleagues from Israel and abroad. I met Paula Heimann for many hours of consultation around this group of patients. She could sense what I meant in presenting the common features of this group, but I did not succeed in conveying these aspects to her accurately at the time. I was much more frustrated when I brought my experiences with this type of patient to a pre-Congress meeting of training analysts. Their immediate reactions were to see these patients as not sufficiently motivated for treatment; or alternatively they thought that I did not know how to deal successfully with the patients' aggression and resistance in the transference.

I tried to better understand the dynamics of those I previously could not sufficiently empathize with. I tried to reach those who had also been very difficult to reach in their previous treatments. This thus became a further incentive for me to become involved in studying the vicissitudes of power in the treatment process.

The last source of my interest in this phenomenon is related to the political arena. On the one hand I was preoccupied with how one could never forget or forgive the tragedy of the Holocaust and always keep in mind the question "Why did the heavens not darken?" when such atrocities were carried out by human beings. On the other hand I felt a strong need to avoid such an attitude, such a position, from becoming one more fanatic and inhuman narrow pathway that might well lead to another tragedy.

Thus, for instance, the inner hardness that certain groups develop in the service of their survival when engaged in an acute ongoing political conflict often is expressed in purposefully avoiding the developing of empathy—so that one does not need to soften and make peace with one's enemies. I see this as one form of social deployment.

As a founding member of Ofek, the Israeli Association for the Study of Group and Organizational Processes, I had yet another opportunity to learn more about the vicissitudes of power in individuals, in groups, in organizations, and in nations. The use of power and the mechanism of deployment seems here too to contribute to the violence around us that we all seem to be so helpless to stop.

Finally, it is the writing of this book that helped me expand my study of the phenomenon of deployment—a phenomenon that I believe needs to be continuously addressed and further understood—clinically, in education, and in the political arena.

1

DEPLOYMENT AS A FORM OF DEFENSIVE CHARACTER ORGANIZATION

This book describes specific obstacles to treatment that we have met in our analytic work with difficult patients. These obstacles are disturbances with a predominantly narcissistic pathology that we have seen in fifteen to twenty patients in the past ten years. Many of these patients had been in prolonged analysis with competent traditional psychoanalysts without any resulting change, or as they would say, "without being touched." While these patients differed from one another in many ways, they had a cluster of specific features in common that we believe constitutes a central psychic constellation. This is characterized by a rigid, set pattern of behavior and attitudes that we call *deployment*.

We see deployment as a form of self organization on the cognitive, emotional, conative, and behavioral levels. Etiologically, such self organization can be viewed as the patients' way of dealing with tensions that are unbearable. These tensions arise in response to threatening feelings such as envy, depression, or anxiety, but especially shame and guilt (Adler 1989, Baudry

---

This chapter was written with Rafael Moses.

3

1989). The deployment is similar to a battle that is experienced as a matter of life and death. It may be a struggle to prove the justice of their cause or their special worth; it may be a battle of wills. Deployment presents itself as a self-programming into a system of attitudes and actions designed to gain self-esteem, power, and control, and to avoid their opposites. We speak of self-programming because we are impressed with the imperative quality that such behavior shows. This behavior seems akin to a robot being programmed to perform in ways that are particularly set and rigidly patterned. Deployment helps defend against feelings that seem to threaten the wholeness of the self. Some deployed patients who feel so unjustly treated view themselves as objects rather than as agents (Shapiro 1965); they tend to deny their own will power and to disclaim responsibility for their actions, particularly for their role in interpersonal conflict in the present and even more so in the past.

WHY DEPLOYMENT?

In using the concept of deployment we place our emphasis on various elements of power. As an army deploys its forces opposite the enemy at the most crucial points, so do we see the patient deploying the forces of his self against the threats from outside and the conflicts within, and against the subjective experience of psychic pain and of other affects.

Reports on the interplay of patient and therapist often leave out the power ploys that are brought into action between the two, as well as the manifold attitudes that powerfully determine one's self-states and directions. Many clinicians have found that our material sounds familiar.

1. The patient uses a deployment of his psychic forces to defend against a multitude of subjective affective states that he fears will overwhelm him in his relations with his important others.

2. He repeatedly reenacts his early conflicts where power struggles of different kinds and rigid patterns of behavior helped to ward off painful affects, particularly shame and guilt.

As with many facets of psychopathology, there is a deployment aspect in each of us. We view deployment as universal enactments that are mobilized by normal, by psychotic, and by neurotic persons. A deployment becomes pathological when a person invests excessive energy in overly restricted ways of perceiving and acting. Patterns of action as well as positions assumed in the past often continue unchanged to the present without relevance to present capacities, needs, and circumstances. The person unknowingly becomes fixed in these positions because of continuing conflicts of motivation and power. A refusal to feel ashamed and guilty requires one to continually ignore certain unpleasant aspects of reality and at the same time to justify one's course of action.

In the treatment situation, deployments are usually not brought up verbally in the session as a problem or as a theme. Rather, they are enacted within the relationship. Therefore, the recognition of manifestations of deployment is a necessary first step. We believe that locating phenomena of deployment and acknowledging their existence lead to a variety of therapeutic implications, which we shall spell out subsequently (Gedo 1988, Levin 1971, McDougall 1986, Moses-Hrushovski 1986, Sandler and Sandler 1978, Schafer 1983).

Such deployment serves to strengthen people from within; thereby they ward off feelings of weakness, of conflict, of worry, and of being blamed and humiliated. They blame those whom they perceive as being responsible for their guilt. A pervasive sense of shame is also characteristic of these deployed patients; they seem to be shame prone. The shame that they need to ward off is felt about issues such as bodily defects and looking different from others, "forbidden" sexual experiences, their past, their parents or siblings, being in need of help, not fulfilling high expectations, and being displaced by a sibling, an event that often assumes the meaning of betrayal and defeat (Morrison 1986). A reluctance to feel shame and humiliation seems to be a predominant force behind this deployment of the forces of the self; as a result, some patients become impervious to shame, and some continue to project their shame onto others, who are then seen as either shameful or shaming. Still others feel shame for behavior or events that are not of their doing, yet at the same time they do *not* feel shame for acts that they did bring about.

The feeling of shame about themselves may manifest itself, among other ways, in a sense of shrinking, of becoming small and helpless—a state that needs to be carefully concealed from others, or in feelings of paralysis, of being unable to speak or to leave the scene, despite strong wishes to hide or run away. The purpose of the deployment is to avoid all these painful feelings by investing immense amounts of energy in holding on to a tough pose and not exposing any possible weakness. The shame that helps maintain deployment as an ongoing process also results in the predictable anger that follows the feeling of being shamed, the "humiliated fury" (Lewis 1987). It is characterized by a strong desire to turn the tables on the shamer. In treatment, it is the analyst or the psychotherapist who is the opponent; outside treatment, this role is usually assigned to a spouse, a parent, or a boss.

Blaming processes used by deployed patients are efforts to shift the direction of shame and guilt away from themselves in order to avoid painful experiences (see also Broucek 1982, and Nathanson 1988). Much denied jealousy and envy can be felt in many complaints. Patients also voice complaints whenever their self-esteem drops because of the success of others. It is striking that many of these patients rarely recall or admit specific emotional experiences of jealousy and envy from their past. Their powerful deployment helps them distance themselves from such events in order to avoid feeling humiliated and weakened. Shame is, to them, such an acutely painful and disorganizing feeling that they have no taste for owning and introspecting it. Shame that remains disavowed often plays a part in the negative therapeutic reactions that develop.

CHARACTERISTIC PHENOMENA OF DEPLOYMENT

Dissociation

In this type of dissociation, which is a central feature of deployment, mental processes coexist but do not become connected with each other. Dissociation occurs between feelings and their motives, between feelings and actions, and between self experiences of the past and present memories thereof. There is a strong tendency to erase whatever has been perceived as humiliating, to rid oneself of overwhelming pressures, and to attempt to thus restore the inner peace that has been disrupted—all by forcefully and instantly severing meaningful connections.

Narrowing the Focus of Experience

Deployment is based on a narrowing of the experiential focus. One aspect of the current experience seems to draw off an excessive amount of cathexis. These patients are so absorbed in their tensions and preoccupations that they are unable or unwilling to consider complexity. A direct exclusiveness of attention with an extreme narrowness of focus and much rigidity is maintained with great intensity under continuous pressure in order to ward off doubts and inner contradictions. Such a one-track-mindedness sometimes has the flavor of a mission—they zealously want to change the world (Lasch 1984). Much force is exerted to maintain exclusiveness in perception, thinking, understanding, and behaving in fixed ways; these patients are constantly, and often unconsciously, on guard to anticipate and to prepare against what they fear most.

The Use of Power

Power is invested in the repeating and enacting of childhood situations and of disavowed feelings or fantasies. To act and enact seems to be the major form of communication with others. These patients are in a constant state of combat-readiness for a perceived impending danger, the danger that their self will be crushed. Power is mobilized to demonstrate, often indirectly, that something is wrong in them so that it will be seen, felt, and, they hope, changed by the others. Power may also be used to show how powerless they are, in order to prove that they are not responsible for what they are being blamed for. The mobilization of all available power occurs when they perceive a seemingly overwhelming force from the other side. Thus, the deployment of many patients programs them to see oppression. They are thus bent on constantly settling accounts from their childhood with their powerful parent, and sometimes siblings, in direct or indirect ways. The use of power often takes place in response to their having been subjected to power abuse as children. This phenomenon is similar to that in persons who were subjected to physical or sexual abuse. As an example, L. perceived her analyst to be a rapist whenever he was perceived as trying to force an interpretation on her or when he seemed to force her to free-associate because of *his* uncontrolled personal needs. Although she clearly understood her need to thus perceive the analyst in the transference, she refused to free-associate or try to see the relevance of her enactments in transference or in life. Rather, this insight now became a new source of L.'s endless accusations that her parents had oppressed her, and the basis for a ferocious fight with the analyst, demanding that he take responsibility for his "rape" of her before she would agree to try to work on it in her analysis. Her behavior had a terrorizing quality; she strongly identified with Jewish terrorists in the Arab–Israeli conflict in that she felt they had no choice but to respond with violence to the Arab uprising. At other times, she would identify with Arab terrorists who used violence against the Jews. Ideology provided her with an opportunity to vicariously identify with toughness and thus disavow her weakness.

Another patient, M., sometimes showed behavior that had the flavor of a psychotic transference. His identification with the terrorists served him as a symbolic message for what he was fighting against. To fight against abuse and aggression became his *raison d'être*. He saw them everywhere, including in his own analysis. The more he came to be in touch with his fear that there was a psychotic element in him, a fear that he would become mentally ill as his sister had been, the more force he needed to deploy in order to ward off the imminent danger and to attack the analyst whom he perceived as the labeler of his madness. Thereby he tried to evade both his fear and the humiliation of becoming deranged. This form of deployment has various functions that become better understood in the course of the analytic process: to continue to see the disappointing parent as a "rapist"; to prepare himself constantly for the parent's suddenly taking him by surprise so that he would not be as shocked as he had been in the past. This was a reenactment of an unconscious memory of sexual abuse. This view of his parent as sadistic also helped him to deal with his own envy and jealousy in response to feeling left out.

N., a woman of 44, was constantly deployed to find a male villain whose faults she continually demonstrated in the analytic hour. Yet she resisted using this as a springboard to look for its conscious and unconscious relevance. She needed to bring her female therapist onto her side, thereby establishing an alliance with her against men. Thus she hoped to correct retroactively the disappointment in her mother—of which she consciously was unaware—who had betrayed her by shifting the focus of her attention to her newly arrived brother. The force she deployed was focused on declaring her perception or feeling to be an incontrovertible fact. When the analyst wished to explore her repetitive perception of a male villain and to see what experiences and fantasies of hers were involved, N. felt insulted, as if she were not being taken seriously or as if she were a child who fantasizes and cannot be trusted to see reality. Consequently, she fled instantly and forcefully into her deployment.

N.'s deployment was similar to that described in Heinrich von Kleist's novel, *Michael Kohlhaas* (or that of E. L. Doctorow's Coalhouse Walker in *Ragtime*) (see also Kohut 1977, pp. 129, 290), whose hero was programmed toward one goal: to see the remedy of the injustice done to him. Like Kohlhaas, she was totally wrapped up in a righteous fight for justice. She could neither forgive nor forget. In her fantasy, she kept experiencing her past and present humiliations and abuse. The warning against forgiving and forgetting became a social mission for her, not unlike that of the reactions of some survivors of the Holocaust, who feel that it is their duty to remember and do all they can so that the crimes against humanity will not be repeated.

A Sense of Entitlement

Entitlement (cf. Freud 1916, Moses and Moses 1990) serves as a defense against humiliation and shame and as an endeavor to retrieve what is felt to have been lost or denied. It is humiliating for such persons to feel needy. Consequently, there is a strong tendency to demand their rights, or, alternatively, a strong wish to be totally self-sufficient and not to need anybody. This wish is often dissociated from its opposite—the wish to be cared for like a baby. Many such patients insist on their right to feel discontented and to complain, and not to be weaned away too soon from their negative feelings. There is a tendency to blame others endlessly—and to blame the therapist in the treatment situation—for their belief that they had not been provided with sufficient space for their real feelings in the past. Their parents had been unable to accept or listen to the complaints they had voiced (cf. Winnicott 1965). Often the parents had needed to deny their own feelings of guilt, depression, anger, and shame (Lidz 1973). As a result, most patients believe that a wide range of their feelings had not been acknowledged. They felt reduced to being considered evil, greedy creatures. They felt particular pain that their parents could not or would not admit their responsibility for their own limitations.

These patients are continually oriented toward registering the imperfections and mistakes of others to counteract their denied guilt feelings and to thus point out where they had been failed by parents, analysts, and others. This trend of belittling others derives partially from envy, so as not to feel so inferior and to feel free from paralyzing inhibitions. Out of shame and the recurring fear of not being understood correctly they had developed, in the past, a strong tendency to conceal their thoughts and feelings. They refrain from expressing themselves directly, which is also a device to obtain power vis-à-vis the others. In therapy, some claim their right to be liberated from having to hold back their "unacceptable" feelings, thoughts, and perceptions. Previously, they had felt hypocritical for wearing a mask, which shamed them once more.

Now these patients want to remove the oppression they feel they had been subjected to and thus lessen their burden. They do not allow treatment situations to be used meaningfully to begin analytic work; they do not wish to see what functions were served by their needs; nor do they see detailed mental landscapes, or their own role in them, or tune in to their feeling states, perceptions, and fantasies. Instead, they demand that their needs be legitimized and gratified. They are on a mission to collect injustices (Bergler 1952, Cooper 1984). They are thus engaged in a battle with their important others. In many respects this behavior also has the character of a sadomasochistic perversion (Socarides 1988), with occasional fantasies of sexual orgies or of being a hermaphrodite. At times their conscious disgust takes the form of nausea. In response to pressures, they feel they have to throw up or otherwise empty themselves of interpretations felt to be indigestible and disgusting.

An interpretation by the therapist that attempts to point out the patients' need to test the therapist, to see if the therapist, like all the others, cannot stand their aggressiveness or contain it, is perceived as criticism. This then brings forth more self-justification for the continuation of their fight. They feel the therapist does not sufficiently appreciate both the difficulty of growing up in such a home and their need for a "parent" who makes *real* space for all their feelings. Such a parent would have enabled the child to grow up to be a feeling, thinking, autonomous person. Instead, they felt treated like a robot, told to eat and sent to sleep. When they are angry, this behavior of their parents enrages them even more. Especially at such a time, they need to be listened to. They were unable to be a model child then, just as they cannot be a model patient now. Also, behaving in a way that pleases the parent unconsciously signifies the sexual submission they so dread; however, to be "themselves," alive, different from the parent in feelings, thoughts, or temperament, is often experienced as an attack on the parent. They also express their need not only to know their own "monstrous" parts, but also to feel that these parts are accepted by their analyst now and retroactively by their parents then. Thus, they want to feel affirmed and confirmed as human beings, complex as they were and are, including their "evil" part.

O. is representative of patients who insist on their need and right to feel depressed and on their need to assert their right to want to die. It was important to O. that the analyst be able to accept hearing about his despair—a despair he could not face alone. O. thus developed a "programming" of this entitlement to affect his therapist and his significant others. Even when not in despair, he would demonstrate his depression to those around him. This all seemed to tie in with his proclaimed right to postpone his real life. Doing so brought him secondary gains. Also, this postponement would bring out the others' intolerance. Thus, he was entitled to express his anger: the others did indeed control his life, no matter how much they denied it. This programming also served to camouflage deeper fears of which he was ashamed, because to fear is to be weak. Cowardice, fear of weakness, and fear of envy were these degrading feelings.

Such attitudes can be better understood in the context of

the traumatic experiences of these patients. For example, the death of a member of the family caused a major change in life-style for a number of patients. They had lost their parent (or sibling) and suffered unfairly thereby. To add to their suffering, the surviving parent behaved as if only he or she had the right to be depressed and to mourn. Thus, following their first traumatic loss, they felt that they had also lost the once-familiar surviving parent, so much had the parent changed. The high conscious or unconscious expectations from the surviving parent often pressured the patient into substituting for the lost member of the family.

Unbearable tension pushed these patients into the role of consoler: to be a good boy or girl, to be the parent for the parent. They felt expected to be loving, appreciative, and grateful, to fulfill the parent's need for them to behave well at all times, no matter how or what they actually felt. In the therapy situation, they often do not use ongoing material for therapeutic work because they are stuck in the role of the "guilty" one, as they felt and were made to feel. To ward off such guilt, some would insist on their rights and their entitlement to special attention and care.

Another illustration of the sense of entitlement can be seen in some patients' attitude toward tidiness. They feel they have a right to demonstrate the mess they are in, and indeed to be a mess. They will not have everything swept under the rug again. They refuse to be seen differently from the way they really feel, nor do they agree to continue to conceal their failures, as they perceive their parents to have done and to still be doing out of shame. Often, this was a way they unconsciously protested against feeling rejected for having been wet and dirty as a toddler. They asserted their "legitimate" right to be held with all their dirt. Only that would make them feel whole! Thus, they now refuse to be made to feel repulsive, as had happened to them as children. The early rejection for their messiness and greediness had become a paradigm for later rejection, engendering shame and guilt throughout their life. If they are to grow with dignity and pride, this situation would need to be corrected for them.

For some of these patients, their messiness demonstrates

their priorities, conveying their view that there are more important issues than tidiness. P. kept returning in his associations to an
incident at age 8, when he had tripped and fallen, hurting his
knee. When his mother saw the blood, she exclaimed: "Watch
out for the rug!" It was the cleanliness that mattered to her, not
that he fell or how he felt! Rather than being soothed when they
were frightened or ashamed, these patients found themselves
rebuffed and further humiliated. Such events came to symbolize
what they felt to be the parent's attitude, to the exclusion of other
more positive aspects of the parent. They will not use their adult
critical faculties to assess the parent's behavior objectively. Other
developmental phases reverberate in these protests, such as when
they were greedy for food (oral) or when their sexual feelings
were considered "dirty" (oedipal). This always led to the same
resentment, and subsequent feelings of entitlement.

Reparative Correction

The wish for reparative correction is a central principle in deployed patients. Their psychic energy is invested in achieving
correction in fantasy or in real life. However, what they unconsciously want to see corrected is very different from what they
consciously wish for. Unconscious wishes for reparation (correction) can be the correcting of a physical or psychic defect felt
to exist; the correcting of unfair and humiliating treatment meted
out to them over the years, thereby correcting a gross imbalance
of power; or the restoring of a harmony that they felt to have
existed before traumatic or stressful events disrupted it. Their
fear of the power of the others—and of their own yearnings for
passivity and submission—sometimes leads them into a counter-
phobic stance with regard to power. To this purpose they sometimes deploy power to overcome their fears and wishes (see The
Use of Power, above).
    M., a 30-year-old married woman had one child, a girl, and
felt that it was essential that she have another one even though

her doctor was very much against it. To her, this second child consciously represented the need to become a fuller mother; also, she feared what intimacy with an only child might lead to. But with two children, if something were to happen to the first child, another one would be there, and if something were to happen to her, the children would have each other. Unconsciously this thinking resulted from her never having felt part of a real home, from a wish to avoid the feeling of envy she had disavowed and her wish to prove to herself that her feeling that something was basically wrong with her, that she had some ingrained defect, was unjustified. Once she became aware of her unconscious motives for correction, she no longer felt the need for another child, which would have endangered her physically. Furthermore, she was greatly relieved not to have to go through with this compulsively pressured planning.

The goal of correction can become a major motivating force for deployment. It is as if a corrective programming comes to be built into behavior and attitudes; psychic wounds that still seem to bleed can thus be forgotten or erased.

Entrenchment is one example of behavior that serves as corrective programming for the self. Armor is created that is designed to establish a new and stronger "identity." Such individuals make considerable efforts to establish themselves as persons with rights and entitlements. They try to disavow frailties, fragmentations, and vulnerabilities from both the present and the past. Behaviorally, they transmit the message that now they are strong, now they will make sure that others will accommodate them, defer to their authority, respect their needs, and adjust to their pace. (We do not use the term *reparation* in Melanie Klein's sense as an attempt to restore internal objects.) Others will now have to adapt to them, not the other way around. The satisfaction they find in erasing the helplessness of the past and in undoing past injuries and injustices seems more important than finding joy and pride in their present life.

Power and force are now exerted to strengthen their armor, to enable them to avoid painful, humiliating, and threatening feelings of betrayal, abandonment, and utter loneliness. They will not let others make fun of them any more; they refuse to be "suckers." These corrective programs are usually turned on in an automatic, unconscious manner, often in response to a loss of self-esteem or security. Within the therapy situation there is a strong tendency to hold onto positions of strength and to distance oneself as much as possible from positions of weakness, frailty, and humiliation. Yet at the same time helplessness is constantly and actively demonstrated.

These patients strikingly need to express their tensions— not in order to understand them but rather to test the therapist, to see if the therapist is strong enough to withstand their pressure. In addition, they insist that others must not inflict pressure on them in return. Often, situations are enacted in which the patients feel unable to trust the therapist's strength. Such patients constantly check out their therapists and watch for signs of tension and fragility. The deployed individual would rather blame the therapist for being too weak than accept the evidence that he, the patient, had unfinished business of his own and proceed to work on it. When the therapeutic work leads to important insights—such as the terror of having caused the miscarriage of a mother—these insights do not seriously change the patients' deep-rooted pattern of pointing out the therapist's frailties. Consequently, they are unable to develop constructive patterns of dealing with their inner tensions. One way they assuage such stresses is by being provocative to others, including the therapist. Then the other's anger serves to relieve tension. It is felt as punishment for both the other and for oneself. Thus, the balance of power is rearranged: the provocation serves as a built-in release so that tension subsides in response to what is unconsciously perceived of as an emptying of the bladder or of the bowel, or a release of sexual tension.

R. was surprised to realize how much of her energy went into avoiding situations where she feared being humiliated, and how this energy was thus not available to be invested in trying to fulfill her goals in life. Often she felt her parents expected her to be a showpiece for them, while her own life had not yet even begun. She felt that her experiential space—the space she needed to be in—did not exist for her. It was as if her remarkably efficient parents were holding a stopwatch over her; she had no time to pause to think or to choose her options. When she did not conform to the high standards and expectations—both conscious and unconscious—set for her, she was paralyzed even more by their shame and her own.

Sexual and physical abuse are often present in the history of such deployed patients, who seem to have "switched on" a form of programming: a fight against abuse that is omnipresent. "I shall not let others silence me anymore," said S., who had been sexually abused. Much psychic energy went into fulfilling the goal of not letting others abuse and intimidate her. She was so intent on not letting them bully her that she was unable to attend to her inner life; in fact, this intent served her to *not* attend to it. She could not find the space to fight for herself or to understand how it came about that she felt so abused. She did not wish to work on understanding what part traumatic events had played in her present condition, or on understanding the role of her perceptions or fantasies as a child. She would not find the space and time to identify the situation that she was now constantly reenacting both in her therapy and in her life. She held on to this position because she both feared and hoped that the "new" other would respond differently from the figures of her past. She had a strong need to maintain control in the analysis, thereby avoiding regression in the service of the ego and minimizing insights for herself on new levels. Often, her fear of appearing contemptible for losing control motivated her to hold on to her programming. Such programming would often develop a life of its own.

The need to hold on to such rigid programming serves two other purposes. First, it protects the perpetrator of the abuse, whom, after all, they also loved, even though they want to tell the world about the perpetrator's crimes and not let themselves be silenced. Second, it fights off change and maintains the status quo. Such persons constantly attack those important to them who make them feel guilty, directly or indirectly. They do not allow themselves to consider their own guilt, or to learn why they cannot face it, all the more because they preconsciously know that fantasy and exaggeration are involved in their perception. They hope to at last find the "corrective experience"—that of being legitimized and not blamed—that they need so desperately in order to avoid feeling evil, disdained, and guilty. Instead, they relive their major traumatic experiences in the treatment situation. When these resistances are interpreted, the fight against the externalized enemy—here the therapist—is often "ideologized": "There is no such term as guilt! Erase it from your terminology!" some say. In many patients, a sort of "political" and "religious" battle ensues in which Heinz Kohut's "tragic man" is used to counteract the zeal of the "guilt-making cult" and what they perceive as efforts to convert them. They want almost to physically "throw up" the induced guilt as they perceive it, through superego representatives, as described by Kernberg. ("Read Winnicott" said a very bright patient, who was not in our profession, to his analyst.) Thus, they hope to rid themselves of the evil that they choose to perceive as being primarily transmitted by such guilt-inducing attitudes. These ideological battles prevent the patients from more meaningfully reaching the traumatic roots at the basis of their deployment.

Corrective programming sometimes shows a strong urge to *ignore time*. For this purpose, the wheel of life would—in fantasy—be turned back to before that point in time where a severe injury to the self experience was felt to have occurred. Some of these individuals feel they need to have unlimited time in the session, or in the therapy, with which they would at last be able to collect themselves and function reasonably well. Some always hope for a magical solution (cf. Smith 1977). The elimination of time also becomes a magic way to erase the chronological differences, which have obvious implications of power, between parents and children, or between siblings. Another "time program" is to symbolically die and be reborn, to start from scratch so that they can imagine themselves now to be physically and emotionally different.

Dramatization is a further characteristic type of corrective program. Its aim is to dramatize what one feels, so that what went unnoticed for so long shall now at last be noticed and felt by others. These persons devote much effort to transforming their fantasies, feelings, and thoughts into a performance, which is to be real. In therapy, they enact a theatrical metaphor that requires the suspension of disbelief. The therapist, a witness to the performance, is asked to join in so that he or she can feel and understand what has been enacted (Boesky 1989). For example, before the therapist's vacation, K. would demonstratively wear two different shoes to transmit the message that something is wrong, to show how divided he feels and that nobody notices this. In one form of dramatization, the patients *become* the feeling that they found so humiliating, so that they could thus avoid experiencing it. Some patients relived their dramatization through the stories of Kafka's *The Metamorphosis* and *The Trial*. To enact the defect makes them feel less miserable and disgusting than to have it. They will thus demonstrate what was done to them. Dramatization may also include a deliberate exaggeration of feelings. Acting a role, or enacting feeling states and fantasies, represents an integral form of dramatization.

T. described how, during her childhood, she was preoccupied with the Holocaust. As an adult, she playacted being in the Holocaust in order to be prepared and not to be taken unawares if the Holocaust were suddenly again to break out. Her deployment consisted of entrenching herself into a fantasy world more real for her than her present-day life. This world, however, was not only a refuge. It was also a creation full of excitement and pleasure, a make-believe designed to console her and correct her disavowed painful experiences. The use of Holocaust images for sadomasochistic aims evoked much guilt and shame, most of it conscious. Later, this turned out to be connected to her sexual conflicts. While disconnecting themselves from aspects of the real world, such patients fervently hope that their therapists will find a way to enter into their split-off world and empathically acknowledge the child's hurts, perceptions, and experiences. These individuals feel compelled to repeatedly reenact childhood situations. Their enactments can often be understood by the therapist as ways of retrieving their feelings that had become frozen in deployments consequent to traumatic events of the past. Much psychic energy was sometimes invested in erasing primal scene fantasies and night situations from their childhood reenacted in the present. Such situations are at times interspersed with preoccupations with the Holocaust.

SUMMARY

In the center of deployment, we view overt or covert power struggles and an insistent wielding of power. These individuals exercise power to manipulate the therapist and others in a variety of "reparative directions." Let us summarize the main psychodynamic factors that relate to deployment:

1. The family constellation of many of these persons shows one powerful parent. The patients themselves often seem to display strong-willed behavior in spite of, or in light of, the unmistakable weakness of their selves.

2. In many of these patients we find passive libidinal longings for merging, which often relate to their fantasy of thus attaining the envied power in a magical way (Socarides 1988). The fear and shame of such longings together with the fear of and anger at the others' use of power, lead to a counterphobic employing of power in the struggle with others. The passive experience of being overcome by painful affects often leads to an active use of sexualization (cf. Goldberg 1975).

3. The passive longings seem to connect with a strong, aggressive, sadistic drive often in response to the experience of

deep, intense shame frequently found in these individuals. Both oral and anal sadistic rage are central (Kris 1976, Modell 1965), and can also be understood as humiliation-rage (Lewis 1987). Whether these sadistic tendencies derive originally from the aggressive drive or from shame and other frustrations (including Kohut's failure of empathy) is not always easy to determine.

4. These individuals try to overcome conscious feelings of shame through an instant, almost automatic way of shaming the other or distancing themselves from the other. Almost before feeling the humiliation designed to be evaded they need to act: they humiliate the other. When they perceive the other as castrating, they set about, preemptively, to castrate him. In many patients, excessive shaming on the part of their parents is a major etiological factor (Levin 1971). Another reason that shame is strong in these patients is that they were often treated as having been children with special talents; yet frequently they felt paralyzed by the fear of disappointing their parents. The enormous glory attributed to them by some parents tended to increase their grandiosity and their dictatorial tendencies. This, in turn, brought about further narcissistic injury to their parents, who then exerted yet more pressure on them.

5. Just as these persons tend to ward off shame and humiliation by turning it against the other, so do they tend actively to turn guilt against the other by blaming him or by exerting pressure to have him at least share responsibility. The parents will often deny their own guilt, and will consciously or unconsciously induce guilt in their children.

6. Deployed individuals show a specific superego–ego ideal configuration that is secondary to their basic conflict of fighting their important others and sometimes the world. As long as their injustice has not been acknowledged, they hold back from committing themselves. They also refrain from accepting responsibility, and sometimes from espousing certain basic values (cf. Rangell 1981).

7. A dichotomy exists in these deployed persons between an often highly developed intellectual part and a stunted emo-

tional part, between their child and their adult parts. Both these parts have contradictory values attached to them, one side of which may be unconscious: the intellectual and grown-up parts are both esteemed and denigrated; the emotional and child parts are concurrently yearned for and disdained.

8. This existing dichotomy or dissociation also makes it very difficult for these patients to accept ambiguity, uncertainty, confusion, and conflict. When threatened with such situations or states, they try to rid themselves of the fear of disintegration, and of unpleasure generally, by externalizing the conflict and by passing their inner pressures on to the other. To act and enact is another way not to feel divided intrapsychically. Power is thereby invested in enactments and in fighting against the other in oppositional ways, rather than in finding ways of dealing constructively with inner tensions and thereby strengthening themselves.

9. Many of these persons had early relationships with one parent, who treated them as an extension of himself or herself. This relationship was a narcissistic one in which they were not related to as independent autonomous people with unique feelings, needs, and perceptions of their own. Perhaps related to this is that one of the central motivations in the deployment is to make the therapist and others experience the child's world and particularly the suffering the child had undergone in it. It is the wish and hope—consciously and unconsciously—of these individuals to be understood at last in all their complexity, and to be responded to in a sensitive and differentiated way. Thus they hope to come to deal with their inner tensions more flexibly and openly. Previously, some had needed to see their love objects as infallible, to hide their own and the other's fallibility. Often these persons are torn between their total love for their loved ones, with a need to remove any blemish or stain on them, and the need to focus exclusively on the blemish by projecting it onto others. Thus they unconsciously split their objects into good and bad ones. At the same time they use all the force at their disposal to dissociate their emotional experiencing and especially their hurt from the conflict.

REFERENCES

Adler, G. (1989). Uses and limitations of Kohut's self psychology in the treatment of borderline patients. *Journal of the American Psychoanalytic Association* 37:761–783.

Baudry, F. (1989). Character, character type and character organization. *Journal of the American Psychoanalytic Association* 37:655–687.

Bergler, E. (1952). *The Superego*. New York: Grune & Stratton.

Boesky, D. (1989). *Enactment, acting out, and considerations of reality*. Panel at the meeting of the American Psychoanalytic Association, San Francisco.

Broucek, F. J. (1982). Shame and its relationship to early narcissistic development. *International Journal of Psycho-Analysis* 63:369–378.

Cooper, A. M. (1984). The unusually painful analysis: a group of narcissistic characters. In *Psychoanalysis: The Vital Issues*, ed. J. E. Gedo and G. H. Pollock. New York: International Universities Press.

Freud, S. (1916). Some personality types met with in psychoanalytic work. *Standard Edition* 14:309–331.

Gedo, J. E. (1988). *The Mind in Disorder*. Hillsdale, NJ: Analytic Press.

Goldberg, A. (1975). A fresh look at perverse behavior. *International Journal of Psycho-Analysis* 56:335–342.

Kohut, H. (1977). *The Restoration of the Self*. New York: International Universities Press.

Kris, A. O. (1976). On wanting too much: the "exceptions" revisited. *International Journal of Psycho-Analysis* 57:85–89.

Lasch, C. (1984). *The Minimal Self—Psychic Survival in Troubled Times*. New York: Norton.

Levin, S. (1971). The psychoanalysis of shame. *International Journal of Psycho-Analysis* 52:355–362.

Lewis, H. B. (1987). *The Role of Shame in Symptom Formation*. Hillsdale, NJ: Lawrence Erlbaum.

Lidz, T. (1973). *The Family and Human Adaptation*. New York: International Universities Press.

McDougall, J. (1986). *Theatres of the Mind*. London: Free Association Books.

——— (1989). *Theatres of the Body*. London: Free Association Books.

Modell, A. H. (1965). On having the right to a life: an aspect of the super-ego development. *International Journal of Psycho-Analysis* 46:323–331.

Morrison, A. P. (1986). *Essential Papers on Narcissism*. New York: New York University Press.

Moses, R., and Moses-Hrushovski, R. (1990). Reflections on the sense of entitlement. *Psychoanalytic Study of the Child* 45:483–498.

Moses-Hrushovski, R. (1986). Interpretation of the past and the present. *European Psycho-Analytic Federation*, 25:15–25.

Nathanson, D. L. (1988). *The Many Faces of Shame*. New York: Guilford Press.

Rangell, L. (1981). From insight to change. *Journal of the American Psychoanalytic Association* 29:119–125.

Sandler, J. J., and Sandler, A. M. (1978). On the development of object relationships and affects. *International Journal of Psycho-Analysis* 59:285–296.

Schafer, R. (1983). *The Analytic Attitude*. London: Hogarth Press.

Shapiro, D. (1965). *Neurotic Styles*. New York: Basic Books.

Smith, S. (1977). The golden fantasy. *International Journal of Psycho-Analysis* 58:311–324.

Socarides, C. W. (1988). *The Preoedipal Origin and Psychoanalytic Therapy of Sexual Perversions*. New York: International Universities Press.

Winnicott, D. W. (1965). *Ego Distortion in Terms of True and False Self. The Maturational Process and the Facilitating Environment*, pp. 140–152. London: Hogarth.

2

DEPLOYMENT IN A SEVERELY REGRESSED DELINQUENT CHILD

BACKGROUND

Sylvia, a young Israeli girl, had been living in an alien world from early in her life. She was brought to a children's home here in Israel at age three weeks and stayed there for four years. Reports from the home indicate that she had had an especially retarded physical, mental, and emotional development. She was very small and thin. Her language comprehension and ability to express herself were limited. She lived in isolation, refusing to play with other children. She displayed rhythmic body movements, especially before falling asleep. She was afraid of heights and would scream in terror when she was lifted up. She was afraid of people; she was afraid of buses. She pocketed whatever happened to come into her hands.

Sylvia's mother, Mrs. Z., was said to have suffered from

This chapter is based on a Ph.D. dissertation written for the Wright Institute, under the supervision of Drs. Nevitt Sanford and Mervin Freedman, and on "Steps in Self-Development" (Moses-Hrushovski and Moses 1986).

epilepsy. Two operations reportedly stopped her seizures, but she still suffered from paralysis in her leg. A social worker described her as a rigid character given to emotional outbursts and strange behavior.

Mrs. Z. had never shown any interest in Sylvia. On the rare occasions that she visited Sylvia in the home, she seemed more interested in herself than in her daughter, on one occasion even sucking a lollipop that she had brought for Sylvia.

Sylvia's father worked as an unskilled laborer in the open market of the town. Occasionally, he would get drunk. The social worker described him as aggressive and cruel. He, too, showed no interest in Sylvia. Although Sylvia showed more interest in her surroundings and began to talk fluently toward the end of her stay in the home, she was still far below her age level in both mental and physical achievement.

When Sylvia was 4 years old, she was placed with a foster family. After her first year there, she was referred to the child guidance clinic through the social worker. The clinic's report on Sylvia included the following:

> Aggressiveness, especially at home. Beats and scratches other children. Destroys objects such as a radio. Tears notebooks and rips apart feather cushions.
>
> Strange behavior and isolation. Plays mostly by herself, talking to herself and to imaginary characters and things. Makes dramatic movements with her hands. Seems not to be aware of her surroundings.
>
> Restlessness. In movement most of the time. Motor disturbances. Nervous movements. Scratches her arms until her skin is scratched and bleeding. Often hums to herself.
>
> Fears, especially at night. Screams, fears dogs, a man standing close by, a bear, a child who wants to cut her with scissors.
>
> Sleep disturbances. Often wakes during the night and sits on her bed swinging her body. Then has difficulty falling asleep again.
>
> Confusion in thinking.

Bedwetting and soiling. Rarely during the day, but usually every other night.

Truancy. Sometimes staying with workers in the fields until five o'clock.

Collects things. Searches in garbage cans, putting what she finds in a bag, hiding it in her bed, and saying that it belongs to her.

Stealing. From the closets of neighbors and from stores.

Psychiatric Observation: The impression one gets is that of a girl who is functioning on a somewhat lower level than her age. Sylvia finds it difficult to understand her relationship with the people around her. There is a disturbance in the process of thinking and in her concept of time. She is perplexed by the reality which she starts to discover. There are early signs that she is turning her considerable aggression inward and may thus be inclined to depression.

Recommendation: Leave Sylvia in the kindergarten for another year and look for another foster family where she might have more guidance and feel more acceptance; child psychotherapy and guidance to foster parents and teacher; reexamination after a year.

Diagnosis: Primary Personality Disorder.

Some months after this report Sylvia's state had deteriorated. She had been left in the same foster home because a better one had not been found. According to the foster mother, Sylvia almost stopped wetting and soiling, but began to steal even more at the foster home, at the kindergarten, and from people in the neighborhood. She ate a great deal, but remained as thin as ever. While she did not participate in the kindergarten, she did show some responsibility in carrying out certain tasks. But she talked to herself, could not concentrate, masturbated excessively, and had no contact with the teacher or the other children. It was at this point, when Sylvia was 7 years old, that she was referred to me for treatment in the child guidance clinic. I saw her for three years, from 7 to 10 years of age, usually twice a week. Then I stopped working for a year, after which I resumed treatment with her for three more years. At the age of 14, Sylvia moved to a room she rented from a cleaning woman at the children's home with whom she had a good relationship. Treatment was terminated when she was 15 years old.

Based on the detailed notes of Sylvia's treatment, and consequent contacts with her, as well as information gleaned from many people with whom Sylvia was in contact throughout her life, her development can be divided into several phases.

PHASE I—AGE 7-9: DEVELOPMENTAL LAGS AND THE FACILITATING ENVIRONMENT

> The individual's maturational processes (including all that is inherited) require a facilitative environment, especially in the very early stages. Failure of the facilitative environment results in development faults in the individual's personality, in the establishment of the individual's self, and the result is called schizophrenia. [Winnicott 1965, p. 35]

Sylvia was extremely flighty, restless, and hyperactive in treatment. When she was given clay, she would cut it into pieces; she would mix paints together messily and endlessly. Her capacity for postponing impulse gratification was minimal.

Much of Sylvia's behavior could not be understood. She was in motion most of the time, passing quickly from one activity to another. Her mood would change just as quickly. Once, while digging in the sandbox and filling it with water, she suddenly turned around and shouted in the direction of an empty candy box: "You are a bad man!" When her therapy hour was due to end, she would keep on washing her hands even though I told her that time was up. Sylvia reacted to being rushed by saying that her foster sister "is not the teacher here." She once came close to me and whispered into my ear: "Maybe some day I'll give you a kiss."

I would follow her, carrying the things she overloaded herself with, opening doors for her, and otherwise being useful. I allowed myself to be used as a "need satisfying object." As D. W. Winnicott (1965) says,

> What matters to the patient is not the accuracy of the interpretation so much as the willingness of the analyst to help, the analyst's capacity to identify with the patient and so to believe in what is needed and to meet the need as soon as the need is indicated verbally or in non-verbal or pre-verbal language. [p. 122]

Or, as Anna Freud (1965) has put it,

> Where the libido defect is due to severe early deprivation in object relations, interpretation of the transferred repetition has no therapeutic results. Instead, the child may answer to the intimacy of the analyst–patient relationship. . . . [On] the basis of this new and different emotional experience, the child may move forward to a more appropriate level of libido development. [p. 231]

One of Sylvia's frequent activities was sawing. When the saw once fell on the floor, she burst into terrifying laughter, which seemed to be one of her defenses against fear.

As our therapeutic meetings continued, there was a long period in which Sylvia constantly sought oral gratification, either directly for herself or through the feeding of dolls. In some fantasy games she acted like a baby drinking from a bottle; in others she would play with the dolls, casting them in different roles, such as the baby she wished to be, the baby she wished to own, her previously envied foster brother, and the like.

"Look, see what I've found," Sylvia announced excitedly, in one of the sessions. "A whole package of cigarettes!" Then, a staff member came in asking about his cigarettes, which had disappeared. Sylvia gave them back after some hesitation. It turned out that she had been smoking them quite expertly. One of the first steps we took to correct this situation was a kind of agreement that if she could not resist the urge to take cigarettes she should bring to our room the ones she took, and we would decide together what to do with them. The room became her cigarette bank, where she saved her "treasure."

To help her sublimate these needs I introduced chocolate cigarettes and provided a nursing bottle. Now Sylvia would begin the session by feeding a doll with the nursing bottle. Then she would switch the bottle to her own mouth. While drinking she would have an inward gaze, as though she were repeating an experience from long ago. Yet it also seemed as though she was now living new experiences that she had missed. She would pour tea into the nursing bottle, first drinking with the nipple, later without it, smiling all the while. We would both have some cookies that I brought. I had to hold these for her, so she could take bites from them from my hand—when she was not too busy painting or doing something else. It seemed that direct narcissistic gratification gradually built up early self feelings in this way.

Sylvia's contact with me at this time was mainly through ordering me around. She was happy to be the ruler and master. "Rena obeys me," she told her foster mother, as she enjoyed the feeling of being an omnipotent queen. It was hard for her to leave at the end of the hour. Often I had to take her firmly by the hand and accompany her part of the way home while talking to her about her anger toward me at what she saw as being suddenly forced to leave. "I didn't come here just to go home again," she would sometimes shout furiously. Then, before I could anticipate what she would do, she would begin pulling toys from the shelves and throwing them on the floor. Although I found these fits of narcissistic rage hard to tolerate, they were useful clues to her vulnerability, to what it was that insulted her. She was able gradually to change direction from acting immediately to feeling and putting her feelings into words.

Sometimes she left cursing. She would take toys with her, although I tried to set limits and insist on the rule that toys belonged to the clinic. But she wanted to ignore the rules since she felt offended by being restricted. Similarly, she would enter other rooms in the clinic while staff members were out, often taking some "treat." Doors had to be locked on the days Sylvia came to the clinic. I tried to put only minimal limits on her behavior, letting her smear, smash, yell, or tear as long as it was not dangerous or damaging, even though I was not always sure whether this acting out helped facilitate the expression of her inner world's feelings and fantasies or whether it enhanced her guilt. During this phase, whenever I had to put a firm stop to some of her behavior while interpreting what I saw as its meaning or intent, Sylvia would become extremely upset.

Her demands and her greed kept growing: she wanted more time, more toys, more food, more sweets. As Melanie Klein (1962) says, it seemed that the small girl "needs these 'good' things to protect her against the bad ones, and to establish a kind of equilibrium inside her" (p. 284).

Sylvia thus transmitted the omnipotent feeling of a baby whose mother was always available to her. She needed me to build up her self-esteem—especially by mirroring her manifold needs—and to contain her immense aggression. I just managed not to break down under its impact.

Sylvia's fear of being alone with me was remarkable. During the first months of therapy, she allayed this fear by opening the door to the playroom, by being constantly on the go, by doing, running, and busying herself. Her difficulty in remembering my name was also striking. But she often came to the clinic on days when she had no appointment to ask if her appointment was that day. When she was told it was three days later, she would say to her foster mother, "Right, that I am going for treatment after I go to sleep and get up, go to sleep and get up, go to sleep and get up?" This was not only an indication of her concrete thinking; it also seemed that the only thing that existed for her at this time was to wait for the treatment. A few months later, she came to one session stating cheerfully that she already knew that my name was Rena.

Sylvia liked fire in all forms. She set fires in our room and in the yard, and did not allow me to extinguish them. She hardly let me take the necessary precautions when I found her playing near the fire as dangerous. She herself would douse them with water. It felt at times as if she were playing with death—as a counter-phobic device—and enjoyed it when she survived.

One day Sylvia came to a session wearing a new red coat. It was the first time that she had a new item of clothing. I told her how pretty she looked and asked who had given her the coat. Disconcerted, she said it was her foster mother. She added that she had two mothers, showing bewilderment about her family relationships. I tried to grapple with her identity problems, which were not surprising given the very real external confusion about who she was, by explaining that her mother who had given birth to her was not able to take care of her because she had been ill. Therefore, she had been at a babies' home for four years. There, her foster mother had chosen her as a foster daughter. I was not at all sure whether Sylvia understood what I was telling her. I was not even sure that she had been listening, because during my explanation Sylvia continued playing without further comment or question.

In talking to her social worker and her teacher, I discovered that Sylvia was actually known by three different family names: her mother's maiden name, her foster family's name, and her biological father's name (the mother and father had divorced and were remarried to each other). Since the father's surname appeared on Sylvia's birth certificate, we decided that it should be used consistently by all concerned.

To help foster Sylvia's sense of identity, we celebrated her eighth birthday—the first birthday celebration in her life! To my surprise, Sylvia did not enjoy it. It was hard to determine if she was not pleased with the presents she had received, or if her tension and anxiety were more related to greed, shame, or feelings of guilt.

At the end of this phase in her treatment, I could see one of her states of fragmentation: After becoming intensely angry at an intrusion by an outsider, she left the session to go into the courtyard to collect dry leaves and stones. Suddenly, pointing at a rock, she asked fearfully if "she" would pursue her. In response to my asking who "she" was, Sylvia said, "The grandmother there." I referred to her inner fear that somebody wanted to punish her, which was externalized. Frightened, she took my hand and pulled me back into the treatment room. Attempts on my part to ask about her fears and fantasies were met by orders that I perform a variety of services for her.

The next phase was characterized by a period of repeated questions, all of which seemed to be pregnant with meaning: "How are people run over?" "Is a foot put in a plaster cast after an accident?" "Does God see everything and punish those who are bad?" "Do people who slander others go to hell?" Part of Sylvia's interest in these subjects related to a home for handicapped children that was near our clinic. I explained to Sylvia that children often feared that their anger could cause terrible results, and that she might very well have such fears of being punished after showing her angry feelings toward me—even more so because her foster mother had fallen and broken a leg after an argument with Sylvia. Guilt feelings from different sources seemed to be involved and intermixed. For example, her mother was paralyzed after Sylvia's birth. Later in the same session Sylvia asked in a faltering voice, "How did it happen that my mother became sick?" This was the first time that she had directly approached the subject of her biological mother's illness. When Sylvia brought up the theme of what might befall her, I told her that she was worried about being punished because she thought that it was her fault her mother was paralyzed, but that in fact she had nothing to do with it. Briefly, I explained that her mother had been born with epilepsy, that her fits were so severe that it was necessary to operate on her after Sylvia was born, and that the operation stopped the epileptic fits but brought on a partial paralysis in her legs. "She is limping, she is sick, poor woman. That's why I was thrown out," Sylvia exclaimed. "She is wonderful. When she gets well, she'll come and visit me."

Although I repeatedly told Sylvia that she had no part in her mother's illness, with much conviction and authority, she could not accept it. She seemed to be communicating with inner voices that shut out my words. She asked seemingly nonsensical questions: "Why do birds peck? Why do lizards bite?" She would pour water on the table, brush it with soap, and drop the foam on the floor. She would do this repeatedly. This activity was apparently one of Sylvia's ways of not being overburdened by her unconscious guilt feelings.

Once, after Sylvia had suggested that I be her baby, she fed both of us instant pudding. As we ate, she told me what sounded like a fairy tale: "My mother was a mother who gave no food to her children." And in a dissociated manner, as if she had violated an inner norm, requiring her to say only good things of her mother, she added, "If I meet her in the street, I'll give her a kiss." Sylvia became more aggressive for several weeks, expressing her psychic pain in games of shooting. During this period, she told me a dream: She saw a limping grandmother coming toward her. She was extremely frightened. Then she remembered that she had to go to Rena. It was a sad dream. She cried until she woke up. These thoughts seemed to be the antecedents of her loyalty conflicts, which she did not bring up until much later: she wondered if coming to see me made her foster mother, her mother, and her grandmother envious and revengeful. These ideas were partly accurate perceptions and partly her projections.

At about this time, Sylvia's foster parents announced that they could no longer take care of her. Another family was found. Fears of abandonment came up in the transference situation, especially because I was now pregnant. Sylvia's feelings of rage and envy, as well as her wishing to be my baby, were expressed and worked on.

It was very difficult working with Sylvia during my pregnancy, because she was determined to settle accounts with the baby I was carrying inside me. At times she would shoot rubber arrows at the doll that she had me hold in front of my bulging belly. Occasionally, she would point the gun in the opposite direction, shooting at herself. At other times, she played games in which she tried to identify with me, becoming a mother—as if that might save her from the bitter experience of being "left" again. "Wherever I go you go," she commanded. "Let's run, so we have plenty of time."

Gradually there was some improvement both in her behavior and in her studies. She seemed to be building up tension-regulating structures. She began for the first time to learn to read.

This phase of treatment ended when I took a year off from work after my daughter was born. Sylvia was 10 years old. During this year, Sylvia was seen by an experienced social worker on a regular basis. This was also the year of Israel's Six-Day War.

PHASE II—AGE 10–12: FEELINGS OF ABANDONMENT AND THE GROWTH OF TRUST IN THE FEEDING ENVIRONMENT

When I returned to work, Sylvia had been transferred to a boarding school. For a variety of reasons, the new foster family had not been willing to keep Sylvia. One reason was related to her sexual seduction by a man in their neighborhood, to which Sylvia responded, however guiltily. This was the last straw as far as the family was concerned, especially since they had wanted to foster a baby rather than an aggressive and difficult girl like Sylvia. Thus, Sylvia was put into Aviv, an educational institution for sexually abused children. In addition to working with her in the therapy sessions, I visited Sylvia at Aviv about twice a week.

After having talked in therapy about some of her experiences during the war—the uproar of tanks moving nearby, the earth seeming to quake and shake, echoing her fright—Sylvia quickly entered her fantasy games, as if for her the Six-Day War was nothing compared with the inner conflicts, urges, and battles she gradually revealed. After some testing of my reliability,

Sylvia became more trustful again and started to tell me the secrets of her sexual episodes with a certain man during the last year. She feared the man and was disgusted by him, but from the way she talked, rubbing herself in a masturbatory manner and getting excited, it was obvious that, at the age of 11, it had given her sexual satisfaction as well.

At this time, a regressive period in her therapy began. Longings for warmth, which had never been fulfilled, awakening sexual drives, and reactions to the change of workers and homes all seemed to have united in Sylvia's craving to be nurtured by me. There had previously been scattered trends of regression, such as talking like a baby, crawling, or drinking from the nursing bottle (especially when being "weaned" from her cigarette smoking). But the regression during this stage was experienced more thoroughly, as if it provided Sylvia with real experiences that she had missed in early infancy.

"Mash the bananas," said Sylvia, when she saw me coming in with the package of fruit she asked for. Turning her sorrowful gaze on me she pleaded, "Take me on your lap. Feed me please!" I hesitated for a moment: should I take this big girl on my lap like a baby, gratifying her infantile impulses? Or would it be wiser to interpret her wishes instead? Then I decided to comply, realizing that it would probably be better to satisfy such strong urges of hers in therapy than let her act them out in injurious ways outside. "When the small girl's early anxiety situations set in, her ego makes use of her need for nourishment in the widest sense to assist her in overcoming anxiety. The more she is afraid that her body is poisoned and exposed to attack the more she craves for the 'good' milk, good penis and children" (Klein 1958, p. 284).

Disappointments and rejections, real as well as fantasized, increased Sylvia's need for love and warmth. In therapy she wanted to be fed, always wanting more food than she was first given. It was as if she were thereby saying that she wanted to be compensated for her real deficits. She was also enacting her deep-seated feeling that what she was receiving was not good enough for her.

"Mash the bananas, cut the pear into small pieces, chop up

the plums, peel the apples; the peel looks like green excrement . . . " I needed to overcome feelings of discomfort in putting Sylvia on my knees. What helped me to overcome them was my remembering a moving scene described by Renee, Sechehaye's (1951) schizophrenic patient:

> I knew what I was yearning for so desperately and I was able to bring out, "because the apples you buy are food for grown-ups and I want real apples, Mama's apples, like those" and I pointed to Mama's breasts. She got up at once, went to the magnificent apple, cut a piece and gave it to me, saying, "Now, Mama is going to feed the little Renee. It is time to drink the good milk from Mama's apples." She put the piece in my mouth, and with eyes closed, my head against her breast I ate, or rather drank, my milk. A nameless felicity flowed into my heart. It was as though, suddenly by magic, all my agony, the tempest which had shaken me a moment ago, had given place to a blissful calm. I thought of nothing, I discerned nothing, I revelled in my joy. I was fully content, with a passive contentment, the contentment of a tiny baby, quite unconscious for it did not even know what caused it. [p. 70]

Once, when Sylvia opened her mouth wide, eagerly pointing at the foods she wanted to be fed with, I completely forgot her chronological age and treated her according to her needs. Often she would say, "It's so tasty. Always bring me this kind of food." She would become furious if an item was missing from the list of fruits she had asked me to bring for the next session. She would throw down the plate like an angry baby whose food had become distasteful. After a while, she would look at me seeking forgiveness. When I pointed out that her anger was that of a baby whose wishes were not fulfilled, she was relieved that I understood, that I was not rejecting her angrily.

Three years later, when Sylvia was 14, she referred to this experience, saying:

> At first I was scared of you, of your face. I didn't know what you wanted from me, and feared that you would harm me.

Then, one day, you took me on your lap and fed me the banana
and applesauce. Then I understood—do you remember?—that
you wouldn't harm me, that you meant well. I wasn't afraid
any more and stopped running away. I shall always remember
it, even when I am 18 years old!

"Yes, I remember," I told her. "I remember very well." "I
was so glad you came to visit me," she said. "Where did I visit
you?" I asked, astonished. "In the baby home," she said, as
though my nurturing her when she was 11 years old had been her
first nursing experience, or as if I had, in her mind, become the
nurse who took care of her as a baby. This seemed to correspond
to Augusta Alpert's (1959) description of what is needed in such
cases:

> To induce regression to the point of traumatic fixation and
> gratify needs with verbal accompaniments, which would serve
> to relate the gratification to earlier intolerable deprivation and
> give it more meaning and cathexis. The regressive need-
> satisfying phase promotes a corrective relationship and the
> revitalization of drive energies, which are then mobilized for a
> higher level of integration and functioning. [p. 182]

This way of feeding Sylvia went on for several weeks. I felt
that the experience would be a fuller one if the feeding could be
accompanied by words that expressed feelings that she had had as
an infant, and which she was now reexperiencing.

While she leaned passively against me, eyes closed, enjoying
being fed, I spoke from what I felt in my countertransference
reactions to her, as well as from what I knew from the records
about her early childhood in the baby home: how a nurse she had
liked had given her a milk bottle; how she had wanted to be held
close, to be fed and cuddled more; how she had always felt that
she had never gotten enough. "Tell me more," she said, hanging
on my words as if she wanted to swallow and digest them as well
as my food, since the former seemed to echo experiences and

wishes from those early years. In this act there was also an element of what Ekstein (1965) describes as symbolic action:

> Symbolic action . . . derives its primary effectiveness not from content but from the soothing tone of the therapist's voice, the repetitive rhythm, the continuity of words, the predictability of voice, words and rhythm. These can readily be understood as interpretation via a symbolic act modeled after the mother's lullaby to the very young child. [p. 155] [Thus,] primitive transference is evoked or maintained, which can serve as the foundation for new and more mature identifications. . . . It is by the continual repetition of such experiences that the secondary process can emerge and extend its dominance. [p. 121]

PHASE III—AGE 12-14: VENTILATION AND REENACTMENT OF PAINFUL EXPERIENCES AND FANTASIES FROM THE PAST IN THE PARTICIPANT-OBSERVING ENVIRONMENT

Sylvia took a corner of the playroom and built a "house of her own" there, insisting that nobody invade it. Having begun to implement her plan, she was full of ideas as to how to furnish her tiny house. At the entrance, she placed a toy piano, which served as a doorbell. There was a light in the corner, which Sylvia turned on to announce the beginning of each session. Soon the house became a stage for Sylvia. She began to produce scenes that seemed to reflect memories, fantasies, and choked-off feelings that had never been expressed before.

Sylvia took the role of her maternal grandmother, who had everything she needed: a small, cozy place, food, light, sweets. It seemed as if Sylvia was enacting a state of self-sufficiency that was a kind of reaction to her previous dependency needs, as well as an identification with the grandmother with whom she had had some contact while visiting her biological mother. One of the scenes she initiated was wanting me to join in blaming the "lazy mother," who took care neither of her husband nor the baby—"the poor little thing." The drunken "father," interested only in his alcoholic beverages, would toss the baby into the air, neglecting both the child and the grandmother. "The baby was dumped in the street," Sylvia said. Then, speaking to the baby she said, "Poor little thing, I don't have any money to give you. Soon I'll be dead—and then, what will you do?" Turning back to her "husband"—whose role I was assigned—Sylvia boomed out: "You really are crazy! Go and look after your wife, so she won't have to go begging from other people in the streets." Lowering her voice, she spoke to the baby again, softly, "Poor baby, now you have spilled hot milk on yourself! Do you have a heart in your chest there?" Turning again to the father, she asked: "Can you feel the pain?"

Sylvia's loud voice during this scene was heard all over the clinic. Staff members came to listen outside the door, to see whether something was wrong. Sylvia did not hear or notice anything. She was totally absorbed in her play. For the next several months, when she continued to playact, Sylvia's passionate expressiveness, richer than ever before in vocabulary and idiom, seemed to flow straight from her unconscious. I felt like I was sitting on a revolving stage, absorbing the unique atmosphere and enacting the various roles she asked me to play. Each of these sessions felt like a volcanic eruption. Out of Sylvia's burning fire from within—from which she had protected herself by displacing her aggressiveness onto others—there grew a common experience for both of us: we could look at it together and work on it.

Sylvia was turning what had been passively experienced into active mastery. From being a victim she became a stage producer and actor. In these episodes, Sylvia convinced me that despite repeated bouts of deprivation and loss, her drives had been smothered but not quenched and could be revitalized. "From the sense of inner goodness emanates autonomy and pride; from the sense of badness, doubt and shame" (Erikson 1965, p. 77).

For her twelfth birthday party, I and a colleague from the clinic went to Aviv. The two of us were the only guests, although all Sylvia's relatives had been invited. Sylvia was physically well developed and looked beautiful, no matter how shabby her dress. She danced gracefully and sang in harmony with the others. When she invited me into her room, I was surprised to see how neatly everything was arranged in her drawers. She took out a small bundle of letters and postcards fastened with a clip, all that she had received in her lifetime, and treated with loving care. They were her private treasure. "Once I waited eagerly to get sweets," she said. "Now I live to get letters!"

This was before the Passover holiday, when all the girls would be leaving Aviv for a week to be with their families. Sylvia asked me to try and persuade her mother to have her for the evening of the seder. We went to visit Mrs. Z., who told us that she planned to go to a relative in Tel Aviv and did not need anybody to "tail" her. When we were left alone, Sylvia took hold of my hand and cried quietly, talking about how mean her mother was. When I responded that her mother was sick, she said that she is sick in her heart and sick in her mind. Helped to express her feelings, Sylvia gradually recovered from the blow.

Sylvia started to ask more questions about her parents' divorce, the father's drinking and gambling, and about the mother's illness. Was it cancer? When I encouraged her to detail her thoughts and questions, it turned out that cancer and crab—synonymous in Hebrew—were confused in her mind. She was confusing cancer with epilepsy and imagining the crab as something crawling within her body. I gave her a brief explanation of the two illnesses (epilepsy and cancer). For the next session, she asked me to bring milk, pudding, and other foodstuffs. As if sensing my reluctance to return to another period of cooking and eating, she said, "Only this once!" She came to the hour in a good mood, and explained, "It's not that I want to go back to my childhood. I want to cook so I can show that I can be a mother! Not like that mother of mine! There are good mothers who cook and make cakes, who have patience with their children. That's the kind of mother I want to become. I'll be a patient mother, but I won't spoil my children so that they will boss me around." According to Erikson (1965), "Adults, when traumatized, tend to solve their tension by talking it out. They are compelled, repeatedly, to describe the painful event; it seems to make them feel better. To 'play it out' is the most natural self-healing measure childhood affords" (p. 215). In this phase Sylvia's mode of mastery changed; there was more play, more imagination, and more thought.

PHASE IV—AGE 14-15: LIBERATION AND SEPARATION AIDED BY THE CLARIFYING AND INTEGRATING ENVIRONMENT

Sylvia brought a storybook to the session about a paralyzed boy, a story that became very central for her. It was about a 10-year-old boy, Dori, who had undergone more operations than he had years, but to no avail. When yet another operation was suggested, he refused. His parents tried to persuade him, but in vain. Then an uncle whom he loved came to visit with a large parcel in his hand. It was a new, big, shining scooter on thick and strong rubber wheels. How senseless could he be, everyone thought. The boy asked everyone but his uncle to leave his room. "Who is it for?" he asked. "For you," answered the uncle. "Do you believe that this time the operation will help?" mumbled Dori. "I don't know. Perhaps. I would try. It's worth it," replied the uncle. Both of them became silent. Finally the boy repeated quietly: "It's worth a try." You can guess the happy ending.

After Sylvia read the entire story to me, we set out to explore the meanings the various parts had for her. There was a constant shifting from certain passages to her own associations, thoughts, experiences—and back again to the story—as if it were a manifest dream that we were working through.

First she picked up on the phrases that reflected Dori's

vulnerability when being pitied. She hated it when girls said she was poor, and she gave an example of such an incident.

The story also triggered her longings for a caring uncle, and old yearnings that her mother would be operated on once more and would finally become well.

She recalled a scene from a movie she had seen about a girl who was so alarmed by a giant snake that approached the carriage she was in that she forgot all about her paralysis, got up and ran away, thereby regaining her health. "This would never happen to my mother," said Sylvia. On our way back to Aviv, she was listening to a song on the radio. "Come back to me from wherever you are" were some of the words being sung in a sentimental way. How she wished that her mother would sing this to her, she said, adding with a smile that she knew that this, too, would never happen to her.

Two days later, I found in my mailbox a drawing of Dori sitting in his wheelchair and a poem:

> When I tell the story of my life tears are streaming
>   from my eyes.
> Three years old, I was thrown away to institutions
>   and to families.
> Take pity on me, you police officer. I have been so
>   miserable all of my life.
> This is a very sad poem about a girl who always
>   thought that she did not get the attention she
>   would like from a good mother or from others.
> It talks loudly to my heart.

Sylvia was at a stage when she did not cry out for pity through her behavior. Instead, she did so frequently through stories and letters.

A new wave of anger against her mother followed. What made Sylvia particularly angry, she said, was that her mother's sickness was not real:

> She can walk all right. It's her behavior which is so annoying. She didn't take care of me in the first place, sending me to a

baby home right away, so how can she be so blaming and
demanding all the time? If I bring her one flower from Aviv she
looks at me as if the whole garden was her due, as if I owe her
something. . . . If I come to her with all my heart, she suspects
that I come for money. If I wear a ring, she says it doesn't suit
me. . . . All the girls like ornaments. My mother is simply
jealous.

Some of Sylvia's complaints were based on reality. Others
sounded more like those of a jealous girl projecting her angry
feelings on her rival, her mother, or like those of an envious
infant projecting his greed on her:

I'll never forget how she chased me away from her house the
moment my brother came in when I was visiting her. "Go
away, run back to Aviv," she shouted at me, so that God forbid
I would not get any money from him. When I meet her on the
street she says, "Why don't you come to see me? Am I not your
mother?" But when I come to visit her, she sends me away! If
she doesn't want me, why doesn't she say so?

At first it struck me as a sad irony; does Sylvia need words to
understand Mrs. Z.'s repudiation? Then I realized that it was not
an unequivocal rejection, which could perhaps have been better
tolerated, but rather a series of double messages, a pulling and a
pushing at the same time because of Mrs. Z.'s own conflicts. This
confusion seemed the most frustrating and unbearable of all.
    "Go away, run back to Aviv," Sylvia mimicked her mother.
"It makes me mad at her even now. I feel like eating her up. She
is so cruel to me. I wish for her death after that of my grandmother. If my father were not asleep, he would have beaten her
up," she continued, thus consoling herself.
    This reminded Sylvia of a teacher who had died of cancer
some years before. Sylvia brought up her worries that somebody
in her family would die and she would become an orphan. We
had talked several times about her fear that she might be punished
by being left alone, linking it to feelings of guilt around the

sickness of her mother, her wishes of death, and her magical thinking that would make fantasy death wishes come true.

In the story about Dori, his mother cried and his father sighed. When the uncle whom he loved came, he agreed to undergo the operation that he had refused until then. "I read the story over and over again," said Sylvia, again bringing up the attraction that the story had for her. When I pointed out her identification with Dori, she listened passively and said: "Yes, I am like Dori. I have a kind of inner paralysis. It's my mother. I keep thinking of her though I want so much to separate from her."

To the next session she brought a composition she was writing for me:

> How would I wish my life to be? I wish my mother would become healthy, would love me and not disappoint me every time I see her. One reason that I want to leave Aviv is that I want to get far, far away from my mother. I don't like her! Because she is sick, she takes out all her anger on me. That's why I want to study far away from her. When I am near her, I can't concentrate. I think about her. I try to understand—but I can't understand her. Nor can I cure her. She is not like the boy in the story who gets healthy in the end. It is true that my mother is paralyzed—but it's with her mind that something is wrong. This is the end of my composition. It's a very sad composition; it moves the heart only of those who know me.
>
> From Sylvia—who is a Coward about her mother.

Shame became the prominent feeling when Sylvia began to talk about herself in comparison to her mother and certain girls from Aviv. She dresses and undresses in a dark room, she said, not like her mother who exposes herself in the streets. When she goes to the theater with girls from Aviv who curse, she sits far away from them so that people won't know she is part of their group. "It's a place for prostitutes. . . . Take me out of this place," she said. "I sit for hours in a dark room, listening to music and imagining that I am all alone. I like darkness."

Now I began to understand what was behind the obscure behavior—staying by herself, not talking—that Sylvia's counselor had told me about some days before. On the one hand, she was eager to be alone as if she could be proud only if she dissociated herself from some evil or dirt. On the other hand, it sounded as if she were hiding some shameful defect. Sylvia's shame probably also had something to do with unconscious fantasies and castration fears about her body, as well as with the prostitution she fantasized about and felt guilty of. But stronger than this were the echoes of phrases she had recently been voicing: "I'll eat her up. . . . I have an inner paralysis, it's my mother. I want to separate from her but I can't." And now she mentioned the tendency to dress and undress in darkness, as if hiding a "defect." All this came together in my mind, and I waited for an opportunity to communicate it to Sylvia.

"You want to be far away from Aviv as well as from your mother," I said the next time Sylvia mentioned wanting to leave. "But it is difficult," I went on. "It is as if she is inside you. When you were mad at her, you said you wanted to eat her up, to swallow her. Little children imagine that they can really do this," I suggested. "Just as they take in food and swallow it, they believe they can do this with their mother." "I would not even want to taste her," Sylvia reacted. "She is so disgusting." By her expression she showed me that the idea was not so strange to her, although it might seem farfetched to some!

"On the other hand, it may be a comforting feeling to have the mother inside you," I continued, remembering Sylvia's fear of becoming an orphan, which she mentioned right after her cannibalistic fantasy. "She does not want to get out. She is strangling me from within, like a cancer," Sylvia responded, pointing at her throat and making a gesture as if she were choking. She sounded as if she were giving birth to a powerful fantasy that had been buried alive in her, and she felt greatly relieved. Verbalizing this fantasy and beginning to understand it seemed to help Sylvia free herself from her mother to some extent, as if the primitively incorporated object was being ejected.

In my earlier years as a therapist, I had needed much evidence before I was able to treat fantasies as strong motivating factors instead of seeing them as faked dramatizations. But now, after meeting the most irrational and weird fantasies in my own analysis and in work with others, I was ready to believe in them. This change in me might have been one of the factors that helped Sylvia come closer to seeing and expressing her innermost fantasies. At the same time, her emotion-laden expressions of her fantasies thoroughly convinced me of their power. Thus a vicious circle had begun to turn: experiencing the validity of fantasies promoted a therapeutic skill of listening and facilitating, which brought forward an increasing number of fantasies.

From her acting the role of the psychologist with other girls in Aviv, I thought that Sylvia was now also more ready to identify with me. Right after the "liberation scene," Sylvia had a brief period in which she played the role of the counselor in school. The staff was smiling, but Sylvia and the girls talked about these meetings, which reminded her of mine and which revealed some of my attitudes that she seemed to have adopted. Seeing my surprised look at the watch she was wearing one day, Sylvia explained that she had borrowed it from a friend. "I need it, when I sit with the girls," she said. "Everyone gets her time, each in turn. I don't tell anything about one to the other. It's personal. It's no one else's business."

This was one of the signs of a general shift in Sylvia's attitude toward the girls in Aviv. Whereas she had previously been centered mainly on herself, viewing reality from her personal point of view, she now became more perceptive of and open to others' points of view and needs. There was more sharing and friendliness. She felt better and wanted to live in her own rented room and set out each morning for work. It was decided to find a place where Sylvia could work close to a mature adult. She rented a room in the apartment of the woman who cleaned at Aviv, to whom she was attached. Sylvia was glad to hear that this was to be allowed, feeling like a graduating student who was leaving home to live on her own.

> There is in every child at every stage a new miracle of vigorous unfolding, which constitutes a new hope and a new responsibility for all. Such is the sense and the pervading quality and initiative. The criteria for all these senses and qualities are the same: a crisis, more or less beset with fumbling and fear, is resolved in that the child suddenly seems to "grow together" both in his person and in his body. He appears more "himself," more loving, more relaxed and brighter in his judgement, more activated and activating. [Erikson 1965, pp. 246–247]

This description approximates my perception of Sylvia as she emerged from the therapeutic encounter.

In the seven years that I worked with Sylvia she had become much more able to cope with frustrations and to satisfy her inner needs in socially constructive, and even creative, ways. Her progressive capabilities far outweighed her regressive patterns. I felt that this was a good time to let Sylvia know that, in three months time, I planned to go abroad for two years. At first, Sylvia expressed the fear of being abandoned, which had been triggered by similar occasions in the past, in the form of anger. But quite soon she could talk more directly about the conflicting feelings that were to be worked through in the last three months of treatment.

SUBSEQUENT CONTACTS

Before ending our last meeting we decided to remain in contact through letters.

Several months after the end of the treatment Sylvia wrote me as follows:

Dear Rena,

I got your letter and was glad to read what you wrote. How are you?

I am very well. How is life in America? I have a story that is similar to what happened between the two of us. It's called "I Was Saved by a Miracle."

In a certain family, there was a deaf-mute and mentally retarded boy. He had a psychologist whose name was Rena. Rena wanted very much to help the poor boy, whose name was Don. She took him to all kinds of parks and showed him all kinds of nice things. She gave him treatment twice a week for a year. Slowly, slowly the boy got better. One day, all of a sudden, when the boy woke up, he could hear and talk. He called our loudly: "Mother, mother. I can talk, I want to talk." His mother wondered who was talking to her. Then she saw that it was her boy. She hugged him and kissed him, saying, "You are saved. It's a miracle, my son." "I am saved by a miracle," shouted the boy excitedly. "Where is my Rena?" Suddenly, somebody knocked at the door. Rena came in. She was very surprised about the boy. The father came and wanted to give Rena a lot of money, because she had saved Don. But Rena said, "Keep the money for when the boy grows up." The boy said, "Rena, take the money, it's yours." So she took it. Rena said she was going to America. Then the boy started to cry and said: "You want to leave me. I am attached to you. Why do you want to go? Why?" He gave her a present and Rena flew far away in a plane. After a year she returned to the house of the child. She knocked at the door. "Yes, come in!" she heard a voice saying. "Does Mrs. Mizrachi live here? Where is the boy, Don?" Rena asked. "I am Don," said the boy. "Who are you?" "I am Rena who went to America," she said. Then they started to meet again. They are still meeting now.

I, too, want you to come back to me the way you came back to Don. Write me a long letter.

This was Sylvia's way of experiencing and containing conflicted feelings such as her anger, when through identifying with Don she did not at first recognize Rena, who had returned, and her longing for the renewal of contact. She expressed it all in a sublimated manner in the story. The letter was a good enough substitute for the real thing, as had been my postcards to her, instead of her being eager for cigarettes and sweets.

Sylvia maintained contact with me by writing me letters for about two years. After she left her foster home, Sylvia worked at different jobs, such as in a laundry or caring for old people. Thus she partially earned her living. She was also given rent aid from the Ministry of Welfare. At age 18 Sylvia married a man she had met at a club. He was a fitter. It was a love match.

Three years later, I met a social worker who worked in the area where Sylvia lived. She had known Sylvia previously and knew of her treatment with me. Sylvia was now 22 years old, married, and the mother of a 1-year-old son.

When I called and asked how she was, Sylvia invited me to visit her. She appeared to be functioning well as a mother. Much of her conversation centered on her father, who had died just before the birth of Sylvia's son. She named her son after him. From her manner of speaking I could sense that a much better relationship had been established between Sylvia and her father. It was important for her to restore the positive aspect of his image in her eyes. She was warm to the boy, taking care of him calmly, while at the same time talking with me, also in a relaxed manner. She could tell him to wait when she was busy with me, yet did not do this in an angry or rejecting way. The house was clean and orderly; neighbors dropped by.

I saw Sylvia three more times. I visited her in the hospital after the birth of her daughter and then again when she went home. My last visit—a follow-up interview—took place when Sylvia was 26 years old. During this visit I was impressed with her ability to handle an emotionally complex situation when her brother came to visit while I was there. She correctly pointed out to her brother that he was patronizing her husband, adding that her husband needed time to get to where the brother already was. She seemed to be in touch with her feelings as well as attuned to those of her husband, even when she definitely disagreed with him, as, for example, about his playing cards, which reminded her of her neglectful father.

Her work—taking care of sick and elderly people—brought her satisfaction. She also earned good money in the process. Sylvia's need to take care of others seemed concurrently to fulfill the desire to achieve respectability and status, and to be gratified by the good things she gave to those for whom she now cared— in contrast to how she had been treated as a child. In times of stress the need for such correction seemed to interfere with Sylvia's ability to be warm and flexible. This was felt when she and her husband were taking care of an adolescent boy whom the municipality had asked them to foster. It actualized her dream to give to others in a way that she had felt would have been satisfying to her in the past. Trying to accommodate to the boy's needs as well as to those of her own children and to those of herself and her husband was too difficult. After the boy was there for a year, the couple decided not to renew this role. All in all, Sylvia seemed at peace with herself and quite happy as a wife and mother.

SUMMARY

Early forms of deployment, as I experienced them in Sylvia's case, will be taken as a lens to focus on the therapeutic processes as they unfolded.

1. *Etiology.* Sylvia suffered from pervasive shame and guilt, particularly around her mother's illness, against which her deployments are enacted through a variety of fixed patterns of action and power ploys. Her self-absorption, also expressed in excessive masturbation since early childhood, is typical of deployed patients. So is her tendency to disconnect from others whenever feeling the threat of being hurt and humiliated.

2. *Drive determinants behind the deployments.* Sylvia was extremely aggressive for a long time. Both oral and anal sadistic
rage, which are central in deployed patients, characterized Sylvia's aggression. But no less important were the humiliated fury
that Lewis (1987) described and the narcissistic rage that Kohut
(1972) described, which were a starting point for reaching the
shaming events, and which then decreased the aggressiveness.
One of the ways Sylvia assuaged her tensions was to be provocative. The anger evoked by the provocations served to relieve her
tensions and to rearrange the balance of power.

Sylvia's rage was an attempt to cope with anxiety and
humiliation. One major source of her narcissistic rage related to
separation issues, which she tried to actively control. It often
took the shape of a battle of wills, for example, in wanting to
decide when to end the sessions and in refusing to accept boundaries. She was building her contact through ordering others
around. In the therapy Sylvia made it clear that she was the
"queen." This corresponded to her need to be omnipotent,
which served to balance her self-esteem and avoid feelings of
failure and depression.

Sylvia was constantly on the go, walking around and collecting things, with me following her, carrying the things she
had overloaded herself with. I found myself serving as a self
object (Kohut 1971) and behaving in ways that fit Balint's (1968)
descriptions of treating patients suffering from a basic fault:
"Apart from being a need recognizing and perhaps a need satisfying object, the analyst must also be a need understanding
object" (p. 181). Empathy was to provide not only for the
patient's needs to be mirrored (Kohut 1977), but also for her need
for distance, for closeness, for anger, to be quiet, to be talkative—
long-term needs as well as short-term needs. Sylvia's sexualized
feelings, utilized to avoid experiencing psychic pain in various
phases, are commonly found in deployed persons.

3. *Action.* Sylvia seemed to defend herself from being
flooded by instinctual stimuli and psychotic anxieties through
action. As is the case with deployed persons, her major form of

communication was to act and enact. Her actions warded off feelings of weakness, conflict, worry, blame, and humiliation. She was extremely flighty. There was an imperative quality to her behavior. Her capacity for postponing her impulse gratification and for building up tension-regulating structures was minimal.

4. *Mechanisms of projective identification.* Sylvia used powerful mechanisms to project parts of herself onto me, to dominate and control me, a mechanism widely used by deployed persons. I took projective identification as one of the methods of communication, trying to return, in a more manageable form, the undigested parts of her experience and inner world that she was, so to speak, putting into me as I experienced it from my countertransference reactions. Later on, when projections lessened, Sylvia became more able to tolerate and contain her conflicting and intense feelings.

5. *Guilt and shame determinants behind the deployments.* On several occasions, Sylvia was ruthless to her dolls because they wet their pants or committed some other minor offense. The fear of being shamed for losing control and face was one of the predominant forces behind the deployments. Her major defense in these circumstances was to identify with the aggressor (A. Freud 1946). As Wexler (1953) says: "By their struggling against overwhelming instinctual expression we have the possibility of fixing ourselves in the patient's psychic structure, perhaps at first as the counterpart and ally of the archaic super-ego, perhaps later as a more differentiated image involving many more thoughts, feelings and values" (p. 169). Like other deployed persons, she showed a specific superego ideal configuration.

6. *Regressive needs.* My decision to respond to Sylvia's regressive needs in the feeding situations was taken on the basis of therapeutic considerations. Direct narcissistic gratification, together with symbolic action on my part, gradually built up early feelings of self and of self-esteem. Many therapists agree about the absolute necessity of a happy infantile experience with a good mother before the patient can begin to grow toward adult

reality (Searles 1965, p. 540). And, as Emde (1990) says, "The special therapeutic atmosphere of shared meaning allows for a reexperiencing of the past such that it is not only less frightening, but becomes a potential source of affirmative continuity" (p. 907).

Sylvia's defenses of quick acting loosened and she became more ready to play.

7. *Enactments and dramatizations—roles of fantasy in converting tension and action to spoken thoughts.* Enactments occurred when Sylvia started to produce scenes from various periods of her life that reflected memories, fantasies, and choked-off feelings that had never been expressed before. Whereas she had previously discharged inner tensions through acting and masturbating, new channels of communication were now open to her in both her inner and outer lives. From being totally absorbed and driven by fantasy—a static dissociated process devoid of resonating symbolic meanings that remains isolated from living and dreaming (as it often occurs in deployed persons)—she now had better access to the use of her imagination, a result of the transformation undergone by her fantasy when it was brought into the "potential space" (Winnicott 1971).

This was a state of meaningful communication, in which insight was given not by explaining but by accompanying Sylvia into her imaginative world and using the language she offered. My role in this phase was primarily to be there, to receive the spontaneous gesture, and to be pleased (Winnicott 1965, p. 76). Sylvia was playacting in order to communicate and ventilate her feelings. Impulses and conflicts previously acted out in an incomprehensible way were put into the form of understandable stories that gave her the satisfaction of creativeness and mastery. It was up to me, as an auxiliary ego, to register her dissociations and help her integrate them into a coherent totality of experience (Khan 1974, p. 249).

8. *Oedipal strivings.* New waves of conflict that surged through Sylvia had the character of oedipal strivings, fear, and guilt. "I want to tell you something. Will you promise not to tell it to anybody?" Expecting a long-hidden secret to be revealed, I

was surprised to hear her disclosure: she loved her father better than her mother. Male counselors at Aviv now became more prominent in her life.

9. *Corrective programs.* Much of Sylvia's psychic energy was invested in corrective programs, a prime motivation in deployed persons. The unconscious aim of Sylvia's corrective behavior was not only to restore internal objects that have been damaged but to restore feelings of self-esteem that had been disrupted from the very beginning of her life. The wish to correct a gross imbalance of power, to correct unfair and humiliating treatment and defects that she had felt to exist almost bodily were other motivations behind the corrective programs. Sylvia wanted to give to others in need what she had so much missed in her past.

10. *Identification and the increased capacity to tolerate affect.* Sylvia said that she would sometimes hear my voice from within her. Her identification with me was noticed in many other ways as well. If the analyst is used as a new person, as a new love object, he or she can also be used as a new object of identification—as happens in children's lives all the time (Sandler et al. 1980). As Anna Freud (1965) says: "It is not the presence or absence, the gravity, or even the quantity of anxiety which indicate future mental health or illness. What is significant in this respect is the ego's ability to deal with anxiety" (p. 156). I feel quite similarly about guilt and shame. It is not the presence or absence, the quality, or even the quantity of shame and guilt that indicates future health or illness. What is significant in this respect is the self's capacity to tolerate rather than disavow and dissociate shame and guilt. It is the person's capacity to experience more widely, more complexly, and more freely his or her present in relation to the past and future, rather than being rigidly deployed in actions and positions fixed in the past. This is what Sylvia to some extent achieved in her treatment.

REFERENCES

Alpert, A. (1959). Reversibility of pathological fixations associated with maternal deprivation in infancy. *Psychoanalytic Study of the Child* 14:169–185.

Balint, M. (1968). *The Basic Fault*. London: Tavistock.

Ekstein, R. (1965). *Children of Time and Space*. New York: Appleton.

Emde, R. N. (1990). Mobilizing fundamental modes of development. *Journal of the American Psychoanalytic Association* 38:881–915.

Erikson, E. H. (1965). *Childhood and Society*. London: Hogarth.

Freud, A. (1946). *Mechanisms of Defense*. New York: International Universities Press.

———— (1965). *Normality and Pathology in Childhood*. New York: International Universities Press.

Gardner, R. A. (1971). *Therapeutic Communication with Children: The Mutual Storytelling Technique*. New York: Science House.

Hrushovski-Moses, R., and Moses, R. (1986). Steps in self-development. *Psychoanalytic Study of the Child* 41:491–513.

Katz, J., and Sanford, N. (1962). The curriculum in the perspective of the theory of personality development. In *The American College*, ed. N. Sanford. New York: Wiley.

Kernberg, O. F. (1987). Projection and projective identification: developmental and clinical aspects. *Journal of the American Psychiatric Association* 35:795–821.

Khan, M. M. R. (1974). *The Privacy of the Self*. London: Hogarth.

Klein, M. (1960). *The Psychoanalysis of Children*. London: Hogarth.

———— (1962). *Love, Hate and Reparation*. London: Hogarth.

Kohut, H. (1971). *The Analysis of the Self*. New York: International Universities Press.

———— (1972). Thoughts about narcissism and narcissistic rage. *Psychoanalytic Study of the Child* 27:360–407. New Haven. CT: Yale University Press.

———— (1977). *The Restoration of the Self*. New York: International Universities Press.

Lewis, H. B. (1987). *The Role of Shame in Symptom Formation*. Hillsdale, NJ: Lawrence Erlbaum.

Moses-Hrushovski, R. (1986). Interpretation of the past and the present. *European Psycho-Analytic Federation* 25: 15–25.

Ogden, T. H. (1988). Playing, dreaming and interpreting experience: comments on potential space. In *The Facilitating Environment*. ed. M. G. Fromm, and B. L. Smith, pp. 255–278. New York: International Universities Press.

Sandler, J. (1976). Countertransference and role responsiveness. *International Review of Psychoanalysis* 3:43–48.

Sandler, J., Kennedy, H., and Tyson, R. L. (1980). *The Technique of Child Analysis—Discussions with Anna Freud*. Cambridge, MA: Harvard University Press.

Searles, H. (1965). *Collected Papers on Schizophrenia*. New York: International Universities Press.

Sechehaye, M. (1951). *Autobiography of a Schizophrenic Girl*. New York: Grune & Stratton.

Wexler, M. (1953). The structural problem in schizophrenia: therapeutic implications. In *Psychotherapy*, ed. O. H. Mower. New York: Ronald.

Winnicott, D. W. (1965). *The Maturational Process and the Facilitating Environment*. London: Hogarth.

_____ (1971). *Dreaming, Fantasizing and Living in Playing and Reality*, pp. 26–37. New York: Basic Books.

3

DEPLOYMENT IN A NEUROTIC CHARACTER

The main part of this chapter comprises the story of Joe, as my first thoughts about deployment began to crystallize while working with Joe, over three-and-a-half years of analysis. It includes detailed exchanges between the analysand and myself, and my own thoughts and feelings, which serve as a basis for my interpretations.

In the final section of this chapter I present some of my working assumptions regarding deployed patients. I have also tried to describe some of the processes from my "analytic laboratory" (Balter et al. 1980), which contributed to the therapeutic process and are elaborated in Chapter 7.

CLINICAL MATERIAL

Some years ago, when I was on a sabbatical in the United States, Joe, a 22-year-old white Jewish man who had been crippled in a serious parachuting accident, came to me for psychoanalytic treatment. Asking him to come for a consultation, I could feel in the three intake sessions that there was good motivation for analytic work. There were indications that he had the capacity to free associate, and there was a good enough rapport between us. Joe's pathology was within the neurotic character range, with depressive, phobic, and hysterical features that I felt made a psychoanalytic venture possible. We decided to begin analysis four times a week even though we knew it was very likely that I would only be in the United States for three-and-a-half years.

My work with Joe felt like a mutual and creative experience: it was open to whatever came up as we focused on his problems of living and on entering his inner life and seeing how his mind worked.

Finally, a more technical point: since more time than usual was available to me during my sabbatical, and since I was very interested in developments within Joe, I not only took more elaborate notes of this analysis than I usually do, but I also indexed them according to criteria such as transference, resistance, memories as they came up from different phases, and other aspects. These notes helped me reconstruct the analytic process with Joe. For reasons of confidentiality (in this case as well as in the others) I have changed details of identification, I hope not at the expense of plausibility and authenticity.

BACKGROUND INFORMATION

Joe could only walk with the aid of crutches. He had been a fanatic amateur parachutist. The accident occurred during one of his parachuting exercises six months earlier and he had undergone one operation. Tall and very thin, his young face was covered with a short beard and he wore his hair in a crewcut. He decided to enter analysis because of his inhibitions, especially in the intellectual sphere, as well as his general unhappiness and distress. In one of the intake sessions he said that he often felt that, whenever and wherever he opened his mouth to say something, his father was always there mocking him and sending him a message of disdain.

Joe left high school a year before graduating because he had failed in two subjects and was depressed. During his therapy, he began and dropped out of courses in computer programming and carpentry, and took and passed high school equivalency examinations. By the time his analysis was completed, he was studying international relations at a university.

Joe's problem, he said, was primarily his father, whom he described as a pedantic, harsh, and domineering man. He did not just talk about this, but was totally focused on seeing and on demonstrating and struggling against this figure. The father was a highly specialized engineer who traveled a great deal. Joe had very few memories of his father from when Joe was younger than 8; not only was the father often away from home, but he also kept a distance between himself and his children when he was home. What Joe had experienced as most frightening and horrifying was his father's tendency to use his power to terrorize and abuse the whole family. Later on, the father became somewhat closer to the family, but he still seemed completely numb to their emotional needs and the world of their feelings. "Children are to be seen, not heard!" was a value transmitted through the father's behavior and words.

Joe had very little to say about his mother, even though his relationship with her was better than with his father. He talked about the miscarriages he knew she had undergone before and after he was born, but could remember no further details about this. He described his mother as a submissive woman, subjugated to her husband, who took out on her children the nervousness she felt in the marriage. This constellation of a powerful father and a submissive wife, or vice versa, is a typical etiological factor in deployed patients. A severe conflict of loyalty is created, in which there is contempt and resentment about the weakness and wretchedness of the mother, who lacks a strong enough sense of pride to assert herself, or to help shield the children from the abuser. The mother is, however, perceived as the kinder of the two parents and she is more sensitive—but she is in need of her children's help. The father is both hated and admired for being as powerful as the patient would like to be. Unable to solve problems and resolve conflicts, these patients deploy themselves into sinking into a fantasy world and thus holding up the progress of their own real lives.

In general, Joe remembered very little from his childhood, only that his family kept moving from place to place because of his father's profession. When he was 8, he contracted a serious form of mononucleosis that kept him bedridden for several months. Lying in bed and taking medication made him increasingly plump. This became another etiological factor for his deployment. Lonely and worried, he soothed himself by masturbating, which in turn increased his self-disdain and drove him into increased deployments, revengeful fantasies, and failures as a way of punishing the others and himself.

Joe had one vivid memory of something his mother said when he was about 10 years old, just before the family left for Africa, where his father had accepted a job. He and his brother Bill, who was two years older than Joe, had found their dog dead near the garbage container. She had been run over by a car; her fur was torn and her belly split open. They were all shocked. The father buried her. Joe remembers his mother saying, "The world is a cruel place!" Fantasies about his mother's frequent miscarriages and a primal scene experience coalesced into one of Joe's core fantasies.

Another memory of his mother from about the same time was about a fight Joe and his brother Bill had. When one of the boys threw out the words "Fuck you!" the mother decided that her sons should know the meaning of the words they were using. So she gave them a "scientific" sex lesson. Joe listened, agape, about how the man's seed enters the woman and develops; but he recalls that she never mentioned how it felt. Was it fun? Beautiful?

Although he had a nicely furnished room at home, Joe often

felt like a stranger there. Just before he began his analysis, he left his parents' home to share an apartment with a friend. About a year after he began analysis, he moved in with his girlfriend, Eileen, with whom he continued to live for several years.

Joe and Eileen had been good friends since high school. They had much in common, but they also quarreled a lot. One of Joe's aims in analysis was to improve his relationship with Eileen. It was Eileen—herself in analysis for several years—who recommended that Joe do the same for his own benefit. What had intrigued him most about the idea was Eileen's description of the value of psychoanalysis. She had said that for everybody there is a "circle" of potential human capacity and energy, and that psychoanalysis helps increase the magnitude of the circle at our disposal.

Moving to Africa when he was about 10 years old was a traumatic experience for Joe. He had no friends; he felt "different" and exposed to shame. He experienced distressful situations at school that caused him to become more dependent on his parents than ever. His younger brother Mark was born when Joe was 11. This added to his distress, and he began to live in his world of fantasies to an even greater extent. In his adolescence he had had fears of amputated limbs, which disappeared after his accident.

THE FIRST YEAR OF ANALYSIS

Joe's analysis began immediately after the three intake sessions. The first sessions centered around his fears of what might happen during analysis. He was always afraid of "what others would think of him"—that he was silly, not serious. The fear of being humiliated filled the first analytic sessions. He talked about lying on the sofa, which disturbed him. It felt as if I was looking at him from above; he thought that if I busied myself in the meantime he might feel less awkward. Though he usually left the session more relaxed, he found it difficult to come to sessions.

Upon arriving at an insight around his jealousy in the transference situation, Joe became excited. Although he had rarely asked her about it, he wanted to run to Eileen right after the session and ask her whether this was also how it had been in her treatment, and whether she felt the same. I noted to myself that there were guilt feelings regarding curiosity and the breaking of boundaries. I waited for further associations. After some moments of silence, Joe began to talk about his wish to build something, to create. He loved drawing, but he felt that he was lacking something important that an artist needs. It was as if he were "not built for creativity."

Joe's desire to be "corrected" or repaired in the analysis, by discovering the "defects" he might have, and his wish to be reborn as a new version of himself that would be strong and creative, colored his analysis from the very beginning.

In the next session Joe talked about a trip that he had taken with Eileen a few days earlier. Both of them liked to travel. They had had "two good days," after which he felt cut off from her for the rest of the last day of the trip and had "sort of broken up" with her. He was terribly ashamed of his behavior—it was horrible; he could not talk about it. I suggested that he try to elaborate more on what he felt. One of my analytical aims was to help him alleviate his shame by encouraging him to talk about it. Another goal was to make more space for him to express his different and confused feelings and feeling states, which he had refrained from doing both because of his tendency to keep feelings to himself and because those he was in contact with were not open to this language.

A short while later he said that he felt like a child who says that he does not want anything, like a baby who wants to cry. "Is this the feeling you have right now with me?" I asked. Joe responded that the image of his mother's depressed face had come to his mind. It was awful. Right then he felt blocked. After being silent for a while, he continued to tell me, with much shame, how as a child he used to shut himself up in his room and sit on the edge of his bed for hours when he was upset. When his mother would enter and ask why he was angry, he would not reply. This turned out to be a basic structure of his deployment: to be offended—to shut himself off—and to make his mother feel guilty. It also seemed that he was identifying with his mother's pose when she was depressed.

Joe then told me that what he had found so difficult to say was that he had become irritated about something Eileen had said when they were traveling. The only way he could express his ill temper was to sit in his car for hours sulking "as if I were still a child sitting on the edge of my bed, refusing any contact." Disconnecting himself when he felt hurt was one of the automatic patterns he had adopted to dissociate himself from experiencing psychic pain. The feeling he transmitted while talking was as if he had had an "accident" and was embarrassed to expose his weakness to me, as if it happened to him and was not in his control. I told him that he seemed to have so much anger stored up inside himself that he could not talk about what it was that irritated him so, first on his trip with Eileen and now with me.

Now Joe remembered the image of the family dog, all fear and self-abasement, with his tail between his legs whenever he had had an accident. The dog would look at Joe's father wanting to be caressed; the father would beat him instead. His father seemed to enjoy it when the dog ran away yelping, pleased to show the extent of his power. Through Joe's strong feeling of identification with the dog, I interpreted his blocking what had been experienced by him as an accident with Eileen: "When you were sitting in your car ill-tempered because you could not deal any better with your inner pressures, you felt needy, wanted to be caressed and pacified. But you were terribly ashamed to behave like a child. So you became immobile," I said, voicing the feeling states that he had intimated, so as to allow them to be reconnected with his experiencing self. Joe now gave some details about what made him feel nervous, which related to Eileen's messiness. Rather than discuss here the anal, sadomasochistic element that was a strong component in Joe's relationship with Eileen, as it was with his mother and father, what I saw instead as a paradigm of the deployment was the humiliation factor related to feelings of shame when he was regressing, losing control, and being mocked and disrespected. Even as a baby, he imagined that his father was mocking him for sucking so eagerly, never able, since then, to control his appetite. Being looked down on and condemned, whether it was experienced or fantasized, was one of the sources of shame and guilt behind his deployments.

In one of the following sessions, Joe told me how much he enjoyed Eileen's taking an active role in their sexual intercourse, but that this also put him under great pressure. He blocked while trying to find words to describe what he felt at those times. I referred to the pressure he was feeling right then, with me, in talking about sex. Continuing, Joe said, "It was as if something awful happened, but I don't know what!" He wished that someone would tell him, "It's nothing! It can be repaired." I asked him to associate to the feeling he had just identified by my repeating it in the same tone in which it had been transmitted to me. A memory came to his mind: While in the bathtub as a child, he had urinated. His mother entered while this was happening and asked him if she should change the water. He felt so embarrassed. This was exactly the feeling he had had with Eileen. "It felt awful to have failed her high expectations," he said. It was then I said that he seemed to fear that I, too, have expectations so high that they exert heavy pressure on him, that he wanted me to console him by saying "Nothing that happens is irreparable." "Eileen's parents are the exact opposite of mine," Joe continued in a reflective mood. When something breaks, they say "Good luck! Take it easy!" They clean up in a matter-of-fact way, whereas my mother tends to panic. "This is so appealing in the atmosphere of Eileen's house," he said. "It will be my attitude when I bring up my own children."

In his first dream, in the fifth month of his analysis, he and Eileen were listening to music in his room along with some other friends. There was much tension in the air. All of a sudden, his father entered with the excuse that he wanted to check the lock. But it was clear that he wanted to see what they were doing. Joe beckoned his father with a finger, as if inviting him to come closer to receive a blow. He felt a kind of strength, as if he had enough courage to tell his father everything that he had hitherto concealed from him. This first dream seemed to symbolize Joe's plan for analysis: to collect his inner strength in order to stop being intimidated by his father, and to tell him whatever oppressed him. This is also one of the persistent daydreams typical of deployed patients: to collect power when they felt powerless to stop the other from intimidating, abusing, and exploiting them.

In the course of his analysis, Joe brought up many dreams and daydreams, which he visualized vividly and which were a prelude to further analytic work. Sometimes he would associate spontaneously, without thinking of the various dream elements. At other times he would associate to the various elements, words, feelings, sensations, and movements that he or I took up. At yet other times he would select some component that caught his attention. A metaphor that I used in one of these hours to transmit the intention of working imaginatively with dreams was "to take each element up with him on a springboard and then to jump into the unknown," which introduced a dimension of play into the work. The analytic work in the hour varied from dream to dream and in relation to the same dream, oscillating from intense consciousness and concentration to relaxation.

Associations to a dream Joe reported, of which he remembered only that he screamed for help in the night, led to guilt for having disturbed his mother's sleep. I felt that he did not want to reexperience here in the analytic session his stressful night situations of feeling lonely and abandoned. I therefore asked him how he felt right then, while talking about his dream. Joe replied that during this long silence he had played with the fantasy that he had gotten up from the couch, saw that I was sleeping, and left the room. It was a sort of a fantasy-revenge that he caught me napping, he said. This was a prelude to primal scene experiences and fantasies that came in abundance later on.

The following session centered on problems of separation

and individuation. Joe and Eileen had had a good talk. This followed a quarrel that lasted for several days. Eileen told him how she could not do anything meaningful when they were apart, that she missed him. He told her that he had never been able to tell her that he was jealous of her. He also found the courage to tell her of his wanting to find out whether it was love or more a question of convenience or guilt that held him in the relationship. In the aftermath of this conversation, Joe and Eileen decided to allow each other more freedom.

While telling me about their good conversation, Joe again felt "kind of blocked." He thought of a hungry dog, starving, the world is bad—he was afraid that I would be repelled by his way of speaking. It seemed that his feeling of being repulsive was also a way to prepare himself so that he would not be taken by surprise when he suddenly felt that somebody was disgusted with him. What was felt by Joe as repulsive were the quarrels that he had with Eileen, through which he relived old experiences.

"It's strange," he continued, "whenever I am embarrassed, my face screws up into an unpleasant smile, as if I were a sadist." When I took up his discomfort with me, he said that he remembered a dream in which there was a white sheet on my sofa instead of the brown plastic cover. He was afraid to soil it. Associations led to a memory from his childhood: His mother had told him to look at the white hand of a relative's baby, so pure and pretty in comparison with his own dirty hand. He had wanted to be like the baby. I linked his blocking in the beginning of that hour with his shame about having messed up, fearing that I would be disgusted by him here. Then I was not sure whether his fear to be messy also related to his unconscious wish to repel me thereby.

Joe, busy with an incident that had just come to his mind, ignored my comment as if he did not want to be disturbed. The incident involved Eileen and himself passing near his parents' home some weeks before. He had gone into the house for a moment and returned holding a yogurt, which he ate without offering any to Eileen. She was hurt. He had eaten it without thinking, casually, as if he were scratching his leg. In that situation, he remembered, he had also had the kind of embarrassed smile he had just mentioned. The feeling transmitted to me was as if he had been caught in the act, and I said so. "Exactly!" Joe responded. "That is what I felt." It sounded as though he enjoyed my having named a feeling state that had been felt as vague and undefined before. "Perhaps now, when you blocked while telling me about your good conversation with Eileen, you were afraid that I would blame you for ignoring *me*, as if that, too, was misbehavior," I suggested. He became pensive and then said that he thought it was true. His mother, he continued, was always offended when he was intimate with his friends and not paying attention to her. I referred to the automatic act, "as if scratching his leg," which embarrassed and shamed him when he was caught. "That's true!" he said. "All kinds of things come up," he continued in an excited voice. "They all have to do with sex!" And he proceeded to tell me what they were.

When he was about 5 years old, he remembered, he had gone into the bathroom with a blue syringe, which he stuck in his navel. His mother came in and shouted at him. To this day he remembers how hysterical she was. He was then silent for a short while, upon which I commented that this is what he might have feared here from me, that I would suddenly alarm him when he was busy talking about sexual games, as if he had messed up.

Another memory came up from about the same time: Joe was playing with his penis beneath the blanket when his mother suddenly lifted the blanket and cried "What are you doing there!" instead of turning around and ignoring it! "This silly woman! She is from the Middle Ages," he exclaimed angrily. I linked the blocking that we noticed during this session with his strong fear of being shamed by me all of a sudden, and of his resulting fury at being shamed. I also thought that his way of reacting to shame was to blame the other, turning the table on the shamer and looking at her with a sadistic smile.

When Joe was totally absorbed in his inner world, ignoring the other, and when he feared being attacked, there was a strong feeling in the air of a child's self-state being reenacted. His shame, his worries, and the guilt that surrounded masturbation, as well as his fear of being disgusting and therefore rejected, came up in the following stage, as did the role that infantile sexuality and aggression had played in the shaping of his development.

THE SECOND YEAR OF ANALYSIS

Several months later, Joe missed an analytic session for the first time. The session to be described followed the missing session; it took place a week before he had to go for another operation on his leg.

Joe told me that the day before he missed the session, he had had an incident with Eileen about which he would talk later. He had heard the alarm clock ringing but had turned it off, wanting to go on sleeping. He was visualizing the moment that he would enter the operating room. (He still had a scar from the previous operation.) "Was I frightened?" he asked himself. He calmed himself, saying that he would be fully asleep during the operation. He woke up from his drowsy state and realized that he was too late for his analytic session. He felt panicky, wanting to put his fist in his mouth. When he realized that he was going to miss the session he called Eileen and asked her—as she had also experienced the "failure" of missing an analytic hour—what to do. She suggested that he call me to say that he would not be able to make it. But he did not feel like doing that.

The incident with Eileen, which he then returned to, was that he asked her to carry him on her back, a kind of game he liked to play as a child. He was shocked when she responded by saying that she might like to have children by him one day and was afraid that if she carried him this might impair her ability to give birth. It was terrible for him to hear this. "I would never say something like that to her!" His regressive pull before the prospect of an operation that frightened him, his anger at Eileen who rejected his request instead of understanding his fear and trying to soothe him, and the intense hurt he had experienced seemed to be related to an unconscious traumatic event that was being reenacted. The missed hour he had felt so panicky about, and the operation he visualized, reminded me of his mother's miscarriages. Might it be, I asked myself, that Joe feels it was his request to be carried that caused his mother's miscarriages?

I said that he needed to be reassured and calmed before the operation, and that he felt he could rely neither on me nor on Eileen to provide relief.

He had such a good memory of his first operation, Joe said, while pondering the details he remembered. He had been hurt along with others . . . lying on the ground. . . . He did not scream. . . . He was the first person to be put in the helicopter, and the first to be operated on. This made him feel pleased despite the pain. He enjoyed being carried on the stretcher. It was great! His surgeon told him he had had a similar accident. This made him feel that such things don't happen only to him, that he need not feel ashamed. Even his father treated him like an equal when he came to visit. But Eileen was spoiling the prospect of the second operation for him because she sat there depressed and distant. He does not want anybody to spoil the operation for him. Joe continued to playact the fantasy of rebirth through the operation. What he was trying to correct through it related to frustrations such as his sibling rivalry. Joe deployed himself in a variety of ways to keep from feeling his envy and jealousy; for instance, by noting and demonstrating his older brother's defects, by considering himself as the smarter and more creative one, by "stealing the birthright" through such playacting.

It sounded to me as if Joe wished to actualize a rebirth fantasy through his operation, hoping that it would free him from all the pressures that had been oppressing him and allow him to be reborn as a strong and happy man. From some highly emotionally charged statements about what helped him or made him feel bad during his first operation, I noted certain feeling signs to be used later to link his frustrations with states of helplessness.

There was another incident he felt bad about: He had woken up in the night and called Eileen, though he knew then that she had difficulties falling asleep. But he could not control himself. He needed to talk with her. He was in a panic. When I commented on his way of relying on Eileen to calm him, he became irritated with me. "For you it's easy to be strong! You, who sleep with your husband!" "You feel that I am harsh here with you and am sending you back to your bed, blaming you for disturbing Eileen," I said. Through the moods that Joe described, he came to reexperience earlier infant and child self experiences and states of being in night situations, which would then be worked through in the transference.

Many examples of how frightening his father was, especially during the time they were in Africa and around the time his mother gave birth, had come up. A week before I was due to take three weeks' vacation, and four months after his second operation, Joe had talked about a time when he and his brother Bill had knocked over an antique lamp while playing. They were frightened of their father's reaction. And, indeed, when he came into their room, he shouted that the lamp should have fallen on their heads. "How do you feel now, here, when you remember this incident?" I asked, since I felt that he was talking about it but was not there emotionally. At this point Joe recalled something that had impressed him greatly. He had talked and talked in his first analytic hour; at the end I had quietly commented that he had opened and closed the session with an apology. This was all I had said in that hour, he said. Recalling that hour, I now reminded him that he had reacted to my remark as if he had been struck on the head with a hammer; he had been under the impact of this comment for the whole weekend, being both frightened and impressed. "Are you afraid of the same thing now," I asked, "that I will similarly bring you down with a blow?" (What he had meant then was that he had been surprised at the scarcity of my words, which pointed to the guilt he was trying to disavow.)

Joe responded that he sometimes felt as if he were playing the children's game "Statues" in his analysis: during the weekend, from Friday to Sunday, he moved around, and when he came back to analysis he would "freeze." "But not now!" he went on. "I don't feel that way now." It was when he first came to my consulting room that I had been more aloof. He had fantasized my having a flat tire so that he could feel strong by helping me. He had perceived my aloofness as humiliating him, as if I were treating him as somebody who had had an accident. His wishing to change roles by making me have an accident, a flat tire, so he would be in the role of a helper, pointed once more to the frequent division he tended to make between those who are above and those who are below. Since then, he had undergone a transformation and felt stronger, he said. Much of what he felt was in terms of steps of rebirth.

He had felt extremely relieved when we talked some time ago about his problem of ambivalence. He realized that when he is angry or wants to hurt someone else it does not mean that he has no capacity to love. Guilt about the feeling of not being able to love led to guilt around sadistic drives.

Joe told me he felt guilty about telling me the sadistic stories about his father; he feared that by so doing he was somehow harming me. But he had to do this so I would see how perverted his father is and how really dangerous the world is.

Joe brought up a discussion with Eileen about a movie in which children were frightened. Eileen thought that if the mother were near the children, the evil would be less frightening. He thought—to the contrary—that one should protect children from being exposed to what is done to their mothers and that children should not be present at such scenes. Then Joe remembered a horrible experience: his parachute instructor severely frightened a black woman and her child. If he could be born anew he would like to be reborn in that situation so he would be able to correct the cruelty that he had not been able to prevent, and thereby also correct his stain of cowardice. He would like to be there again, but this time in the role of a strong man who would stop such tortures. Tracing this feeling of fear and guilt led to a real experience when he felt helpless and ashamed of being passive in such circumstances, letting cruel deeds take place without his being able to stop them. He felt, as do many deployed patients, that only if he could go back and undo the wrong behavior could he feel more self-respect. Primal scene fantasies were intermixed with other fantasies as well as traumatic experiences. Joe recalled an experience at home that enraged him: His younger brother asked his parents what the difference was between collision and accident. They smiled at each other when his father told his brother that he had been born out of a collision. But there was no accident. "How could they bring in their sexual affairs when they were asked about such a frightening theme as accidents and collision?" Joe hated their way of being closed to the child's feelings and their teasing manner. Was he an accident? he wondered, remembering that he had heard that he was unplanned.

Another incident from Africa came to Joe's mind. He remembered exactly that he was sitting at his desk, doing his homework, and listening to his father tell his mother in the kitchen about how people used to drop dead bodies off a high cliff. Vultures would swoop down at the bodies before they reached the ground. He could still hear the sounds that his father made imitating the vultures. "It's awful! Why does he tell such horror stories in such a cool way? He is a sex maniac! A rapist!" He then remembered that he had been frozen to the chair while his father was speaking. "Maybe I was cruel in telling you about this?" he asked me. Maybe it would depress you?" "You want me to feel how it feels to be left all alone when such frightening scenes come to your mind," I said. "And perhaps you also want to punish me before I leave on my vacation, leaving you all alone in the cruel world."

Joe needed me to feel with him before he could be ready to figure out which were real elements of sadism and which were his fantasy, as well as what were the functions behind his fantasizing. He spent many hours dealing with perceptions, feelings, and fantasies where the sadistic element colored everything he saw. The central analytic dynamics at that point in the analysis consisted of Joe's internalization of frightening aspects of his parents. He oscillated between identifying with his mother—experienced as vulnerable and damaged—and with his father, whom he perceived as a pervert and a rapist. Joe was preoccupied with rape both in his dreams and while he was awake. He felt ashamed and guilty about these preoccupations. Gradually, he became more aware of the sadistic pleasure he derived from seeing and talking about these forms of rape. It also gave him some counterpower against his father. With much shame, he told me that he had sometimes tortured his dog as a child—not that he enjoyed beating the dog. He would shove a stick in his direction and frighten him. The sadistic play that Joe described so shamefully resembled sexual intercourse as perceived by his child part. Then he asked hesitantly whether I was a survivor of the Holocaust. If I were, he said, it would be awful. That would make him a real sadist. He had never suffered directly from any war, so how could he tell me about the torture he had experienced, as if he had been in the Holocaust himself? I wondered whether his feelings of guilt related to sadistic fantasies toward me that he could not feel free enough to talk about. I asked whether there was anything he felt reluctant to talk about here, right now. Not that he was aware of, he said.

While talking about his guilt feelings, Joe remembered how preoccupied he had been with God already in the first grade. Later, in Africa with his family, when he did not fast on a day of fasting, he was tortured by shame that he did not have the courage to at least face God and confess.

THE THIRD YEAR OF ANALYSIS

In the following months, memories of archaic fears came up. Joe remembered that, when he was about 7, his parents took him to visit friends who had a daughter of his age. It was a room full of carpets—no wall was bare. On one wall there was a bulge. He touched it and became terribly alarmed. In fantasy, he visualized a kind of crocodile that suddenly opened its mouth. As it opened, he could see teeth. He ran to the bathroom and, sitting on the toilet, he was terribly afraid that the crocodile's teeth would pull and bite him. These fears came up when Joe feared that something might happen to him when he felt exposed in the analytic situation in the context of sadistic happenings. He had had this fear for years. In his adolescence he had fears of amputated limbs, which disappeared after his parachuting accident. Fears from earlier developmental phases now connected up: Joe would tell his mother that he was going to the toilet, "so that she would know, just in case."

Joe's words elicited in me echoes from various traumatic experiences that had come up in his analysis, particularly from the year when his mother had had one of her miscarriages. He was 7; he had seen her running to the toilet in panic; his grandmother had said that it ended in a miscarriage and not in a birth. This was one of the repetitive themes that came up in a dissociated way.

In one of the following sessions, Joe said that he felt something important was happening to him. Now, when he thinks about how angry he is with his mother for making him feel guilty, he realizes that, actually, he makes others feel guilty too. For example, when he used to sit on the edge of his bed for hours, he wanted to make his mother feel bad by demonstrating how wretched he was. And now when he tells me about the cruel world, he is doing the same to me, perhaps because of his doubts as to whether I am on his side. Gradually, he started to see more the role that he played in the tensions at home; his belief that all his troubles stem from his father's despotism stopped being the objective reality.

Joe remembered that he was 7 years old when he decided to be sad rather than happy, to make his mother feel bad. To decipher some sources of the psychic pain that caused him to make the deliberate decision, I asked what else came up from his seventh year, and he spoke in more detail about the tensions at home. He recalled vividly how he refused to stay alone in his bed; one of the pieces of "cognitive dissonance" that came up was: "Why are my parents together in their bed and we, the children who need it more, are forbidden to sleep together? It's unfair!" Joe also remembered how he would cry outside his parents' room to make certain that they did not sleep peacefully, "so they'll know they are bad!" He felt neglected and betrayed. Gaining more empathic understanding about his child parts, he began liberating himself from sinking into his fantasy world. The more he talked about his feelings, fantasies, and behavior with me and others, the less was he driven to hate the other and see the other as all black. After this, he gradually began shedding his role as a victim. Now he was able to better see his own part in creating the role of a miserable person for himself.

Joe also remembered how, while sitting on the edge of his bed for hours on end, he used to have a fantasy about his father: In one of his aggressive moods, his father pushed him until he fell and broke his skull. Joe's satisfaction in this fantasy derived from the fact that at last everyone could see the kind of a sadist his father really was. Even his mother felt sorry for what his father had done to him. Yes, even his father felt miserable and was sorry that he had mistreated his son.

A series of dreams that followed brought us close to Joe's primal scene fantasies, which were the major topic of our sessions during the following months.

Primal scene fantasies and feeling states could be seen and felt (a) from the background given to this dream; (b) from the manifest dream taken as a poem; and (c) from the associations to the various dream elements leading to the latent meanings, for example, linking the childish excitement and forbidden games he felt guilty about to his castration anxiety in a meaningful way. Some new memories came up, as if seen through a fog: Joe as a 3-year-old lying in a baby crib and screaming louder and louder in his head, as if not wanting to hear the weird sounds of his parents that seemed amplified.

Vague memories about fears of death came up in this context. It felt as if he needed to remember to breathe so that he would not die. In one of the following sessions, Joe recalled how he liked to fall asleep before his parents went to sleep, when a light was still on in the hall, and "when it was calm and safe." Thinking about the noises, he said, reminded him of a story he had read long ago and had enjoyed. It was about a cave. Because of an earthquake and rains, one part of the cave had become separated from the other. The people who lived there became blind. And, as happens with blind people, their other senses become so sharp that they could hear every sound. "I am like that," he said. Therefore, when he hears the noises that his parents make when they eat, he finds it unbearable. He always puts on the radio so that he will not be able to hear them.

After reflecting on what we were talking about, Joe said he had never before realized that his resentment against his parents' noises might be related to what they did in bed.

He had told me at the last session how beautiful he thought the line of birds sitting on the television antenna was. But Eileen spoiled this for him when she told him that they were fighting for space to sleep. He had thought they were being loving to each other.

Contradictions that Joe's child-self found between love and sex were now brought up. In the last part of his analysis it became possible to interpret the expression of primitive and disturbing versions of the oedipal configurations, his longings, his jealousies, his sudden feelings of betrayal—his being at a loss because of the undigestible sights and sounds of his infant- and child-selves.

Joe shared with me one of his self-observations at this time: When he goes for walks now, he can look to both sides and derive much enjoyment from what he sees. It is as if a new dimension has opened up for him.

Another aspect of Joe's working through his castration anxiety was when more conflicts came up around his curiosity. He remembered how, as a little child, he had been curious to see what his mother was hiding under her skirt. He and his mother rested together after lunch in her bed. Both were under a blanket. And, while she was reading, he slowly lifted up her skirt. He could not remember what he saw. But anxiety was in the air. I told him, "It is too frightening to remember."

Another memory came up: Joe asking his mother, whom he saw lifting her arm in the hall, whether she had hair in her armpit. He knew that adults have hair under their arms, but he asked anyway. When she said that she did, he asked whether she also had hair under her other arm, even though he knew the answer. Then he ran after her and begged her not to tell anybody what he had asked. "It's a secret," he told her. When she entered the hall he could hear the adults explode with laughter. He was so ashamed! (We talked about how what adults enjoy and laugh about is often felt by the child as extremely humiliating.)

"I asked even though I knew," he repeated again, as if to prove to himself and to me that he was not as big an idiot as he felt he was. Why did he make a fool of himself? He knew what was under her arms! "Yes," I said. "But you were not sure what was under her skirt." "Yes," he replied, stammering in his acute anxiety and embarrassment. I thought that, without talking about it directly, he understood the mechanism of displacing upward what was too frightening for him about anatomical gender differences between the sexes below. I took up his childhood wishes to see, to touch, and to know what was exciting and repelling, wonderful and terrible—as he had experienced in a dream—and noted that he still feels inhibited whenever such humiliating laughter rings in his mind. Sexual games with friends from childhood and adolescence, interlocked with pregnancy fantasies, now opened up for further exploration.

In one of these sessions, Joe was cracking his finger. When I pointed this out, wondering what he was expressing thereby, he was surprised. He had never talked about it. "It's a kind of addiction. I've been doing this since the eighth grade, just as some children smoke to look like adults." Then he talked about a photo taken when he had mononucleosis, when he was 10, in which he looked like a woman with a big belly. He was surprised to see it. Shame about his body-image from various developmental stages now appeared. The following night he dreamt he was a little boy, naked in his mother's bed. He embraced her belly and her breasts and felt a pleasant sexual feeling mixed with a little disgust. Her head was leaning over his. It felt as if a warm cloud enveloped him.

Associating to this dream, Joe remembered that he had slept in his mother's bed when he was about 15. While playing with this memory for a while—wondering whether it was real or a fantasy—Joe tended to think that it did happen during one of his father's absences. He felt guilt and shame about his incestuous wishes, which he could now tolerate better, also in the transference. At about the same time, he dreamt that he met me in the street and said: "Hello, I saw you in my dream last night." There followed more talk about oedipal wishes and feelings of being deprived and of jealousy. It was now several months before the end of his analysis, and also just before he was to go on a three-week business trip. He felt good about this trip. His only fear was that if he had any dreams, he would not be able to discuss them with me. This led to further reconstruction of childhood night situations, especially his feelings of loneliness and his fear of having "accidents."

While going back and forth from the present to the past in one of these sessions, Joe recalled something he had not remembered for years: He was about 4 years old and in a preschool kindergarten. A French child came into their class and was standing on a table showing a frog. Wanting to see the frog, Joe, without noticing, pushed a little boy who was also standing on the table. "The boy fell. . . . There was lots of blood. . . . He cried terribly. . . . It was awful!" The kindergarten teacher shouted at Joe, saying he could have killed the boy. "Until then I had been good! Suddenly I was bad! Everyone hated me!" After that he was afraid of falling—afraid *he* would be pushed. I took up the trauma that he felt when he was so suddenly and severely blamed, and also dwelled on the cognitive dissonance: "Being good and liked! Suddenly being dropped and perceived as evil, hated!"

"It was my jealousy that should have been blamed," said Joe, as if surprised at the direction that his story had taken. "Everyone admired the French boy . . . what he did . . . how he talked . . . what he said." The way Joe was talking and the words uttered formed themselves into the following words: "Your feeling of jealousy toward somebody who was admired caused the accident," I said. "What comes to mind when you stay with this feeling now?" Joe replied that it sounds familiar but nothing comes up. Whereas identified feeling states did often bring up images or new memories, this time an inner resistance was clearly noticed that interfered with the process of disclosure.

Joe's experience a year before came to my mind, when Eileen had refused to carry him lest she would not be able to bear a child, and I said so. This reminded him that he had wanted to hit his mother when she used to suddenly become hysterical. "They said that I must be careful," came a foggy thought or memory. "She has a child in her belly!" A thread of the fantasy, that he caused or wished to cause his mother to miscarry, began to be woven into the fabric of the hour. Joe's resistance to his feelings of guilt was expressed thus: "How will it help if I understand? I want to get off this planet, to stop the world!" A scene from a movie about a pregnant mother who miscarried then came to his mind. In the scene an infant's voice said: "At age one hour—I had just been conceived. One month—I have eyes. Two months—I am beginning to have limbs. Four months—they killed me." This memory, which kept coming up in his analysis in different contexts, served later on as an important source of reverberations.

Joe's jealousy and envy at the birth of his younger brother Mark when Joe was 11 came up in many contexts, as did fantasies of his having harmed the baby even prior to his birth. He also had fantasies and fears of his brother's revenge. One of the images that haunted him was a baby's hand coming out of his grave. For several months he brought up experiences that he and Eileen had had with abandoned kittens and puppies they were taking good care of. When it rained he would worry they might get wet. This formed one of the many avenues to work on his problems with wetting and "accidents," which became related at this stage to what would happen when he was excited, even as an older boy. This threw light on his keen concern about the attitudes of his parents around the bed-wetting of his young brother. Behind his wish to pay for the brother's psychotherapy, which his parents refused, was a condensed corrective wish: Had his parents realized that there were emotional reasons for his own bed-wetting in the past, he would have been saved so much suffering. Also, it corrected his feelings of unconscious guilt of having damaged his little brothers. Talk of feeding the infant animals with warm milk and honey when they whined, even late at night, revived feelings and fantasies that enabled him to reconstruct baby parts, infant-self states and feelings from childhood night-situations: He had felt abandoned, his emotional needs were not being related to, and he was exposed to frightening primal scene experiences.

Another stressful event that shocked Joe occurred when one of the kittens was dropped due to the carelessness or clumsiness of a child who was eager to take care of it. Joe presented this as a disaster, as a trauma for them all: Eileen, himself, and the kitten. It felt like a dramatization of a traumatic feeling state that preoccupied Joe. It was as if Joe's terror at having dropped something and someone had become united with his fury at those who had miscarried. It was an incident both real and symbolic.

Then came one of Joe's resistant sessions. He began by disputing the approach he thought I represented. "What is the aim of psychoanalysis?" he asked. "To make me happy? To give me the capacity to enjoy life? To make me feel better? I don't want to be happy! After all the years that they made me suffer. My satisfaction is in my misery. This is what adds power to my claim that I am right, that the world is bad." I reacted by saying that he put all his efforts into feeling bad, as if demonstrating that there is no other way he can get through to people except by showing his misery, that he felt helpless vis-à-vis inner accusations, that he was trying to externalize.

"The world is shit!" he went on, returning to a recurring theme. "Even after I end my treatment, the kittens will shiver in the winter. The puppies will whine." He explained that he refused to be shut off from real suffering. "You are protesting against the me who ignores your suffering," I said. "What comes up today in this context?" As Joe proceeded to associate, it sounded to me as if one of the arguments he was reliving through what he said was that he was not crazy, as he was sometimes made to feel. "I know what I am saying. I am not making things up when I talk about suffering." What had made him furious so frequently was that all kinds of perceptions he had had were denied or mocked.

I brought up his resentment at what he saw as my ignoring objective reality, as if I disrespected what he said. Taking it back into our relationship, I asked whether he felt that I treated him as if he were crazy, making up things. Joe then explained his complaint about the noise his parents made. He had thought that they were very inconsiderate—and even crazy—when they made these noises. He could not fall asleep. When he once told them that the noises disturbed him, they blamed him for still being awake, as if it were his problem, "as if I were the one who was crazy—who was wrong." He had remembered this incident the night before, when a friend who slept in his and Eileen's apartment put on her light late at night and was inconsiderate in other ways. He also felt that I too did not realize fully enough how inconsiderate his parents were of him. Negative transference toward me appeared as he distrusted my alliance with him. "There is nobody in the world who can really understand me," Joe said in despair. Moments of despair came up when he felt humiliated and could not talk about it to anyone. The more I was able to listen to despair without despairing myself, the more he could feel and be with these difficult states.

Eileen, Joe, and some friends had gone to see a beautiful movie. Afterward they talked about good and evil. Joe now realized that it was his problem that he often saw the world as bad. For so many years he had seen it as *their* problem, which had turned into a question of life and death. Now he became even more convinced that much of the badness was in him. It had calmed him that it was not his fault but theirs. My interpretive focus at this time was on his difficulty in giving up his vengeful fantasy consolations from the past. Space was given to Joe's difficulties in giving up his pacifier when he was about 4 years old as well as other consoling devices. He could now empathize with the difficulty while not being so ashamed of it anymore.

Having achieved the capacity to take more distance and reflect upon his modes of behavior, Joe said that it was funny how he sometimes thought he was God—especially when he was so often preoccupied with preparing the list of children's rights, wanting to adapt humanity to what he thought.

More material about Joe's feelings of guilt, which he had tended to disavow, emerged in the following sessions, mixed with fantasies about the death of his miscarried "siblings." Joe realized how guilty he actually felt for his aggressive fantasies and his oral greed, which came up in various contexts. One of Joe's ways of correcting his "badness" was to become a vegetarian. Another way was to correct his father's horrible mistakes by being the opposite: "My father acted on his drives, torturing my mother physically like the bull in the fairy tale who could not refrain from drinking." Joe, in contrast, was "in control and considerate of others' rights and feelings." Gradually he became more tolerant of his "badness" and a softening of his deployment into his fantasy world occurred.

I was fascinated by the various kinds of enactment that enabled Joe to work through what he had been unconsciously preoccupied with when he perceived the world as threatening and bad in emotionally meaningful ways. I even began to wonder whether his parachute accident—caused, as he explained it, by turbulence that took the air away from underneath—might not really have been an enactment of his fantasies, as well as punishment for his unconscious guilt.

One of Joe's reactions to concluding his analysis was to perceive it as another miscarriage. Much anger was expressed that I was leaving him—dropping him before his time. He would like to at least get some compensation, something he could take with him in case he needed me or made mistakes. In his fantasy it looked like a book or a painting that he could carry with him. It was as if he wanted to be given something created by both of us. It also had the feel of a transitional object.

In one of our last meetings before ending his analysis, Joe talked about the progress he had made. He felt that the "circle" of his inner strength had grown, and that this was "a good feeling." It was not only that he had much more energy to do things. He also felt that something was emotionally alive in him even when it did not take the form of the completed work of art that we would have wished it to be. "Now," he said, "there are more and more cracks in the theory that my parents are the cause of all my problems." Now he could see that his own suspicions, fears, greed, and envy had also played a significant role.

"I am also more willing and able to stop myself in time," he told me. "I am no longer automatically driven to repeat previous patterns of detaching myself and feeling hatred as I used to do." Another change that Joe had mentioned was that, "all of a sudden, poems took on meaning." Joe began to understand the text of plays he had previously been reluctant to read, thinking he would be unable to understand them. He felt stronger and enjoyed studying at college, but was still sometimes bothered by bad moods.

There was an agreement between Joe and me to maintain a follow-up relationship through the mail for as long as he felt like doing so. For several years I would send him a greeting card on the eve of the New Year, and he would write a letter telling me how he was doing. He was happily married. He and his wife were raising their son, who was relaxed, curious, very communicative, and still nursing at the age of 8 months. He completed his B.A. in international relations and political science. One of his professional duties was to take part in international conferences. A most satisfying experience, described in his last letter, was his participation at a conference that had almost exploded due to the tensions surrounding a tragic international incident. The fact that the conference could be brought to a peaceful close despite the stormy discussions and confrontations, and that there were "tears in the eyes of many participants" as they departed, proved to him that, "this is the only way: to meet and to talk!" This, he thought, is the most important thing we have to do today!

SUMMARY

How did I experience the therapeutic process with Joe? I view his treatment as an integrated entity made up of several threads:

1. The process of free association in the analytic situation, which allowed him to immerse himself in the process of regressing and using his power of imagination to re-create the inner world of his childhood. "It is when playing—and only when playing—that the individual child or adult is able to be creative and use his whole personality. It is only in being creative that the individual discovers the self" (Winnicott 1971).

I was impressed how Joe remembered almost nothing in the beginning of his analysis, except that his family moved around a lot. From there Joe developed his ability to bring up lively memories of his developmental history, through their reenactment in the analytic situation with me, integrating them into a coherent explanatory narrative. The process of free association also served the aim of promoting continuities of thought, affect, memory, and sense of self (Kris 1983). Through reconstructions the successful exposure and reintegration of early etiological traumata in the analysis, especially those traumata revolving around miscarriages and primal scene experiences, allowed Joe's ego to be strengthened (Rangell 1981).

2. Interpretations of Joe's feelings and behavior as motivated by unconscious instinctual libidinal and aggressive drives and defenses (primarily externalization and projection of conflicts) were an important part of my therapeutic work. Working through the conscious and unconscious elements of his Oedipus complex, lived out in dreams and in the transference, enabled Joe to become more tolerant and aware of his impulses and to move toward greater and more mature integration.

3. No less important than interpreting the oedipal and preoedipal dynamics that led to Joe's castration complex was the central role that shame played in Joe's pathology and in the "deployment" (Moses-Hrushovski and Moses 1989) that he used in order to protect himself from these feelings of shame.

Joe's deployment can be seen in the fact that his whole personality was focused into a system of attitudes, roles, and positions designed to protect his self-esteem. His efforts, and much of his power, were geared toward (a) attempts to avoid feeling and remembering emotional events that threatened the integrity of his self; (b) attempts to actualize in reality or in fantasy the unconscious wish to go back in time and correct both the damage he had fantasized to have caused as well as his self injuries; and (c) attempts to be compensated for the mental suffering that had been inflicted on him in the past and had caused his self-effacement.

Joe lived in constant great tension, as if his life were a continuous battle. Shame was such an acutely painful and disorganizing experience that he wished it would end quickly; he had no taste for introspection with regard to shame.

There was a constant effort to avoid some unknown "accident" or catastrophe that might occur if he let go and gave up control. The problem was not so much the repression of his feelings; it was more his refusal to admit whatever he perceived as weakening or humiliating into his experiential space. Since Joe was under pressure to "cleanse" the stains of shame and regain the state of harmony that he had lost, his creative inner space had been restricted.

For a long time I tried to contain his feelings of psychic pain, which were unbearable to him. I deciphered the vulnerability that motivated him to act quickly in order to keep from feeling. Toward the end of Joe's analysis, what he felt in the session toward me often opened up the road to fuller emotional and verbal expression. He was able to move on to new experiential landscapes.

Placing the problem in the context of child behavior, so the conflictual parts can be felt and not only understood, often enabled me to introduce empathy with Joe's child part, which had been dissociated. Feeling less ashamed of his "childish" part enabled him to begin a dialogue with it instead of reenacting it.

Joe's realization that his need to prove his righteousness was a question of life and death for him was another step toward making him more interested in exploring what the catastrophe was, the occurrence of which he was so completely attuned to without having any idea of what it was. By being able to reach meaningful situations he was now freer to meet a growing range of feelings and tolerate to a larger extent feelings of humiliation, shame, and guilt. He was no longer compelled to be in full control—a state of affairs that had prevented his loosening and opening up. Eventually Joe came to remember several states that he had experienced as "worse than death." They usually came upon him suddenly, when he felt crushed, diminished, or help- lessly exposed to humiliation and shame (Mitchell 1988).

In many respects Joe's analysis took place under the sign of the wish to correct painful experiences from the past through fantasy acts. He loved parachuting from a plane, as it allowed him to fantasize reentering his mother's body and emerging strong and undamaged. This was a fantasy play related to oedipal and preoedipal unconscious wishes. It was also a way to repair the damage that he had unconsciously felt his mother caused him.

Another wish to be corrected was also enacted in Joe's analysis, in that he viewed each hour as part of the transformation he wanted to undergo in the direction of being cleansed and legitimized. This presented a good opportunity to work on his self-image, which was rigid and inclined toward resisting change until special attention was paid to this area.

His satisfaction in finding that he could recover, through the analysis, some of the feelings that he had frozen and almost lost seemed to increase Joe's inner strength and our working alliance. This enabled him to invest in psychic work instead of remaining addicted to a fantasy life devoted to correcting his past failures and humiliations.

REFERENCES

Balter, L., Lothane, Z., and Spencer, J. H. (1980). On the analyzing instrument. *Psychoanalytic Quarterly* 49:474–504.

Kris, A. O. (1983). The analyst's conceptual freedom in the method of free association. *International Journal of Psycho-Analysis* 64:407–411.

Mitchell, S. A. (1988). *Relational Concepts in Psychoanalysis: An Integration.* Cambridge, MA: Harvard University Press.

Moses-Hrushovski, R., and Moses, R. (1989). *"Deployment" in self-defeating persons—a specific configuration met in the treatment of self disorders.* Presented at Austen Riggs, Stockbridge, MA.

Rangell, L. (1981). From insight to change. *Journal of the American Psychoanalytic Association* 29:119–125.

Winnicott, D. W. (1971). *Playing and Reality.* London: Tavistock.

4

TREATING A SELF-DISORDER IN A HOMOSEXUAL YOUNG MAN

Daniel was 28 years old when he came to me for analysis. His aim was to clarify his sexual direction, for he did not know whether he was homosexual or heterosexual. He saw the problem as a lack of desire and he did not bring it up until a year later. Otherwise everything was "OK." He was "OK" with his family; he went through everything "OK" in the army; and at work they thought he was "OK." His lack of emotional content was striking.

Daniel described his father as someone who did not talk about personal matters and was not interested in becoming emotionally involved with others. The father was often very busy with his computer business. Daniel was ashamed of many facets of his father's behavior. In addition to showing a remarkable lack of tact, the father would often explode in inexplicable rages. In addition, Daniel felt he ate loudly and grossly and wore shabby-looking clothes. As far as Daniel could remember, he had never called him "Dad," since he did not perceive his father as such. He always envied children who spoke with pride about their parents. His embarrassment about his father's behavior kept him from bringing his friends home. All Daniel's efforts went into ignoring his father and distancing himself from him, both in his everyday life and in his analytic work.

Daniel portrayed his mother as a bitter woman, who made her bitterness evident to all and made them feel it was their fault. She was unable to find a job, although she had a B.A. in education. Daniel always had the feeling that he had to choose between his parents. Among the two, it was his mother for whom he felt he cared more. It was not until later in his analysis that the intensely domineering nature of his mother came up. Whenever he or other members of the family had opinions or feelings that differed from hers, she would become so offended that he felt he could only survive psychically by complying with her, without saying what he felt and wanted or even thinking it.

Daniel perceived himself as a feather blown about by the wind, with no direction or backbone of its own. He had few memories of his childhood. He did remember that he enjoyed being the first son and grandchild, until his sister was born when he was 4 years old. At age 7, he remembered, there was a split in his mind: at home he liked to play with his sister, but at school he felt ridiculed when playing with girls. Children teased him, and called him "Daniella." When he was 9 he underwent an operation on his bladder. For a long period all he remembered about the operation was the good side, the presents and attention he had received, and the relief he felt after many months of pain and difficulty while urinating. It was not until much later in his analysis that the worries and the shame involved in his urinary problem, and the fears and the guilt about having such a problem, came up.

School was a dreadful experience for Daniel. Socially he felt he did not belong, that the other children were of a higher social class; educationally he often felt behind the others, even though he did well enough to be accepted to university where he received his B.A. degree in accounting. He was so busy with studying to avoid failure that often he felt he functioned like a machine. And he did not know what to do with his free time.

The first time Daniel was free of his mother's apron-strings was when he went into the army, where he often felt "like the shell of a peanut floating on the water." Not knowing what was expected of him there, he tried to shirk duties whenever possible.

For quite a long time after he began his analysis Daniel would enter the room hastily, almost running to the sofa. He transmitted a combination of "eagerness to get the right food" together with an embarrassment to be seen in his "weakness." His facial expression was frozen, his body was tense. Everything was said in a monotonous tone, without expression or affect. He would talk briefly about his activities but found it hard to relate to his feelings.

His massive defense was his passivity. Actually, what he would like to do was to sleep on the sofa until I reached some conclusion about his problem. His fantasy wish was that I would enter his body, press some button, and change the direction of what had gone wrong with his life. One opening for understanding his passivity and dependency was made in a session primarily devoted to his fears around the analysis. The expression of his feelings and associations led him to traumatic experiences he had had before the bladder operation. He remembered how difficult he had found it to urinate, the horrible pressure he had felt. In the transference situation, I was the physician who had the tools, who could help him, while he had suffered helplessly under the doctor's care. There were many opportunities to identify passive yearnings, which were condensed in his passive position, and to work them through. Thus, when Daniel said that he would rather have me prick him with a pin to release his tensions than talk, I linked his difficulties in free associating to the traumatic experience of his operation, when he had to wait passively to be treated by others. Then he remembered how careful he had to be not to urinate after the catheter had been removed. At other times, he saw me as his mother, "the boss," who expected him to report his whereabouts to her. He realized that he had been passively resistant to his bossy mother and that he reacted with this behavior everywhere.

One recurring theme was the frustration that Daniel felt with his only friends. They were a couple and he felt all alone when he was with them. He asked himself how he had reached this state where he was so alone while they were together, had a home, and a child. He had not been guided properly—that is the reason for his being retarded; this left him frustrated and betrayed. He felt that his "abnormality"—that he was alone—"stuck out." There was a continuous wailing in the hour, saturated with despair.

In the transference situation, I became a woman trying to seduce him. He had to increase his control in order to avoid the possible dangers. I pointed out that he was making efforts in the direction of being in control to avoid all kinds of dangers—dangers that turned out to be related to his conscious efforts not to wet, not to play sexual games, not to masturbate in public, not to be aggressive, not to say things he might regret. And now I was telling him to take the opposite direction, to give up control!

I acknowledged how difficult and confusing this must be. Rather than waiting for him to bring these things up, I related to his various feeling states and ways of dealing with them, as they were transmitted in the transference and inferred from behavior and associations in the analytic situation (Sandler and Sandler 1978). For a long time he continued to perceive me as the expert who should diagnose his illness and cure him while he was asleep. Various feeling states such as wishing to be the baby and to be fed, a fear that he was going to die, and a suspicion that the physicians hide the information from him—all seemed to be condensed. In the analysis we could feel and understand how he unconsciously repeated the experience of being operated on by the doctor, who assumed all the responsibility for his well-being. I felt that heavy pressure was being exerted on me to do something to alleviate Daniel's state of suffering and to give him back the peace of mind he had lost. Much of this suffering related to the severe shame, the subject of which he was reluctant to open up and explore. Thus he felt miserable and rejected (Levin 1971).

I pointed out that by passing his inner pressures on to me he was trying to rid himself of them, and also make me feel what he had felt when he had had experiences that he could not discuss with his parents then—and with me now—without the fear of being ridiculed. Daniel then remembered that his mother used to claim that he would often pressure her to help him relieve his boredom. From the context of these hours we came to understand that his boredom was a reaction to envy and jealousy. Later on, the pathological boredom became related to passive wishes that he had to deny.

Daniel was deployed to see injustice everywhere, that the "good guy" gets less attention, love, and appreciation than the "bad guy." This was his experience at work, and this is what he experienced in analysis—where "other patients get more" from me than he does. And, he remembered vaguely, this was also how it had been at home. But Daniel's memories were not experiences that he lived and could revive. They were more like fleeting pictures that he viewed as if he were an outsider. One such memory was of the time when his grandmother visited the family from abroad for several months, to see his newborn sister. Memories of the unbearable tension in the home, especially between his mother and her mother-in-law vis-à-vis his father's attention, and his fear that it would end up in a catastrophe, came up in his analytic hours. Moreover, the pressure from his mother to take sides in this ongoing battle led to a further shutting-off of his feelings.

Although with time Daniel attained a better understanding of his pathological boredom, his monotonous and expressionless way of speaking continued. It sounded to me like everything he was saying had the same value or lack of value—as if he were not expecting me to listen anyway because I was not really interested in him or in what he had to say. When I pointed out this quality of his speech, Daniel's tendency was to state that it was true: neither I nor anyone else was really interested in him. At times I related to his lack of trust, wondering to what kind of experi-

ences it related. At other times I related to his way of turning
feelings into facts, as a way of collecting ammunition for his
battle, so to speak, and thereby getting me off his back.

Another motivation behind his "toughening" was to avoid
a traumatic fall. It seemed safer to harden oneself than to soften
up or to come emotionally close—only to then be dropped again.

Daniel's set-orientation of placing on others the responsibility for taking away his pain was his way of saying that this
could not be left to him because he was powerless. It was also a
way of regaining what he felt he had lost, namely, the soothing
parent whom he had perceived as turning away from him, especially after his sister's birth. Gradually he came to realize that his
power was actually invested in various entitlements. For instance, he felt that he was now entitled to receive the care that he
had needed so badly in the past, especially when he had been so
envious. Accounts of several events were found to be related to
this sense of entitlement. He was wronged both because he had
been forced out of his place as mother's special favorite whenever
his father returned home from long business trips, and also after
the birth of his sister. He felt, too, that he had always been "the
good boy," who did not make any trouble. How could it be that
his selfish sister came to be favored? This injustice had hurt him
so much that he could not get over it. A great deal of his energy
was invested in proving his point and trying to make others feel
what he had felt; only then he could feel that he was understood.
In my countertransference reactions, I felt something that Daniel
seemed to have evoked in me, something that I thought could be
used for exploration toward a better understanding of a covert
transmission: "My feeling is," I said, "that I am a bad mother;
that my food is no good." Whereas what Daniel wants is a
mother who guesses what he needs and provides it willingly.

In my relations with Daniel I felt that I was coexisting on
two levels: talking about the child who was felt to be and was in
fact sulking, but also treating him as an adult, a partner with
whom I shared what I experienced at that moment. Daniel

suddenly remembered a moment when he asked if he could nurse at his mother's breast as his little sister was doing. His mother let him suck, but he knew that it was not the milk he wanted. From the manner in which he talked, I could sense his shame and guilt around his "baby wishes" and his need to satisfy them at the time. This was one of the only experiences in the entire analysis that he hurried to ask his mother about, to see if it had really taken place. His mother confirmed the incident, telling Daniel that one brief suck at the breast had been sufficient for him. Daniel then brought forth some of the fantasy wishes and frustrations he had experienced as a child with his child's thinking: Just as the mother provides care for babies by filling them with milk, she fills the hunger of grown-ups with sex. Daniel, who was exposed to stimulating states by his seductive mother, felt that he was too big for the good milk and too little to approximate the closeness that he witnessed between his mother and his father. Thus he felt especially empty and abandoned in the evenings.

There was a strong need to feel that I was listening patiently and without contempt to his claims before he could give them up. From Daniel's associations I gathered that one of his unconscious intentions was to irritate me to the point where I would lose control, so that the balance between us would thereby be restored. He wanted to feel that he was not the only one who behaved shamefully, like a child, but that I, his analyst, was not that controlled or "perfect" either.

Daniel continued to complain: He lived a "dog's life." He got up, went to work, and ate. He worried about how he would occupy himself in the evenings, when he had nothing to do but go to sleep. The fear of this void was constantly threatening to him. Gradually it became transformed into fears, worries, and doubts, which he began to unravel: Should he look for a girl? But he was not attracted to girls at this stage. Then his heart would start pounding from fear that he would not be able to fulfill a girl's expectations.

I tried very hard not to be infected by Daniel's despair, to be guided instead by the manifold signs of the context in order to reach the "erased" experiences that were the source of this despair. When he expressed his wish to leave the country, I pointed out that "doing something" was his way of distancing himself from his distress. I showed him that he had a need to seek the correction of what hurt him so much outside of himself, so that he would not have to examine it; that he was waiting for changes to "come by themselves."

Daniel had a strong tendency to dissociate himself from his emotional experiencing. He literally wished to get out of his skin, to erase emotional experiences that were painful and hurting. Just like his desire to leave his body behind him when he wanted to free himself from the shame of his body and his family, Daniel also wanted to escape his country, as if by so doing he could free himself from his internalized object—his critical mother—whom he could never please. "Abroad," he said, "there is flexibility, there are open spaces, where one can run and move as one wishes—even naked—without being pressured all the time and looked down upon." At this point, he talked about his tendency to shunt aside all irrelevant details and to say only what is purposeful. I pointed out his tendency to maintain control and his need to shut out all his weaknesses to avoid being humiliated. Then a fleeting memory came to him that his mother—who ran a kindergarten for several years—had transferred him to someone else's kindergarten because he once took off his pants in front of the other children.

One of his unconscious fears was that if he lost control he would go into the street naked and be ridiculed and punished. Although this fear was related to Daniel's exhibitionistic drive, which came up in different phases of his analysis and was a source of previously disavowed guilt, it was no less related to his strong need to liberate himself from all the pressures and restrictions weighing on him, and his wish to take off his masks. It was also a provocation against his mother, a fantasy act that he often employed to relieve his tensions regarding her, whom he perceived as both seductive and punitive.

In the second year of his analysis, when Daniel felt more

prepared to talk about the disappointments that he had previously preferred to forget or erase, he decided to open up a topic that he found extremely shameful: his masturbation fantasies and the conflicts they evoked in him. For several weeks he struggled with himself over whether to reveal his secret or not. From the way Daniel described his struggles to reveal or not reveal, I noticed a strong element of seduction. He would show me something and then conceal it, as if he wished to stimulate my curiosity. When I pointed out to him that this is what he had been unconsciously doing, Daniel brought up the dangers he saw in his mind: he feared losing his only source of satisfaction, lest he be like a baby who holds something in his hands and screams with despair when he is suddenly deprived of it. This was also how he experienced his castration anxiety in these sessions, which was tied to conflicts around pacifiers. Daniel also feared that he might become ashamed of something that he did not feel ashamed of while he was alone, only because he was afraid that I would be repelled by it and ridicule him.

The intensity of his guilt, shame, and worries could be felt from the way he divided his life into two periods: before he began masturbating and afterward. Before, he did not have to conceal anything from his mother; afterward, he was always afraid that she would find the stains of semen which proved his "sin." In conjunction with Daniel's feelings in the transference situation that he might provoke my rejection of him, he remembered that he had always been cautious and fearful lest his mother distance herself from him, as indeed she had done when he had an accident in kindergarten and soiled himself. He also remembered that his compulsive masturbation was used as a sleeping pill—to shut off noises from his parents' bedroom, which enraged him. Moreover, he could remember how excited he was when he discovered that he could magically actualize his wish to become an attractive athletic male by imagining such a person while masturbating. Later in the analysis, when he brought up his homosexual impulses, he had the exciting revelation that his wish had all along been that he become an attractive man; that thus a heterosexual rather than a homosexual drive was behind his physical attraction to men (Socarides 1988).

Daniel's anger was turned against me: I appeared in his masturbation fantasies looking him over critically and thereby spoiling his fun. In the course of his analysis we came to see this as serving as a punishment for him in order to keep from suffering unbearable guilt; it was also a punishment imposed by his mother, whom I represented. Later on, his fear of punishment became more clearly related to severe castration fears. It seemed "miraculous" to him that he could fall asleep after masturbating without feeling any guilt or shame; but when he awakened the next morning he felt like a leper. When Daniel would bring up his powerlessness vis-à-vis his compulsive masturbation, he would complain that I should have been able to remove the "cancer" of his addiction to masturbation. He was too weak! The power that he eventually attained in overcoming this addiction became a criterion of the success of his analysis.

At this stage Daniel decided to leave his parents' house to live on his own. He could no longer stand the tensions between his parents, which he had tried to ignore until then, and he wanted to become independent.

While talking about an experience he had one night when he masturbated in order to fall asleep before his parents began their arguments and to avoid hearing their irritating noises, he vividly recollected being worried about having masturbated so much that his muscles would degenerate, and that his excessive activity would cause him to have cancer. The growth he had removed from his bladder was now linked with the fantasy that he had brought this upon himself through his masturbation, accompanied by the shame and fear that he would never be able to be loved and to be potent as a husband. He also remembered how he had panicked and had wanted to run to the police when one of his parents' quarrels reached the point where his father threatened to take out a revolver and shoot his mother. This was now like a breakthrough. Details of the stressful situation, which had been partly repressed and partly denied, came up in the hour in a fluent and vivid way. For a very long time, Daniel remembered, he had gone about with the suspicion that his father might murder his mother or himself, and with the feeling that his father owed him, Daniel, a debt for his not having gone to the police. Daniel was proud he could now speak of this irrational thought without being overwhelmed with shame.

In one of the following sessions, Daniel reported a dream of which he remembered only a part: he and I were talking intimately while somebody was intruding. From associations to the dream he came to express his envy of his "rivals" in the psychoanalytic institute and of my family, and his fear of losing his special place in my life. At the same period, dreams and reenactments in connection with a sadistic officer in the army led to a reconstruction of fantasies and fears around his primal scene experiences. Daniel remembered that, while any small noise or low voice in his home would awaken him, a tank passing nearby in the army would not wake him up. He could remember the envy that he felt when his parents were together in their bedroom and he was alone. He felt this loneliness particularly in the evenings, when he would be overcome with shame and guilt about the sexual games he had played with his sister. When these feelings were revived in the transference situation, he was able to attain a better integration of states that had previously been dissociated, and achieved greater tolerance toward his feelings.

It was shortly after these hours that Daniel established his first love relationship with a young woman, for whom he felt what he had "never been able to feel before." "Why did I have to wait thirty years for this happiness?" he asked.

Since the aim of this chapter is to focus on specific segments of the analytic work, I have so far covered the first two years of Daniel's analysis. I shall now mention some relevant subsequent developments in Daniel's analysis and life.

Daniel's girlfriend left him after about a year for a variety of reasons. Instead of expressing his feeling of great pain, he was preoccupied with fantasies of revenge. If only he could find another girl right away, so that the one who had broken off with him would be sorry! Or perhaps he would now turn to the other sex, which is what he in fact did. Previously, he had only had fantasies about men that he wanted both to be with and to become like, but had not had any actual homosexual encounters. After I interpreted this act as one that allowed him to protect himself from experiencing his deep hurt and rejection, he burst into tears, sobbing loudly in his analysis for the first time.

Whereas previously I had been the supporting mother from whom he expected blessings before each difficult test, after his experience of being abandoned I turned into the disappointing mother who punished him for his disloyalty by refusing to guide him—or who had even failed to equip him properly.

Dreams from this phase threw light on Daniel's oedipal struggles. For instance, he had dreamt that wanting to go to a meeting with the woman who was his boss, he instead went to the university, where he had a seminar that he had been given permission to be absent from that particular day. Luckily, he saw a pilot with a small plane, who flew him to the meeting with his boss, so that he was almost on time. He felt greatly relieved that she was not angry with him. Associations led him to recall a movie whose essence was competition for a very prestigious job leading to murder resulting from intense envy. I commented on his recently losing his prestigious relationship with his girlfriend, and that before that he had been displaced in his mother's affection by his sister. Daniel's dream seemed to reveal his murderous impulses toward her. He then realized the deep disappointment and hurt behind his aggressiveness, and the fact that his homosexual activities at this stage were linked to revenge. Through these activities he was transmitting the wish to do without women, to ignore them as if they did not exist, to pay them back "in the same currency" in which they had punished him. In this phase he attacked me in various ways, such as making fun of what I said and expressing his wish to hit me and to end the analysis.

Daniel now began and ended several relationships with men—both emotional and sexual—that were enactments (Stoller

1974) brought into analysis. Daniel then began the long process of working through his unconscious guilt feelings and shame, which were linked to sexual games with his sister, and to the humiliations that he had tried to correct through these enactments. One such correction was that he could now take me with him while he repeatedly tried to overcome his severe shame about all those years when he had felt lonely and alone. His attempt to be "purified" through relationships with respected individuals was another correction: he became attached to a male friend who had similar inclinations but was not ashamed of them. Daniel felt that if such a person, with a Ph.D. in philosophy, who was humane and sensitive, was "like him," then he, Daniel, must also be OK. After a short time, Daniel realized that he was not so much attracted by the sexual satisfaction. Rather, this man was the kind of twin brother he had always wanted to have, to enjoy unfettered and interesting conversations with a man who related to him as an equal and did not have contempt for him. At this stage Daniel could accept and understand the different unconscious wishes that came up around this relationship: his search for a male figure to identify with, which he so lacked because of his detached and distant father; revenge against a woman because of the severe narcissistic injuries she had caused him, by leaving her behind for a relationship with a man. The central meanings behind Daniel's homosexuality were uncovered and worked through: the defense against incestuous wishes and castration anxiety; the search for masculinity through both magical visual identification and sexual intercourse (Socarides 1988); fury at his seductive mother; and a sexualization of affects as a way of controlling unbearable feeling states (Goldberg 1975).

Daniel's fascination with homosexual men gradually decreased, and he began to reestablish relationships with women. Now he felt less ashamed with them, less offended by them, and more loving toward them. One of his best experiences with a girlfriend came when he could share with her—as previously with me—some of the "shameful" events of the distant and not-so-distant past—and still feel accepted by her.

He and a friend went to see the film version of Eugene
O'Neill's play *Long Day's Journey into Night*. He was so happy to
see that his was not the only family with many tensions and
shameful episodes. For the first time he enjoyed a film without a
great deal of action; he could view what was happening in one
room without feeling that he had to escape from it.

When I met Daniel several years after his analysis, he was
the happy father of two children and appeared quite satisfied in
his marriage, work, and social relationships. He said that he was
more relaxed, freer to develop and follow different interests, and
less pressured by expectations. I could see that this was so. Daniel
also mentioned that he now felt young and calmer, in contrast to
the feelings he had had before analysis—that he was old and had
to constantly hurry to accomplish some unknown goal to keep
from being humiliated.

There was also improvement in his symptoms: his self-
esteem was increased, there was less intensity in his feelings of
shame and guilt, and there was no longer the strong need to be on
guard lest he be caught in his lies. Though his capacity to feel and
contain tensions grew—and he no longer had to discharge them
immediately through activities and sexualization—there still remained a tendency to sexualize affects.

What I experienced as the most striking change in Daniel
was the more lively expression he had on his face. Unlike the
severe dissociations through which he had protected himself in
the past, it seemed that there was now more contact between his
feelings and thoughts, his imagination and his actions. Through
exploring his sexual identity, Daniel was now able to experience
more of the real self, which had been hidden so deeply that it
seemed to be almost dead.

REFERENCES

Goldberg, A. (1975). A fresh look at perverse behavior. *International Journal of
    Psycho-Analysis* 56:335–342.

Levin, S. (1971). The psychoanalysis of shame. *International Journal of Psycho-Analysis* 52:355–362.

Modell, A. (1975). A narcissistic defense against affects. *International Journal of Psycho-Analysis* 56:275–282.

Sandler, J. J., and Sandler, A. M. (1978). On the development of object relationships and affects. *International Journal of Psycho-Analysis* 59: 285–296.

Socarides, C. W. (1988). *The Preoedipal Origin and Psychoanalytic Therapy of Sexual Perversions.* New York: International Universities Press.

Stoller, R. J. (1974). Hostility and mystery in perversion. *International Journal of Psycho-Analysis* 55:425–434.

5

SHAME, GUILT, CORRECTION, AND ENTITLEMENT IN THE DEPLOYED PATIENT

Joe (Chapter 3) was the first patient whose deployment intrigued me. He was sensitive, caring, responsible in many ways, yet so extremely stubborn and wrapped up in his power struggle with his father—as well as with any other adult who was emotionally unavailable—that nothing else in his life seemed to matter. "The only thing left for me after all the years that I have suffered as the victim of power abuse and humiliation," he said once, although it was very often transmitted, "is to document the causes of my suffering so that justice will be done and other children will perhaps profit once the adults can feel, understand, and change." Joe's strong determination was to prove how the "others" had wronged him and his siblings. Only this would make him happy! After all the years of torture, how could he forget? Nor did he feel he should forgive! For, "Mankind forgives scoundrels and rapists too quickly!" He did not want to become immune to suffering as everyone around him seemed to be.

Joe's deployment into the narrow desire to document his suffering was not merely a defense, such as rationalization; nor was it a fight that would prevent him from having to feel his troubles. His anxiety, his rage, his envy and sibling rivalry, and his guilt relating to both oedipal and preoedipal conflicts had already been worked through with some personal change and growth. But there was a political element, a kind of mission, that was strongly and continuously felt until the end of his treatment: to fight for the emotional rights of children, so they would not fall prey to abusers. It was not simply a character resistance; it was a deployment that I later saw in other patients—a specific configuration of a narcissistic disorder.

These deployed patients were like soldiers who had to wait until the war was won before they were able to begin their own lives. Until then there was no taste for introspection of what they felt, thought, or wanted from life. Obstacles to their real and full self-participation in the analysis and in life directed me in my clinical work.

The *psychic energy* of such patients is largely invested in (a) being constantly on guard, prepared for accidents or catastrophes that might occur if they let go and give up control—they would be trapped; (b) dissociating themselves from emotional experiencing by putting aside feelings in general, especially those feelings that are unpleasant, confusing, or contradictory; (c) focusing on the problems in others while attempting to avoid feelings and remembering events that threaten the integrity of their own self; (d) trying to prove their rightness and worth, and obtaining legitimization for feelings and deeds that cause them unconscious guilt; (e) attempting to actualize in fantasy the wishes to correct and receive compensation for the mental suffering inflicted on them in the past, which was the cause of their self-effacement and self injury. Such patients attempt to erase the disintegrating feelings aroused whenever they perceive the danger of being ridiculed and humiliated.

Like Joe, the other patients described in Chapters 1 to 4 almost all exhibited a *one-track-minded orientation* owing to their *vulnerability*, which narrowed their perceptions and actions. Just as people under the pressure of hunger primarily tend to see food and think about how to get it, these deployed individuals under the pressure of an often unidentified and unexpressed insult, constantly orient themselves toward perceiving an insult and dealing with it.

All the deployed patients I have seen use the mechanism of *dissociation* in a manner similar to what Kernberg found to be characteristic of patients with character pathology and borderline personality organization (Kernberg 1970). Their aggression takes the form of the humiliated fury that accompanies the shame as described by Lewis (1987), although oral roots of demandingness and anal masochistic elements are strongly present.

A *pervasive sense of shame* is also typically seen. The deployed patients feel crushed, diminished, and helplessly exposed to humiliation and shame. Shame is spread over everything: their body, their past, their family. The pain of shame is so acute, and such a disorganizing experience, that they are anxious to do anything to avoid feeling it. Their feeling of shame is similar to that what Grunberger (1971) has described:

> Each time the child is confronted by an instinctual impulse that has not been narcissistically enhanced and integrated, this want of narcissistic confirmation will renew the pain of his narcissistic wound. He is reminded of his paradise lost and in contrast to his earlier narcissistic omnipotence he has a searing sense of inadequacy and insignificance and fantasy that can be compared with shame. Shame that the ego feels before its ego ideal. [p. 224]

The deployed patients experience shame as worse than death. A basic aspect of this shame involves a split in their self, which is reenacted in the transference situation when they simultaneously experience themselves as shamed—desiring to hide because they feel ugly, bad, worthless—and as shaming, identifying with the "shamer" (Morrison 1986). They endeavor to shame others through contempt and disrespect, seeing the world as evil and wanting to leave it in many self-defeating ways.

As with shame, the feeling of *humiliation* is also central to deployed patients: they feel humiliated and want to humiliate in turn. Underneath their deployments is the fear that something is wrong with them, and they perceive this as a self defect. A common metaphorical theme was the humiliating image of the *self as damaged*, the experience of having been traumatized in some irreversible fashion by events in one's past, for example, having been crushed in an earlier relationship with caretakers (Mitchell 1988). There was a strange mixture of power and powerlessness in these deployed patients. On the one hand, there were signs of a weak sense of self when some of them described themselves as feeling like a feather being blown about by the wind with no direction or backbone of their own. On the other hand, they indicated powerful tendencies to be in control and to control others, which might have been caused by the specific configuration of their pathogenic background.

Reconstructions and other information allow us to infer that the deployed patients described suffered not only, or even primarily, from what they fantasized about their past, but rather from actual abusive experiences—always modified by what they perceived and fantasized. They were dominated by the *sense of nothingness* described by Franz Kafka in his *Letter to His Father* (1966):

> As a father you have been too strong for me. . . . I was quite obedient; but it did me inner harm. . . . If I were asked what was your influence on me—it would be difficult to answer. It is so because of some fear which I still feel, a feeling of zero which often takes hold of me. Even now, writing I feel inhibited. [p. 6]

The feeling of being treated like a piece of furniture that can be moved from place to place without being asked—where there is no chance of being listened to or taken seriously as a feeling human being—was one ingredient of the home atmosphere that froze the deployed patients internally and drove them into such deployments as retreating into fantasy life while hiding their real self, assuming roles in which their real selves have become lost, or acting compulsively to prove their worth and restore their self-esteem, while at the same time satisfying their need for revenge. Even though they are sensitive people, many of them became hardened in their battle, as if it were a question of life or death. Since they were under pressure to avoid further bullying and oppression from abusive authorities, teachers, and parents as well as to cleanse the stains of shame and regain the state of harmony which they lost, their creative inner space was restricted.

There is a special mixture of shame and guilt that characterizes them. As Adler (1989) says, the role of guilt feelings in such patients is significant, though not easily detected. Adler has found that both borderline patients and those with narcissistic personality disorders experience intense guilt in addition to humiliation and shame. They exhibit an archaic primitive superego in which guilt is experienced in a harsh all-or-nothing way and is readily projected onto the therapist, who is then viewed as malevolent and angry. This unadmitted and disavowed guilt has been found to be one of the major motivations behind the deployments that direct such patients in their treatment as well as in their lives.

Another element that drove my deployed patients into self-defeating patterns was their excessive *sense of entitlement* (Moses and Moses-Hrushovski 1990). Their conviction that they had the "right" to be consoled, supported, and corrected—instead of being rebuked and criticized as happened in the past—increased their inner passivity and self-pity, which further weakened them.

The entire personality of the deployed patients I have seen has been focused on a system of positions, roles, and attitudes designed to protect their self-esteem. Since these attitudes were assumed in the past and have remained rigid and unchanged, they hindered real self participation. Some typical positions enacted by deployed patients were: having an attitude of contempt toward others' "low standards," adopting the role of victim, seeming cooperative externally but not yet being appeased, feeling they had been wronged, postponing what has to be done until justice has been effected, and assuming the role of righteous counselor. In all these positions deployed patients were sitting on the fence and refrained from investing themselves in either their analysis work or their lives until real inner collaboration with the analyst was achieved in the working alliance. A central difficulty in the analytic work with many deployed patients, apart from their ability to build and maintain a good enough working alliance with the therapist, is related to the task of free associations. They claim that, since they have spent their whole lives trying to gain control (not to wet, not to be aggressive), they find it frightening to be expected to go in the opposite direction, that is, to give up control and free associate.

Their major form of communication was *to act and enact*. This protected them from being drowned by instinctual stimuli and allowed them to distance themselves from unbearable distress. Thus, Daniel (Chapter 4) ran through life speedily, trying to leave out his frozen and chaotic emotional life. His wish to disown parts of his self was so desperate that he embodied it in the strong desire to "get out of" his skin, to "leave" his body, his family, his country.

All the deployed patients I have worked with also presented a massive use of *projective identification*, that is, of freeing themselves of contact with parts of their own minds by exerting pressures on the other. Projective identification was one aspect of the omnipotent balance that such patients needed to establish in order to protect the power imbalance they suffered from.

The analysis of my deployed patients has mostly taken place under the sign of their corrective motivation through dreams, fantasy wishes, and acts. In every case, the satisfaction of trying to undo past injuries—at least in their fantasy—seemed more important than enjoying their present lives.

Joe loved to parachute from airplanes, as if this allowed him to reenter his mother's body and to emerge strong and undamaged. It was a fantasy play related to unconscious oedipal and preoedipal wishes. It was also how he tried to repair the damage he felt, unconsciously, that his mother had caused him. What intrigued Joe most about psychoanalysis was the notion that there is a circle of potential human capacity and energy, and that psychoanalysis helps increase the area of that circle that was at a person's disposal. It seemed as if he wished to give birth to a new version of himself, a stronger and more creative one. Through his care for abandoned kittens, he reenacted feeling states that he then became more ready to explore, express, and work through—feelings of his own suffering that were also intermixed with feelings and fantasies about the children that his mother had miscarried.

Daniel's whole being shrank into the position of the pitiful person whose set was to wait for something to happen to correct the injustice before he could begin his real life. His feeling of entitlement was that he had the right to be soothed instead of rebuked when he had accidents or failed. In the effort to reparatively correct his self-image, he was driven to display his failures in order to obtain what he craved so much: to be treated in a way that would make him feel that he was neither evil nor repellent, but rather worthy and loved. He was preoccupied with the fantasy wish of correction, with waiting for his "rebirth," at which time he would mystically enter a new body and be transformed into an attractive person.

As part of the consoling reparative function, Daniel utilized his passivity and self-pity to force me, his analyst, as well as meaningful others, to take responsibility for his plight. It was the task of myself and these others to correct Daniel's situation by acknowledging our role in the injustices done him, to feel sorry for this, and to compensate him for what he had suffered in the past (Moses-Hrushovski 1986).

Since my deployed patients were unable to contain existing tensions such as shame and guilt, they built a *corrective program* into themselves, tending to perceive each session as part of the transformation they wished to undergo in the direction of being cleansed and legitimized. Gradually, they came to differentiate between the times when they were using their position of *being a victim* to enact the childhood situations to be corrected, when it was more a battle against those who had wronged them, and when they were mobilizing the role of victim in order to prevent themselves from being accused of aggressiveness, envy, or greed.

But it is not until the major sources of their disavowed guilt is reached and worked through (Adler 1989, Sandler and Sandler 1987) that the deployments soften, the sense of entitlement decreases, and the direction of their psychic energy investment changes from a self-defeating into a self-developing one.

Because deployments are often ego-syntonic, it was difficult for both the patient and others to distinguish when certain tendencies and positions were part of their identity, their real self, and when they were deployments against feelings. This was particularly true in the case of Daniel, who redefined his identity while examining his homosexual tendencies, after his physical attraction to men changed in consequence of his working through his conflicts and feelings from frozen and encapsulated states of the past. Thus, the recognition of these patients' deployments and their transformation back into the feelings and feeling states that have been erased in the service of their self survival, is essential to the process of searching for their real and complex identities.

REFERENCES

Adler, G. (1989). Uses and limitations of Kohut's self psychology in the treatment of borderline patients. *Journal of the American Psychoanalytic Association* 37:761–787.

Grunberger, B. (1971). *Narcissism*. New York: International Universities Press.

Kafka, F. (1966). *Letters to His Father*. New York: Schocken Books.

Kernberg, O. (1970). A psychoanalytic classification of character pathology. *Journal of the American Psychoanalytic Association* 18: 800–822.

—— (1987). Projection and projective identification: developmental and clinical aspects. *Journal of the American Psychoanalytic Association* 35:795–821.

Lewis, H. B. (1987). *The Role of Shame in Symptom Formation*. Hillsdale, NJ: Lawrence Erlbaum.

Mitchell, S. A. (1988). *Relational Concepts in Psychoanalysis: An Integration*. Cambridge, MA: Harvard University Press.

Morrison, N. K. (1986). The role of shame in schizophrenia. In *Essential Papers on Narcissism*, ed. A. P. Morrison, pp. 51–57. New York: New York University Press.

Moses, R., and Moses-Hrushovski, R. (1990). Reflections on the sense of entitlement. *Psychoanalytic Study of the Child* 45:61–77. New Haven, CT: Yale University Press.

Moses-Hrushovski, R. (1986). Interpretation of the present or the past. *Bulletin of the European Psychoanalytic Federation* 25:15–25.

Sandler, J. J., and Sandler, A. M. (1987). The past unconscious, the present conscious and the vicissitudes of guilt. *International Journal of Psycho-Analysis* 68:331–341.

6

COUNTER-TRANSFERENCE WITH DEPLOYED PATIENTS

THE PHENOMENON OF COUNTERTRANSFERENCE

I consider countertransference to be everything the therapist feels while working with the patient—his or her emotional reactions to the patient's feelings, attitudes, activities, fantasies—in other words, the therapist's overall resonance to the patient's personality and presentation.

In recent years the totality of the analyst's or therapist's personality has received increasing attention. Today, therapists and analysts are perceived of as delicate analytic instruments (Balter et al. 1980), for both research evidence and clinical observations leave no doubt that, although it is difficult to isolate and identify the most salient dimensions of this force, the therapist's personality can be either a positive or a negative force in the therapeutic encounter (Goldberg 1989, Hamilton 1990). Gill's position (1987) is that the basic integrating point of view of psychoanalysis should be that of relations between people: "Person seems to me on the one hand to encompass self, object

127

relationship and interpersonal theories, and on the other to be relatively free of the connotations these terms have acquired in our battles" (p. 20).

As Strupp (1971) says: "The patient reacts to the therapist's overt, but also to his nonverbal hidden intentions, and the therapist reacts to the patient's reactions to him. It's truly a transactional process" (p. 322). What seems to matter most is the readiness to regard our attitudes as part of our analytical instrument and as a crucial part of what influences our work (Hurwitz 1986). Indeed, it is surprising that despite the widely accepted notion that attitudes are always part of the overall picture (Bergin and Strupp 1972, Greenson 1967, Rogers 1969, Strupp 1971, Will 1987), so little is known about them. Perhaps this is because we take it for granted that therapists always have the "right attitudes"—attitude here meaning much more than the therapist's style. Bennett Simon (1989) says, on the basis of his analytic experiences with four analysts, that the personal style and character traits of the analyst do matter considerably.

There are personal attitudes such as tact, emotional involvement, aloofness, and the exhibition of hope or resignation. There is an attitude of affirmation (Schafer 1983), which may affect the entire analytic process and its outcome. Weigert (1954b) discusses the importance of flexibility in psychoanalysis. Compassion for the patient, although it must be restrained, is an essential attitude if the analytical work is to be successful (Greenson 1967, Racker 1968). Adler and Buie (1979) speak of the reliable capacity to sustain, which is an inherent part of the therapist's personality. Most crucial is the provision by the therapist of adequate support to keep the experience of aloneness within tolerable bounds as the underlying issues, including the patient's rage, are examined (Adler and Buie 1979). Attitudes may also refer to one's relationship toward the use of feelings in the analytic situation and toward one's use of imagination in the attempt to work as creatively as possible.

Hurwitz (1986) compares the difference in the attitudes of his two analysts in terms of their effects on him. Dr. X's appearance, tone of voice, and style consistently served to activate painful fantasies of being judged; his interpretations often sounded like pronouncements to Hurwitz. In contrast to Dr. X's sarcastic and condescending attitudes, Hurwitz found that the attitudes of Dr. Y, whom he did not experience as aloof, distant, or guarded, led him to feel a degree of relaxation and freedom from anxiety that he could never experience with Dr. X. Hurwitz also discusses Guntrip's experiences with his two analysts— Winnicott and Fairbairn—who also differed greatly in their attitudes. Guntrip (1975) described Fairbairn "as being an essentially nonrelating mirror analyst, a technical interpreter who consistently stayed at an oedipal level." He described Winnicott "as more spontaneous, more intuitive, and more willing to engage in a personal relationship, much more in touch with and able to organize archaic experience" (Hurwitz 1986, p. 460).

Although there are some precise transcriptions of verbal exchanges between patients and therapists, such transcriptions rarely provide information about what the therapist was feeling and thinking, or about his or her attitudes during the sessions recorded. There are not many analysts like Searles (1965), Weigert (1954a), Will (1987), or Winnicott (1947, 1951, 1960), who are able to write about their subjective interventions in a direct and simple way.

There are several reasons that might account for the reluctance of therapists to specify all the emotions they feel during the therapeutic process. One is that—powerful as they are—emotional factors such as feelings and attitudes are often transmitted by tone, gesture, and other expressions that are not easily translatable into words. But the "partners in the enterprise" can usually detect traces of these feelings and attitudes even when the therapists themselves are not quite aware of them or endeavor to ignore and conceal them.

Another reason why therapists do not usually relate their own feelings may be connected with humility or defensiveness. According to Greenson (1967):

> When one describes in detail what one does in psychoanalysis, one reveals not only a great deal of one's intimate involvement

with the patient, but also a great deal of one's personal life in general. There is a feeling of exposure and vulnerability in revealing how one analyzes. Since much of the patient's material is highly instinctualized and evocative, and since the analytic understanding of a patient depends on a special empathic intimacy with him, shame, hostility or fear reactions may arise when exposure of his situation is called for. [pp. 4-5]

In the panel on countertransference, chaired by Tyson (1984), Renik summarized the development of psychoanalytic ideas on countertransference since Freud, that is, first the expansion from a narrow focus on the analyst's unconscious responses to a view that encompasses preconscious and conscious responses to the analytic situation as well (Bion 1967, Klein 1967, Thomson 1980). As Limentani describes it, the analyst's thinking and cognitive processes are constantly under the ebb and flow of his own mental and emotional reactions. While he may sometimes be clearly aware of it, at other times it is felt only on a subliminal level (Limentani 1977). The analyst as he listens to what the patient fantasizes is at his best related to the creative process in literature, music, and art (Kris 1950).

A second development described by Tyson has been the shift from Freud's limited definition of countertransference as the reactions of analysts to patients' transferences, to a broader usage that includes virtually all the analyst's feelings about, and attitudes toward, the patient, as well as their many and varied determinants.

The third direction in psychoanalytic thinking about countertransference—as Tyson pointed out—has been a change in emphasis concerning methods of dealing with it as a phenomenon. In this connection, the fourth development has been an increasing tendency to regard countertransference as an important source of information. Thus Loewald (1986) says: "If a capacity for transference from its most primitive to its most developed form is a measure of the patient's analyzability, the capacity for countertransference is a measure of the analyst's ability to analyze" (p. 286).

Sheldon Roth (1990) describes and illustrates four different forms of countertransference: (a) empathic countertransference, in which the therapist unconsciously shapes and amplifies actual and/or potential facets of his or her personality in response to the transference demands of the patient; (b) unique countertransference, when the therapist and patient have an unfortunate ready-made fit between their personalities that provides marked built-in resistance to the working through of the patient's major transference conflicts; (c) situational countertransference, which relates to the therapist's own special circumstances and those of his or her milieu and surrounding culture; and (d) characterological countertransference, which Roth uses to describe the therapist's built-in attitudes toward the world in general—attitudes that do not relate to the patients.

Paula Heimann, one of the pioneers in the use of the analyst's countertransference as an instrument in clinical treatment, pointed out how countertransference could be utilized as an important tool in psychoanalysis, making a sharp distinction between this and pathological countertransference responses. Heimann (1950) includes in countertransference all the feelings that the analyst experiences toward the patient, for she considers this emotional response to be closer to the psychological state of the patient than the analyst's conscious judgment. The crucial factor in the treatment then becomes the analyst's apprehending these countertransference feelings, that is, containing them, analyzing them, and finding some way to impart their significance to the treatment (Fromm 1989).

How analysts allow themselves to have and experience countertransference, and then to work the feelings through and transform them into useful interventions and interpretations, is one of the many questions that have been raised in the literature. Brenman-Pick (1985) suggests that the real issue of truly deep versus superficial interpretation resides not so much on the level addressed as on the extent to which the analyst has been able to work through the process of countertransference reactions internally. Searles (1965) found that his achievement of an integrated

view of a patient toward whom he had previously been responding on two or more quite distinct and conflicting levels,
was a prelude to the patient's own improved integration. There is
still considerable controversy about the uses to which countertransference information can be put, for example, whether it
should be shared with patients or used only as a diagnostic index.
Ogden (1979) formulates the task of the therapist as needing both
to experience and process the feelings involved in projective
counteridentification.

One of the issues relating to the working through and
transformation of countertransference experiences into useful
information and interpretations depends in part on the objective-
ness and validity of our reactions. Can we analysts trust our own
feelings? How can we safeguard against using our countertransference reactions in a "wild" way? One of the necessary conditions for both of these issues is our capacity to be separate. When
the analyst has a strong sense of self he can be more flexible in
shifting from total identification with the patient to the detachment and separateness that allows one to use one's judgment in a
differentiating way.

Loewald (1986) says that "a significant part is played by the
observations of one's visceral reactions to the patient's material."
If the fantasies and thoughts stimulated by this material are sifted
and appraised judiciously, analysts can process it within themselves and put it to good use for analyzing the nature of the
patient's communications (Loewald 1986). Racker (1957) says
that "true objectivity" is based on a form of internal division that
enables the analyst to make himself (his own countertransference and subjectivity) an object of his continuous observation
and analysis. "Then the observations inferred from the analyst's countertransference may be translated into the realities of
the patient and the patient's inner work" (p. 315). Critically
checking the interpretations based on countertransference reactions against a multitude of other feeling signs transmitted in
actual data from the analytic situation is another way to obtain
validity and reliability (Heimann 1960).

There is within us a delicate mechanism of reality-testing

that guides our power of judgment when we are monitoring our inner reactions and allows us to make the necessary differentiations.

Another issue concerns the neutrality of the analyst as opposed to his emotional involvement. Whereas previously many analysts thought that we should stand by reflectively, without becoming emotionally involved, more analysts now accept the role of the analyst as a "participant observer" (Greenson 1960, 1966, Jacobs 1989). For we analysts work not only with the ego; it is also the w'ego (the we-go) (Emde 1988, 1990.)

The image of the analyst who turns into a blank neutral screen for the patient's projections is no longer accepted. Many feel that scientific neutrality cannot exist in work based on a mutual relationship between the analyst and the patient. Moreover, it is not even desirable to remain aloof and uninvolved because it is only when we are emotionally involved—with the necessary control—that we can reach the wide range of patient feelings and respond to it; it is only when we involve our own feelings and imagination that we can create a climate based on emotional receptivity, participation, and communication—a climate that enables us to reach emotional insights and depth. "For most, if not all, patients in analysis the analyst's emotional investment acknowledged or not by either party is a decisive factor in the curative process" (Loewald 1986, p. 285).

Thus, questions such as those that Rogers (1958) asked himself are relevant:

> Can I be strong enough as a person to be separate enough from the other so that I shall not be depressed by his depression, frightened by his fears, swallowed by his dependence needs? Am I strong enough to be present emotionally as fully as possible, yet not be overwhelmed? Can I be strong enough to feel the patient's fears and depression, yet not be too profoundly terrified by his unconscious terror, fear and rage? [pp. 11–12]

As Heimann (1950) states,

> The emotions roused in the analyst will be of value to his
> patient if used as one more source of insight into the patient's
> unconscious conflicts and defenses; and when these are inter-
> preted and worked through, the ensuing changes in the pa-
> tient's ego include the strengthening of his reality sense so that
> he sees his analyst as a human being, not a God, nor a demon,
> and the "human" relationship in the analytic situation follows
> without the analyst's having recourse to extra-analytic means.
> [pp. 83–84]

Heimann refers to the school of thought that not only acknowl-
edges analysts as having a wide range of feelings toward their
patients, but also recommends that they should even express
them openly at times. This view is based on the idea that such
honesty on the part of the analyst is helpful and in keeping with
the respect for truth inherent in psychoanalysis (Stein 1989).

According to such new conceptions the dynamics of transference and countertransference are influenced by both real factors of the therapist's personality (Greenson and Wexler 1969)
and internal forces of feeling and fantasy, by both events from the
present and from the past, by real perceptions as well as displace-
ments and projections, and especially by the complex interactions among all these elements (Berman 1991).

DEPLOYED PATIENTS AND
COUNTERTRANSFERENCE

In recent years, some of my colleagues and I have experienced
difficulty in our analytic work with patients who present a
unique defensive configuration that I call deployment. These
patients, who had been in analysis with very competent traditional psychoanalysts, claim that with their former analysts—even though they learned to understand their problems
better—they were not touched or did not profit. The patients in
question—twenty-four in all—had disturbances with a predom-

inantly narcissistic pathology. They exhibit deployment, a form of self organization on the conative, emotional, cognitive, and behavioral levels through which they deal with pressures and tensions, primarily of guilt and shame, that they are unable to bear. These forms of deployment are not merely defensive styles, character resistances that we meet in neurotics, but represent rather a way of life that these patients strongly identify with, deploying forces against the subjective experience of psychic pain and other affects. Their prime motivation is to change the other rather than themselves. Deployments are seen as self-programming into a system of attitudes, roles, and positions aimed at protecting the deployed patients' self-esteem, consoling them for the humiliation they have suffered, and correcting injustices. Deployment relates to the total organization of the self that prevents patients from investing themselves fully in the breadth and depth of what really matters.

I shall focus now on the countertransference dilemma, evoked by some characteristics exhibited by deployed persons, that I have experienced in my analytic and therapeutic work, and that has been similarly experienced by some of my colleagues in different and unique ways.

In deployed patients, patterns of action and positions that have been assumed in the distant past often continue unchanged to the present, with no relevance to present needs, capacities or circumstances. As Schwartz (1987) writes: "States of fixity and flexibility in action and intrapsychic structure need to be more thoroughly explored by psychoanalytic observers" (p. 117).

The following are some characteristics of the deployment that evoked specific countertransference reactions in me:

1. The deployed patient is constantly on guard to prevent being trapped again, or taken by surprise. They invest immense amounts of psychic energy in entering and maintaining a tough stance, often to such an extent that they act outwardly and hardly feel anything inside. It is as if they prefer deliberately to ignore a variety of disturbing feelings in order to avoid weakening. In

such circumstances, in which the patients try tenaciously to hang on to their control, there is not enough space for either themselves or for me to be free enough to feel, think, or regress in the service of the ego; or to be imaginative enough to reach a deeper understanding of the unconscious or disavowed experiences that remain hardened. At times I found myself being didactic (e.g., trying to explain to them the importance of giving up control in order to reach their real feelings), which would only revive their vulnerabilities from the past and increase the need to be deployed. It was only when I gained empathy for their strong need for control, as a question of life or death for them, that I could recognize and acknowledge the difficulties involved in their having to give up their control, which in turn enabled the patients gradually to be more spontaneous and free.

2. The blaming processes used by deployed patients are efforts to shift the direction of shame and guilt away from themselves in order to avoid painful and humiliating experiences. Even when this function was understood, it was hard to remain calm and wait for the patients' readiness to take responsibility for their parts, their feelings, their thoughts, their actions, and their fantasies. By turning their shame and blame against the other, the other became the focus of attention. They deliberately rendered themselves dependent on the other in order to obtain the care they felt entitled to, thus weakening even further their sense of self and their capacity to apply problem-solving approaches (Volkan and Rodgers 1988).

I sometimes felt it impossible to be constantly blamed and shamed and still utilize enough empathy (so craved by deployed patients) to learn from the feelings induced what these patients have experienced and to put into words what they had needed to disavow. When they constantly point out what is wrong in the other, exaggerate it, dramatize it, and thereby deploy themselves even further into demanding what they feel they are entitled to, it is not easy to refrain from reacting angrily. At times my colleagues and I have felt that to allow ourselves not only to feel our anger but to voice it in a way that would contribute to a better understanding of these patients' dynamics would enable us to regain our openness and to be more fully receptive to our patients.

3. The compulsive repetitions of these attitudes and behaviors are related to the fantasy wish of deployed patients that if only they could be empathized with repeatedly, no matter how they behaved, this would correct their experience of being accepted only on condition that they fulfill the other's expectations. They need to reenact a complaining relationship with the analyst, emphasize their victimization, and their mistreatment by the analyst as well as by everyone else to the end. They wish to complain endlessly, and they feel that the analyst can tolerate it in order to correct their experience with parents who took complaints as an indication of their being evil. They feel entitled to obtain what they had missed and to be absolved from guilt for their rage (Coen 1989). They feel strongly that they will only cease to feel themselves to be evil once they can feel accepted for what they are—no matter what they do. Only then would they be ready to take on responsibility and live in reality rather than in fantasy. It was difficult not to be terrorized by the heavy pressures on the one hand, yet not distance myself emotionally from them on the other hand.

4. The fight against abuse that is omnipresent relates to the sexual, physical, or psychological abuse that is often part of the history of deployed patients. They are extremely vulnerable. Their tendency to discern offenses and to speedily offend others in order not to feel overwhelmingly offended endangers all that has been built up in their treatment (Fraser 1981). A serious difficulty in treating them is that they live the abuse in the transference relationship to such an extent that it may turn into a "transference psychosis."

Fighting for their cause both directly and indirectly, and also fighting against the abusive world, does not leave them enough free space to experience what is happening in their present lives in its overall complexity, breadth, and depth. One of my countertransference feelings was that if only the deployed patients who play a power game would "change their gear" and stop their "games," everything would be so different. In fact, such an attitude would only offend them, because they would then feel that they are not being taken seriously. Also, what may seem easy to me is not at all easy for them.

5. Another requirement conveyed through the enactments of deployed patients, especially those who suffered from sexual abuse, is not to be silenced anymore. They want to feel that the analyst in the analytic situation, and the meaningful others in their life, can take their constant complaints and whining without being repelled by it and without taking it so personally as to feel guilty for their inability to help, and thus themselves become helpless and despairing. Unconsciously, the patients are driven to exert pressure on the analyst, through numerous vehicles, to be on their side and not collude with the abuser—be it a parent, a sibling, a relative, or a stranger. To feel the despair they experienced in the past now in the present and yet preserve hope is often a difficult task. To constantly cast us in the roles they need us in, without our acting on them, is quite demanding.

6. Another characteristic feature of deployed patients in the analytic situation is that they communicate more through enactment than through the content of their free associations (Boesky 1982, Rangell 1968). Therefore, I had to rely almost exclusively on my countertransference reactions to try and identify the patients' feelings and fantasies, and to then transmit them in such a way that the deployed patients could both recognize and accept them.

I felt that these characteristics of the deployed patients required new thinking on my part. For instance, a deeper understanding of their sense of entitlement (e.g., that others must always accommodate to their needs) enabled me not only to overcome my impatience and irritation at what at times seemed to me *chutzpah*, but also facilitated my using these deployments to find meaningful ways of reaching the sources of their having become stuck in open or hidden power conflicts. As Gill (1984) says, "The compulsion to re-experience and re-enact the past is a major motivation for the selective attention with which the patient experiences the present as he constructs his plausible understanding of it" (p. 165). One of the most common roots of this conflict relates to the deployed person's vulnerability to being designated as the crazy person or pervert in the family. The repetition compulsions are therefore designed and enacted in order to force the others to finally own up to their responsibility for making the deployed patients act crazy or feel egocentric and evil. This would then also decrease the amount of guilt that deployed patients feel compelled to disavow as long as they are carrying the others' guilt in addition to their own.

When I came to view enactment as a special form of remembering, as a legitimate vehicle of communication rather than primarily as acting out, in its derogatory meaning, a different emotional climate began to be created. This was an affirmative climate rather than one where patients once again seemed not to measure up to expectations, a reexperiencing of their past trauma.

THE PSYCHIATRIC HOSPITAL SETTING

At the Austen Riggs Center, I had the opportunity of studying the complicated dynamics of deployed patients in a hospital environment, clinically and theoretically. The intense countertransference that I experienced while working with four deployed patients, as therapist or interim therapist, taught me much about the feelings, attitudes, developmental frustrations, and traumatic experiences of patients that might otherwise have escaped my comprehension.

The four patients I will discuss to illustrate my countertransference reactions are John, a psychotic patient, 35 years old;

Jim, a 30-year-old schizophrenic patient who had been at Riggs
for several years; Mary, an 18-year-old who came to Riggs after
several suicide attempts; and Bryan, 20 years old, who suffered
from depression.

John

At one of our first meetings, John arrived with a library book
from which he enthusiastically read me a passage. I shall present
this experience in some detail as I have felt its impact in my work
both with John as well as with other patients. The passage in
question reads as follows:

> In a psychiatric clinic a physician observed a mentally ill
> woman for several months. For over ten years she has to go to
> a window every morning and stare into the courtyard. She no
> longer experiences anything; she is unapproachable, motion-
> less, rigid and mute. The physician begins to devote even more
> time to this woman. He hovers around her, appears late at
> night and early in the morning and tries to start a dialogue with
> her. Everything seems hopeless. One evening the physician
> suddenly turns to the woman who is standing at the window as
> usual and tells her with great urgency that he had observed her
> without interruption all night and all day. He himself cannot
> explain how he came to react in this manner. The woman is
> completely astonished and turns around to speak with the
> physician. She is completely changed and the next morning
> begins working in the laundry. The physician has succeeded to
> establish a dialogue. He loosened up the playful aspect of his
> omnipotence fantasy—to attempt the most improbable thing
> of all: to reestablish a dialogue with this unapproachable pa-
> tient. He found a dialogue which allowed the sick woman to
> abandon her rigidity. He did not suddenly take the sick woman
> unawares or trick her: instead he succeeded in establishing a
> dialogue.
>   Society and all members who see themselves as normal
> regard perverts with the same rigid look with which the

woman stared into the courtyard—they are emotionally unapproachable, rigid and mute. In my comparison, as absurd as it may sound, they are the pervert. [Morgenthaler 1988, pp. 141–143]

This passage symbolized for me the truth that I could only establish a real dialogue with patients when I was able to leave aside the rescue fantasies that I had at times. When I could free myself from rigid, impersonal attitudes I made a constant attempt to establish an emotional climate in which the patients felt that they were being treated respectfully—a climate in which reciprocity and the common human sides were both recognized and felt (Balint 1968).

In the meetings that followed John told me that he had been hospitalized in seven psychiatric hospitals for varying periods of time. But he had never been able to open up or talk about what he felt. All that the former hospitals had been interested in, he felt, was in giving him medication that would numb him. Austen Riggs, he said, was the first hospital where he felt a different approach. For many sessions he feared that he would be tricked, but he also hoped that, this time, something good would happen to him. In his fantasy he played a double role: that of the woman in the passage from the book who had given up yet who still, somewhere, hoped to be approached in an unconventional way; and that of the physician who desired to establish a dialogue with the sick woman, but in vain.

In the sixth month of treatment, John announced that our best therapy hour was the one in which I had said "John, right now, I feel psychotic!" This statement was an expression of my confusion about when he actually meant what he said and when he was acting manipulatively in order to blur his meaning and mix me up. But, when he heard what I had said, he looked relieved and happier than I had ever seen him. "That was the first real thing you said today! It was a personal 'I.' It was so real." Upon which I laughed. "And your laughter is like a hug for me!

For now I see that you can feel and understand what was driving me crazy!"

John referred to this moment as the best hour he had had in several different contexts (Moses-Hrushovski 1992). He did not primarily stress his parents' blame to disavow his own guilt for acting crazy; rather, he was expressing the hope that what had not been acknowledged by them in a real way could perhaps at last be felt and understood. Then he would not be driven so automatically to demonstrate the others' faults, and would be more willing to acknowledge his own part in the "defeating and self-defeating race" he had been running for so long.

Jim

From the very beginning of my work with Jim, a 30-year-old schizophrenic, I was able to figure out and untangle a mixture of his feelings, feeling states, and fantasies that had a complex impact on me. The working through of my countertransference reactions with Jim enabled me to tease out those elements that were relevant to opening up, understanding, and reconstructing development phases and issues that he had reenacted in his treatment.

At times I felt myself responding to Jim as if he were a hungry baby—and as if I were not giving him the food he was so eager to have. Early on he made it clear to me in various ways that he needed to see me more than the regulation four hours of treatment a week. For quite some time, he insistently demonstrated how difficult it was for him to be on his own every weekend—namely at the Riggs Inn with other staff members and patients, but without therapy. I would feel guilty. I felt I was rigidly following some norm without being able to respond to Jim's unique pace and needs. I was very worried that he might harm himself as he feared and threatened he would. Jim's eagerness to come to the therapy session, his coming to his early morning sessions carrying his breakfast without having had time to eat it, demonstrated that it was not that food for which he hungered, but mine. This paralleled what he felt at home, where it had been his nanny's food that he preferred, or that of his father, who unlike his mother at least saw that he was "hungry" and sent him for psychotherapy, although he was not able to provide the right food himself. All this was done with the intent of making me feel worried and guilty, especially before I "left" him for the weekend or for my vacation (Roth 1990). Although this was Jim's way of punishing those who he felt were betraying him, there were other motivations as well: he needed to keep reenacting situations until I would feel what he had felt when he was distressed and had nobody to hold him, to understand, to care. But precisely what situations he was thus reenacting was not clear to me for a long time.

There were times when I felt the need to be close as if he were a very sick child who could not be left alone, who kept calling out to me because he was worried and lonely, but who also used his illness to possess me exclusively and to control me. How to be receptive to Jim's emotional needs, which he felt were rarely attended to, and to mirror them (Kohut 1977) without letting him captivate me with his manipulativeness, was a constant problem for me.

The strong sense of entitlement that Jim transmitted in so many ways—and which was often trying for me—was centered especially around his entitlement not to be left alone when he threatened to commit suicide. At times I was so exhausted by Jim's fantastic demands that I felt what Winnicott (1947) has termed hate in the countertransference. It was only after two of his psychotic regressions, which I experienced with him, that I was able to regain more of my empathic capacity to cope with his emotional needs.

In endeavoring to understand exactly what in my behavior and attitudes might have contributed to his psychotic episodes, I asked Jim whether his anger with me had to do with my "letting" his parents take a trip to India. I thought that he would be able to deal with his feelings here—whether his anger was related to my pressure on him to let them go. "Yes, you did not read my mind," came his clear response. Since this came in the midst of his confused utterances, I was quite surprised. "You hoped," I continued, "that I would be sensitive enough to understand that even though you are 30 years old there is a baby part in you emotionally which you are ashamed to acknowledge." Thus, it seemed that through his psychotic episodes Jim was letting me know that I had underestimated his baby parts that were hidden behind his loud protests and demandingness. My not having focused on them verbally sufficiently might have been due to my fear at the rage he directed against me and to my feelings of guilt. As he told me later on, Jim's experience of my being able to feel with his neediness, which he never could admit, and with his terror of being utterly alone in the world—during and after the psychotic episode—brought him some relief. Moreover, the fact that he could experience me as someone who was able to tolerate his despair—as well as his anger—without abandoning him, brought about a change in our relationship.

These were the times when I most appreciated the supportive atmosphere of the staff in the open hospital, in which the staff's spirit of mutual concern, care, and interest in each and every patient was an important therapeutic component. The feeling that I too was being contained, and not left alone with this heavy responsibility, enabled me to contain Jim at the most trying times. It allowed me to provide enough of the feeling of safety needed for my being with Jim in states that he had hitherto had to repress or disavow.

Jim's acknowledgement that I could "feel" with him, together with the support of the rest of the staff, allowed me to move from feeling disturbed, angry, and manipulated whenever I felt Jim's strong sense of entitlement to not be "abandoned" by me for the weekend, to an empathic understanding of the "needy baby parts" of Jim, who had felt totally betrayed and deserted for so long. After his second psychotic regression I could also see and feel how insulted and shamed he felt every weekend when I left, as if what he had exposed to me during his sessions was so repulsive that I had to reject him. Working on my countertransference (Boyer 1989), I felt that the way to deal with Jim's demandingness had been unconsciously to remove myself emotionally. To not distance myself, yet not be terrorized by his heavy pressures, became possible when I could come to be in touch with some of my personal dissociated parts. This, in turn, made it easier for Jim to reach emotional experiences in specific situations of his childhood that he had previously split off through his deployment.

Mary

Mary, an 18-year-old who came to Riggs after several suicide attempts, made suicide threats that worried me. Although I assessed them to be only threats, I also felt that one can never be sure. Mary's militant apocalyptic fantasies reminded me of those who must destroy everyone about them in order to eradicate their own intolerable pain (Ostow 1986). The nature of Mary's suicide attempts was—so I found myself thinking—to wait for somebody to rescue her. She would say: "It's not so much that I am depressed. I need you to prove to me that life is worthwhile." I was struck by a "freezing" that Mary showed whenever I gave her an interpretation in a certain hour. Although she was inviting some response on my part, it seemed as if she was also pushing it away speedily and aggressively so that I felt there was an unidentified panic reaction underneath. When Mary brought up her fear of being "trapped" with everybody, including me, I suddenly asked her whether she had ever been given enemas. She said immediately that she well remembered her childhood constipation, age 7 or 8, when her mother had regularly given her enemas. I then asked how she felt on those occasions. She remembered experiencing some pain, but suffering mostly from the humiliation inflicted on her. When I asked Mary about the enemas, it was an intuitive act; it was not based on clear signs of which I was conscious at the time. But Mary's responding to my question by bringing up meaningful associations, becoming somewhat less guarded and more ready to loosen up in subse-

quent hours, told me that, even when my countertransference
instrument was operating on a subliminal level alone, it could be
used productively.

Bryan

One of the countertransference reactions that I felt impeded my
analytic work was my difficulty in establishing and maintaining
boundaries, such as ending the hour in time. When I reflected on
this after a therapy hour with Bryan, a 20-year-old who suffered
from depression, I thought about the extreme shifts that I often
felt with him—at times so close and intimate and at other times so
distant and detached. I was not always able to identify the specific
circumstances that seemed to bring about such shifts. I asked
myself whether my adopting the role of his lenient nanny was
not just a role enactment (Sandler 1976). Was I also unknowingly
colluding with Bryan against the strict "Mother Riggs"? In this
connection I thought of the split that Bryan enacted—to be
gentle and cooperative with one caretaker (myself) but to be
contemptuous and oppositional against the other (Riggs). After
monitoring some of my critical reactions to certain staff members
and sharing them in one of our morning conferences, I achieved
a more differentiated view of what was being reenacted in this
split. I could alert myself to my personal parts, and then the
enacted split became a source of insight for working on Bryan's
disavowed inner conflicts. Moreover, by coordinating my experience with those of the rest of the staff, I was able to contain the
bitter disappointment with which Bryan was trying to deal
through the split. As Gabbard (1988) says: "The patient's internal split often begins to mend at the time that the staff's
cleavage heals." I will now report part of a therapy hour with
Bryan that took place at this phase.

   I asked Bryan about the quick glance he gave me after which
he avoided looking at me. He responded, with pain, that it was
terrible for him to be so close and then, all of a sudden, to be shut
out of the intimacy of the hour, left all alone, when it was over. "I

get lost then . . . I have to prepare myself for avoiding this blow."
Associations led to night situations when he had been very close
to his nanny but had to leave her room when her husband came.
It seems that through my difficulties in putting limits on Bryan
I was enacting a kind of complementary countertransference
(Racker 1957): the lenient nanny versus his strict mother.

I found that I continued to run over in time at the end of the
therapy sessions with Bryan, although I had decided to hold to
the time limits. I tried to understand my personal motives behind
it. I now began to write down whatever came to my mind, as
freely as it came, after each hour—while continuing to reconstruct the process of the hours themselves as precisely as possible.
I would write down all my feelings, fantasies, and thoughts, as
they came, until a point when I felt some closure in myself. This
often signified exhaustion—a sign that the inner work should be
continued later, when my scattered feeling states and fragmen-
tary thoughts would come together again. Then I would find
myself shifting, from these levels of resonating, back to Bryan as
he was in the hour and letting him be his separate self.

Writing down in a freely associative manner was a procedure that often helped me to reach new territories that unknowingly had their impact on me. It also helped me make peace with
whatever was puzzling or irritating me. While repeating the
echoes that were reverberating within me I would feel that
different layers were touched. The deepest resonance that I felt
around these hours came when I suddenly remembered the tears
I had in my eyes when Bryan mentioned the mother of one of his
friends. "How can one go on living as if nothing happened! She
lived hiding in her own house in Germany after the Gestapo had
taken over . . ." But Bryan, too, lived in exile in his own home
after his nanny had left and his parents behaved as if nothing had
happened.

An important aspect of Bryan's pathology, which became
better understood toward the end of his treatment, threw new
light on the meaning that abandonments had for him. The inhuman element of being suddenly abandoned by his nanny was

represented by the symbol of Germany. Everything else stopped being real to him. Life turned into a battlefield. He fortified himself with the attitude that one should not and could not forgive or forget until wrongs are acknowledged and corrected. This became a kind of mission for Bryan. This occurred when he was 6 years old. After that, he did everything he could to oppose the values of his parents and to avoid letting them or his teachers discipline him.

I knew that much of Bryan's opposition was based on having felt insulted and envious when his younger brother was born after he (Bryan) had been the favorite for years. Still, from the way he talked about his feelings and fantasies, a new dimension was added: an unconscious identifications with the Holocaust survivors, which added to the fuel feeding his constant power struggles in life. This also struck chords within me. It had been an overidentification with a strong emotional element in him that contributed to my difficulty in maintaining boundaries.

I also remembered Bryan's deep resentment—joined by mine—as expressed in the sessions, when values such as efficiency and high achievement took on more importance than what really mattered: his sadness when he talked about his parents always being tense and in a rush to do things, to achieve accomplishments at the expense of being relaxed together and emotionally available to each other. He was always being hurried—to finish everything quickly and to grow up fast! In one of the sessions I mentioned the need to work on a certain problem that came up relating to his contempt. "Work?" he asked. "I thought we are playing," he said. "It is playful work," I commented. He smiled. Some sessions later when I commented on his power struggle with me in the past few sessions, Bryan responded that although he knew that he did this everywhere else, he had not been aware of doing it with me. Nor had I been aware of it before I began working on my countertransference. Afterward, however, I found myself not only freer to set limits when I so chose but also freer to arrive at an increased depth in our understanding. The hunger strikes that he had previously enacted, as well as the anal holding-on to his entitlement to demonstrate and dramatize the previously concealed messiness, also came to acquire different meanings after these sessions.

I shall now illustrate a particular interactive process between the patient's transference and the therapist's countertransference that has been made possible by the safe environment of a psychiatric hospital. After several good therapy sessions, which both Bryan and I felt were productive, I was surprised when he returned from his vacation in terrible shape, trembling, not disclosing to anyone what had happened to him, and anxiously pacing around the room in his therapy hour.

It turned out that he had had sexual intercourse with Ann, another patient. This is itself was against hospital rules, but the main problem was that neither of them had used contraceptives.

First I felt annoyed at Bryan's lack of responsibility and his need to act out in this manner, rather than to talk in therapy about his drives and conflicts. But remembering some similar experiences in my own family helped me regain my capacity for empathy to some extent. After this memory of mine, I felt again able to immerse myself in whatever came up and was transmitted in the hour, able to listen to Bryan's tones, melodies, tensions, as well as to his words. All in all, it sounded to me as if Bryan had enacted a situation in which something terrifying happened as a result of his having been left alone.

I could sense his anguish as he was pacing in the room agitatedly, uttering some fragmented sentences from time to time: "I should die . . . I want to cry . . . but can't. . . . I wanted to feel close . . . to be a man . . . I did not mean to impregnate her. . . . I am the murderer of the baby which will be aborted. Ann said that she enjoyed it. Still, I feel that I did something terrible . . ."

From the guilt I felt at not having given enough space to his sexual impulses toward me in the previous therapy sessions—impulses that were in the air but were not talked about—as well as from other clues that had somehow escaped my attention, I suggested that what he did with Ann was something he wanted to do with me—perhaps thereby protecting me! Bryan nodded sadly and said that it had also been because he liked Ann; he was not only using her. "Perhaps I wanted a child from her. . . . But we don't want it actually!" In later sessions Bryan could talk about his forbidden feelings toward me and fantasies he had felt ashamed and guilty of. But in this session he insisted that all he needed was to be helped to stay with his anxieties—not to understand!

"When would one know whether Mary was pregnant? I did not tell anybody else but you. . . . She feels paranoid about it," were some additional worries he voiced in this session. Then, after some silent moments, he asked me for the first time in his treatment to hug him. Embarrassed at this request, remembering well that I am his therapist, not a friend or a parent, I refrained from hugging him even though I knew that this was what he usually wanted most when he felt so anxious. Instead I gave him my hand. After a few silent moments he said that, when he had really needed it as a child, he never got a hug or even a hand; only words.

My giving him a hand, the difficulties of not knowing, the frustrations of not being able to tell anyone else on the staff about Bryan's predicament—all evoked strong feelings in me and struck echoes in me that were not yet clear in words.

I was conflicted between being loyal to Bryan and Ann—not to "expose" them in public—and following the policy of the hospital with which I usually identified (i.e., to share this information with the rest of the staff in the morning conference). My compromise was to call the clinical director after this session and to ask if she could see me for a few minutes. I then told her briefly about the incident and the emotional context within which it had occurred.

My intense gratitude for the director's calm listening and brief reply—"I trust your clinical judgment"—said in her warm and responsive way when I asked her opinion on the problem of "touching," giving a hand to the patient in certain circumstances, showed me how anxious I had been, and how quickly I could recover and regain my self-confidence—when I felt trust and support. It was several therapy sessions later that Bryan reached a deeply hidden memory of sexual abuse as a child, which until then he had been careful to refrain from telling anybody.

As Searles (1965) says, it seems that therapists must integrate their different views of their patients and respond to them as single persons who can possess different personality facets, before patients are able to subjectively integrate these different heretofore more-or-less dissociated areas into their conceptions of themselves.

SUMMARY

When we regard countertransference as the total responsiveness—conscious and unconscious—to the patient, and when we conceive of the countertransference as a delicate analytic instrument (Money-Kyrle 1956), there is a shift in emphasis—from the analyst's interpretation as the analytic tool, to the analyst who interprets his or her countertransference, feelings, ability to "be with" a variety of distinct feeling states, attitudes, and inner activity. I consider all kinds of attitudes on the part of the analyst (as described in Chapter 7) of paramount importance in treatment, especially in that of deployed patients. To take into consideration the complexity of their capabilities, levels of discourse, and intentions when any of the clinical issues are worked on is one of the many attitudinal elements that contribute largely to the therapeutic atmosphere and the working alliance. To take into consideration the patients' symbolic messages or intentions to change the world so as to make it more sensitive to their feelings and allow individuation without ignoring the aggressive drive and countershame strategies, creates a different quality than to focus predominantly on the aggressive drive, a quality that can affect both the patient–analyst relationship and the therapeutic outcome.

REFERENCES

Adler, B. (1988). Personal communication.

Adler, G., and Buie, D. H. (1979). Aloneness and borderline psychopathology: the possible relevance of child development issues. *International Journal of Psycho-Analysis* 60: 83–96.

Balint, M. (1968). *The Basic Fault: Therapeutic Aspects of Regression*. New York: Brunner/Mazel, 1979.

Balter, L., Lothane, Z., and Spencer, J. H. (1980). On the analyzing instrument. *Psychoanalytic Quarterly* 49:474–504.

Bergin, A. E., and Strupp, H. H. (1972). *Changing Frontiers in the Science of Psychotherapy*. Chicago: Aldine Atheron.

Berman, E. (1991). *The professional affinity between the analyst and the analysand and its influence on transference and countertransference*. Reported to the Israel Psychoanalytic Society, June.

Bion, W. R. (1967). *Second Thoughts*. London: Heinemann.

Boesky, D. (1982). Acting out: a reconsideration of the concept. *International Journal of Psycho-Analysis* 63:39–55.

Boyer, J. B. (1989). Countertransference and technique in working with the regressed patient. *International Journal of Psycho-Analysis* 70:701–725.

Brenman-Pick, I. (1985). Working through in the counter-transference. *International Journal of Psycho-Analysis* 66:157–165.

Coen, S. J. (1989). Intolerance of responsibility for internal conflict. *Journal of the American Psychoanalytic Association* 37:943–964.

Emde, R. N. (1988). Development terminable and interminable. *International Journal of Psycho-Analysis* 69:23–42.

_____ (1990). Mobilizing fundamental modes of development: empathic availability and Therapeutic action. *Journal of the American Psychoanalytic Association* 38:881–915.

Foster, B. (1987). Suicide and the impact on the therapist. In *Attachment and the Therapeutic Process*, ed. J. L. Sacksteder, D. P. Schwartz, and Y. Akabane, pp. 197–204. New York: International Universities Press.

Fraser, S. (1981). *My Father's House: A Memoir of Incest and of Healing*. Garden City, NY: Doubleday.

Fromm, M. F. (1989). Impasse and transitional relatedness. In *The Facilitating Environment: Clinical Applications of Winnicott's Theory*, ed. M. G. Fromm, and B. L. Smith. New York: International Universities Press.

Gabbard, G. O. (1988). Splitting in hospital treatment. Mimeographed. Topeka, KS: The Menninger Clinic.

Gill, M. M. (1984). Psychoanalysis and psychotherapy: a revision. *International Journal of Psycho-Analysis* 11:161–179.

—— (1987). The point of view of psychoanalysis: energy discharge or person. In *Attachment and the Therapeutic Process*, ed. J. L. Sacksteder, D. P. Schwartz, and Y. Akabane, pp. 17–41. New York: International Universities Press.

Goldberg, A. (1989). A shared view of the world. *International Journal of Psycho-Analysis* 70:16–20.

Greenson, R. R. (1960). Empathy and its vicissitudes. *International Journal of Psycho-Analysis* 41:418–424.

—— (1966). That "impossible" profession. *Journal of the American Psychoanalytic Association* 14:9–27.

—— (1967). *The Technique and Practice of Psychoanalysis.* New York: International Universities Press.

Greenson, R. R., and Wexler, M. (1969). The non-transference relationship in the psychoanalytic situation. *International Journal of Psycho-Analysis* 50:27–40.

Guntrip, H. (1975). My experience of analysis with Fairbairn and Winnicott. *International Review of Psycho-Analysis* 2:145–156.

Hamilton, N. G. (1990). The containing function and projective identification. *International Journal of Psycho-Analysis* 71:445–453.

Heimann, P. (1950). On counter-transference. *International Journal of Psycho-Analysis* 31:81–84.

—— (1960). Countertransference. *British Journal of Medical Psychology* 33:10–15.

Hurwitz, M. R. (1986). The analyst, his theory and the psychoanalytic process. *Psychoanalytic Study of the Child* 41:439–467.

Jacobs, T. J. (1989). *The interplay of enactments: some of their roles in the analytic process.* Panel: Enactments in Psychoanalysis. San Francisco, May.

Kernberg, O. F. (1970) A psychoanalytic classification of character pathology. *Journal of the American Psychoanalytic Association* 18:800–822.

Khan, M. M. R. (1964). Ego-distortion, cumulative trauma and the role of reconstruction in the analytic situation. In *The Privacy of the Self*, pp. 59–68. New York: International Universities Press, 1974.

Klein, G. S. (1967). *Peremptory Ideation: Structure and Force in Motivated Ideas.* Psychology Issues, vol. 5, Monograph 18/19. New York: International Universities Press.

154   Deployment

Kohut, H. (1977). *The Restoration of the Self*. New York: International Universities Press.

_____ (1979). The two analyses of Mr. Z. *International Journal of Psycho-Analysis* 60:3–27.

Kris, E. (1950). *On Preconscious Mental Processes: Psychoanalytic Explorations in Art*, pp. 303–318. New York: International Universities Press, 1952.

Limentani, A. (1977). Affects and the psychoanalytic situation. *International Journal of Psycho-Analysis* 58:171–183.

Little, M. (1951). Counter-transference and the patient's response to it. *International Journal of Psycho-Analysis* 32:32–40.

_____ (1981). *Transference and Countertransference*. New York: Jason Aronson.

Loewald, H. W. (1960). On the therapeutic action of psychoanalysis. *International Journal of Psycho-Analysis* 41:16–33.

_____ (1986). Transference–countertransference. *Journal of the American Psychoanalytic Association* 34:275–289.

Loewenstein, R. G. (1958). Remarks on some variations in psychoanalytic technique. *International Journal of Psycho-Analysis* 39:202–210.

McDougall, J. (1978). Countertransference and primitive communication. In *Plea for a Measure of Abnormality*, pp. 247–298. New York: International Universities Press.

Money-Kyrle R. (1956). Normal countertransference and some of its deviations. *International Journal of Psycho-Analysis* 37:360–366.

Morgenthaler, F. (1988). *Homosexuality, Heterosexuality, Perversion*. London: Analytic Press.

Moses-Hrushovski, R. (1992). Transference and countertransference. *International Journal of Psycho-Analysis* 73:561–576.

Moses-Hrushovski, R., and Moses, R. (1989). *"Deployment" in self-defeating persons—a specific configuration met in treatment of self-disorders*. Presented at Austen Riggs, Stockbridge, MA.

Nacht, S. (1962). The curative factors in psychoanalysis. *International Journal of Psycho-Analysis* 43:206–211.

_____ (1964). Silence as an integrative factor. *International Journal of Psycho-Analysis* 45:299–302.

_____ (1965). Interference between transference and counter-transference. In *Drives, Affect, Behavior*, ed. M. Suhur, pp. 315–322. New York: International Universities Press.

Ogden, T. H. (1979). On projective identification. *International Journal of Psycho-Analysis* 60:357–373.

—— (1989). Playing, dreaming and interpreting experience: comments on potential space. In *The Facilitating Environment: Clinical Applications of Winnicott's Theory*, ed. M. G. Fromm, and B. L. Smith, pp. 255–278. New York: International Universities Press.

Ostow, M. (1986). The psychodynamics of apocalyptic: discussion of papers on identification and the Nazi phenomenon. *International Journal of Psycho-Analysis* 67:277–285.

Parson, E. R. (1988). The difficult patient: psychotherapeutic strategies, conceptual, diagnostic and therapeutic dimensions (special issue). *Journal of Contemporary Psychotherapy* 18 (12).

Pick, J. B. (1985). Working through in the counter-transference. *International Journal of Psycho-Analysis* 66:157–166.

Racker, H. (1957). The meanings and uses of countertransference. *Psychoanalytic Quarterly* 26:303–357.

—— (1968). *Transference and Countertransference*. New York: International Universities Press.

Rangell, L. (1968). Symposium: acting out and its role in the psychoanalytic process. *International Journal of Psycho-Analysis* 49:195–201.

—— (1979). Contemporary issues in the theory of therapy. *Journal of the American Psychoanalytic Association* (Supplement) 27:81–112.

Rawn, M. L. (1988). Classics revisited: some thoughts on Strachey's "The Nature of the Therapeutic Action of Psychoanalysis." *International Journal of Psycho-Analysis* 69:507–520.

Reich, A. (1951). On Counter-transference. *International Journal of Psycho-Analysis* 32:25–31.

Renik, O. (1984). Panel: countertransference in theory and practice. Chaired by R. Tyson. *Journal of the American Psychoanalytic Association* 34:699–708.

Rogers, C. R. (1958). The characteristics of a helping relationship. *Personnel and Guidance Journal* 37:6–16.

—— (1969). *Freedom to Learn*. Columbus, OH: Merrill.

Roth, S. (1990). *Psychotherapy—The Art of Wooing Nature*. New York: Jason Aronson.

Sacksteder, J. L. (1989). Psychosomatic dissociation and false self development in anorexia nervosa. In *The Facilitating Environment: Clinical Applications of Winnicott's Theory*, ed. M. G. Fromm, and B. L. Smith, pp. 365–393. New York: International Universities Press.

Sandler, J. (1976). Countertransference and role responsiveness. *International Review of Psychoanalysis* 3:43–48.

Sandler, J. J., and Sandler, A. M. (1987). The past unconscious, the present unconscious and the vicissitudes of guilt. *International Journal of Psycho-Analysis* 68:331–341.

Schafer, R. (1959). Generative empathy in the treatment situation. *Psychoanalytic Quarterly* 28:342–373.

———— (1983). *The Analytic Attitude.* New York: Basic Books.

Schwartz, D. P. (1987). Intrapsychic structure and interaction. In *Attachment and the Therapeutic Process*, ed. J. L. Sacksteder, D. P. Schwartz, and Y. Akabane, pp. 117–136. Madison, CT: International Universities Press.

Searles, H. F. (1965). *Collected Papers on Schizophrenia.* New York: International University Press.

———— (1979). Transitional processes and therapeutic symbiosis. In *Countertransference and Related States: Selected Papers*, pp. 503–576. New York: International Universities Press.

Simon, B. (1989). *Is there a psychoanalytic technique? From on the couch (with an N = 1 (x^4) from someone now behind the couch.* Presented at Austen Riggs, Stockbridge, MA, January.

Stein, S. (1989). The influence of theory on the psychoanalyst's countertransference. *Scientific Proceedings of the Australian Psychoanalytical Society* 16:33–45.

Strupp, H. (1971). Towards a specification of teaching and learning in psychotherapy. In *Brief Therapies*, H. H. Barten. ed. New York: Behavioral Publications.

Thomson, P. (1980). On the receptive function of the analyst. *International Review of Psycho-Analysis* 7:183–204.

Tyson, R. L. (1984). Panel: countertransference in theory and practice. Chaired by R. Tyson. Reported by Owen Renik. *Journal of the American Psychoanalytic Association* 34:699–708.

———— (1986). Countertransference evolution in theory and practice. *Journal of the American Psychoanalytic Association* 34:251–275.

Volkan, V. N., and Rodgers, T. C. (1988). *Attitudes of Entitlement.* Charlottesville, VA: University Press of Virginia.

Weigert, E. (1954a). Counter-transference and self-analysis of the psychoanalyst. *International Journal of Psycho-Analysis* 35:242–246.

———— (1954b). The importance of flexibility in psychoanalytic technique. *Journal of the American Psychoanalytic Association* 2:702–710.

Will, O. A. (1987). Human relatedness and the schizophrenic reaction. In *Attachment and the Therapeutic Process: Essays in Honor of Otto Allen Will, Jr.,* ed. J. L. Sacksteder, D. P. Schwartz, and Y. Akabane, pp. 263–297. Madison, CT: International Universities Press.

Winnicott, D. W. (1947). Hate in the countertransference. In *Collected Papers: Through Paediatrics to Psychoanalysis*, pp. 194–203. New York: Basic Books, 1958. (Also *International Journal of Psycho-Analysis* 1949, 30:69–74.)

——— (1951). Dreaming, fantasizing and living. In *Playing and Reality*, pp. 26–37. New York: Basic Books.

——— (1960). The theory of the parent–infant relationship. *International Journal of Psycho-Analysis* 43:585–594.

Wolstein, B., ed. (1988). *Essential Papers on Counter-transference*. New York: New York University Press.

7

THE ANALYST'S ATTITUDES IN TREATING DEPLOYED PATIENTS

This chapter is based on the treatment of twenty-four patients (ten women and fourteen men) who entered psychoanalysis or psychoanalytic psychotherapy because of depression, psychosomatic complaints, phobias, or sexual disturbances. Common to all these patients was a self disorder, strongly expressed through the forms of deployment I have described. Most of these patients had been in previous psychoanalytic treatment yet claimed that they had "not been touched"; while they now understood much more, nothing much had changed in their emotional experience. And as Bollas (1991) writes, "The life of the true self is to be found in the person's experiencing of the world" (p. 9). Psychoanalysts and psychoanalytic therapists have been increasingly confronted with patients who do not fit a classical model of analyzability. Parson and Schachter (1988) claim that the successful treatment of these patients requires a systematic technique derived from a different psychotherapy model.

An unquestioned assumption in psychoanalysis has been that achieving a cure demands the development and resolution of the transference neurosis. But in the so-called narcissistic disorders, a transference neurosis is either entirely absent or present in only a vestigial form. We now view the analytic setting and the analytic relationship as a major element in the curative process (Cooper 1987, Modell 1990).

Viederman (1991) distinguishes between the climate of analysis, which is the prevailing emotional tone of the relationship in part created by the analyst, and the weather, which approximates the usual transference vicissitudes. I agree that the analyst's attitudes have a strong impact on the atmosphere and analytic work with all patients; but it is of cardinal importance in working with deployed patients. The climate of analysis comprises all the attitudes of the analyst that contribute to the therapeutic ambiance of the working alliance, the mental landscapes patients construct in treatment, and the quality of the entire therapeutic process. Duncan (1990) states,

> It is difficult to define what I term "atmosphere." There are remarkably few references in the literature of psychoanalysis to atmosphere. . . . Atmosphere does exist in the sense that it is a separate and real psychoanalytic entity, phenomeno-logically separable from such established psychological phenomena as affect, countertransference and projection, and as much entitled to full conceptual status. [p. 6]

There is a difference in climate when a patient says whatever is on his or her mind, merely complying with the "basic rule," and when the same patient feels that the climate created allows it and encourages it in a real way. As we know, it is also important for all of us to be alert to what we transmit not just verbally but also nonverbally. It cannot always be ascribed to resistance when patients who have been told to say whatever they feel about their analysts do not feel free enough to do so. Especially when we are criticized, it is crucial to note whether we can listen empathically or whether we respond in a retaliatory way because of our own vulnerability, either by cutting ourselves off emotionally or by remaining silent. One of the attitudes that is central to creating the psychoanalytic situation is the "analyst's attitude." The analyst's attitude is understood by Kris (1952) to consist of undirected fantasy—thinking, providing access to preconscious ideas and affects, "a regression in the service of the ego." Stone (1981) characterizes it as follows:

> The analyst maintains anonymity (as far as possible); he gives no affective response to the patient's material or evident state of mind, nor opinions, nor direction, not to speak of active interest, advice. To the extent that it does not become equated with coldness, aloofness, arbitrary withholding, callousness, detachment ritualization or panicky adherence to rules for their own sake . . . it is an integral, indeed, central element, the rule of abstinence without which there is no analysis. [p. 99]

While the concept of the analyst's attitude as clarified by Schafer in his book *The Analytic Attitude* (1983) is widely accepted by analysts, and although many analysts briefly refer to the great impact that attitudes have on the analytic process, the multiple and discrete attitudes of the analyst that play an important role in the analytic workday have received very little attention in psychoanalytic literature (Compton 1987). Francis Baudry (1991) defines the term *attitude* as being closer to the level of observation; it refers to ego–syntonic mind sets that lend form to the analyst's perception and shape his view of the world and therefore his responses to other people. Baudry states that normally one does not think of the character and attitudes of the analyst as a component of analytic technique. He suggests that it is relegated to the art part of psychoanalysis, those subtle, unfathomable, intuitive aspects of the professional behavior of an analyst that provide much of the frame and background of the analytic relationship. Arlow and Brenner (1988) suggest that psychoanalysis depends on the attitudes, goals, or setting of priorities that frame and color our observations. Nacht (1964) proposes that the progress of analytic therapy is related to the influence of the analyst's deep inner attitudes, and that these attitudes comprise more than interventions or verbal interpretations: "It is the nonverbal relationship which gives it substance and significance" (p. 300). Perhaps speaking of attitudes in terms of the analyst's attitude, as if it were one unit, may have contributed to the dearth of further research on attitudes and attitudinal elements of the analyst. Attitudes may be conscious, preconscious, or unconscious. Stone (1981) writes that, "Most important attitudes are imparted nonverbally, by the timing and duration of silence, by tone of voice and rhetorical nuances in interventions, by facial expression at the beginning and end of the hour, by the mood in which realities are dealt with (p. 109). But, as Klauber (1981) says, "what happens between the patient and the analyst is still quite mysterious . . . the personal fact or what makes a successful analyst may be even more difficult to study" (p. 197).

According to Compton (1987) a mental attitude refers to a readiness to respond in a particular, distinct way to the stimulus, such as an object (a real thing including actual persons), concept, or situation. Attitude is important in determining relationships with other people and may be inferred from the observation of such relationships including the relationship that compromises the analytic situation (Compton 1987). He concludes that a theory of attitudes remains to be developed within psychoanalysis.

In the material that follows, I have culled out of my clinical experience attitudes and attitudinal elements—much of which exists only subliminally—that I have found closely woven into the clinical fabric of my work with deployed patients. My descriptions are not intended to be comprehensive, but, rather, to set the stage for continued exploration and conceptualization. As Gardner (1991) writes, "Through the fuller self observation of the analyzing mind in motion we have a chance to learn more about our art." (p. 870).

In the chapter on countertransference, I specify some of the attitudes that contribute to the clinical climate and facilitate a fuller self-participation and self-exploration on the part of the patient. These attitudes include the affirmative attitude (Hrushovski 1970, Schafer 1983), flexibility (Rosenfeld 1987, Weigert 1954), compassion (Greenson 1960), emotional involvement (Loewald 1986), emotional availability (Emde 1990), the ability to provide a safe background (Sandler 1960, Sandler and Sandler 1978), the objectivity and neutrality that is not to be confused with the attitude of the detached scientist (Gill 1954, Goldberg 1989, Loewald 1960, Stone 1981), the attitude of hope (Ornstein 1989, Wallerstein et al. 1989), the belief that we can help (Fromm-Reichmann 1950), and the attitude of mutuality (Adler 1980, Fromm–Reichmann 1950). The enjoyment of one's work and one's controlled enthusiasm for it is yet another attitude that has been mentioned as having significant influence on the other (Greenson 1962, Katz 1967). Our readiness to regard these attitudes as part of our analytic instrument is crucial to the outcome of our work (Hurwitz 1986).

THE AFFECT-FOCUSED APPROACH

In my analytic work, I try to shift the emphasis from the interpretation that is given, to the analyst who makes the interpretation. The tone of voice in which an interpretation is offered and how the interpreter feels toward the patient are of no less importance than the interpreter's words.

> Tact, basic rapport and its fluctuations, the breadth of life experience and imagination, the manner in which intercurrent events in the patient's life and before, during and after the analytic hour, are handled, all are important ingredients of the therapeutic action without which even the most correct interpretation may remain unconscious and ineffective. [Scharfman 1979, p. 630]

The verbal articulation of the analyst is only a small part of what is lived during the hour. What the analyst feels, thinks, understands, selects as problems to be worked on—his or her inner activity—has much more impact than the words articulated. We are constantly selecting things to say from an enormous range of choices, and what we say is often based on intuition (Tucket 1982).

With this focus, more attention can be given to the ways in which we analysts use ourselves, for instance, to how we use our feelings, thinking, and imagination to empathize with patients. This allows us to learn and share more about ourselves as the "analytic instrument" (Balter et al. 1980, Grolnick et al. 1978, Isakower 1963, Jaffe 1986), as well as about the working model that the analyst slowly builds up within himself. Greenson (1978) is one of the few authors who explicates this process:

> As I worked with the patient day by day I had slowly built up within myself a working model of the patient. This consisted of her physical appearance, her affects, her life experiences, her modes of behavior, her attitudes, defenses, values and fantasies. I listened to the patient's words and transformed her words into pictures and feelings from her memories and her experiences. . . . By shifting the working model of the patient into the foreground, the rest of me was relatively deemphasized and isolated. [pp. 155–156]

Although it is widely accepted that nonverbal communication plays an important role in our clinical work, it is difficult to spell out specific sources of nonverbal data that lead to our understanding and interpretations. It is easier to describe the ideas expressed, the plot, and the words spoken in the session than to discern the distinct and complex feeling states and qualities conveyed nonverbally.

> For it is the nature of feelings that they are like millions of sparks that spin around within us and that only when they are kindled in the relationship they become clear and convincing. When the session ends, these sparks tend to fade and disappear,

as if a light has been turned off and ceases to exist. Often it needs the imagination and creative resources of the analyst to bring the felt feelings and fantasies back to life. [Moses–Hrushovski 1987]

Affects are major roads to the unconscious. But, unlike associations, affects are not inherently connected to word representations nor—even as dreams—with visual representations (Rangell 1967). Adatto (1957) said, "An affect when clearly understood constitutes psychoanalytic shorthand equivalent to the lengthy historical reconstruction of certain aspects and vicissitudes of a patient's early life" (p. 252).

I find myself using a variety of lenses and feeling antennae in order to grasp signs of the feelings, feeling states, and emotional constellations not given verbal expression in the hour. Behind the definition of intuition as "a well informed guess" (Eiserer 1959) is the notion that we need reliable signs and signals in order to perform the intuitive act. "Relationship is a semiotic skill: it involves the interpretation of signs, an enterprise of endless subtlety" (Levenson 1983). "Few are proficient in the complex task of decoding nonverbal communications," says Dorpat (1991), "such as those transmitted via projective identifications, acting out, somatic disturbances, body language as well as the affective components such as the tone and timbre of the voice in ordinary human vocal communication" (p. 131).

The concept *sign* embraces two notions, which are not necessarily inseparable: (a) the idea that a sign indicates the actual presence of something, as opposed to a symbol, which merely refers to or represents that thing; (b) the idea that a sign can be understood directly, without symbolic interpretation. A baby's cry is understood and responded to directly, and so, probably, are the tones and inflections of speech that indicate the speaker's affective state (Rycroft 1968). Tuckett (1982) suggests that we can learn much about the unconscious relationships between ourselves and our patients, particularly about the kinds of transference repetitions and enactments, by being more systematic in our thinking about the whole range of signs and signals used in the psychoanalytic interaction.

TUNING IN TO SIGNS AND SIGNALS

In each session, I first try to find the essential nature of the current theme.

> First the analyst tries to discover a theme which will give interdependent relevance to all that the patient is saying and doing. This unifying theme is his explanatory hypothesis and its discovery requires close application to detail and a good deal of logical thought. Much of this is done preconsciously with an effortlessness. . . . he can only achieve the necessary analysis and synthesis because he is at various levels of consciousness matching the patient's experience and modes of operation with his own. [Klauber 1981, p. 116]

Watts (1975) illustrates the non-active functioning that conveys the attitude of effortlessness in the following way: "listening without straining to hear; smelling without strong inhalation; tasting without screwing up the tongue; and touching without pressing the object" (p. 43).

I find myself listening to the music accompanying the words and trying to match its emotional tones and melodies with words. I try to paint and sculpt the scenes that came up in the session in words, so they can be seen, sensed, and felt in all their complexity and subtlety—enabling them thereby to come to life. I felt a process similar to that described by Paul Klee as happening in himself when he "began [his painting] by relating lines, shades and colors to each other, adding a stress here, removing a weight there to achieve the feeling of balance or 'rightness,' after which every artist strives" (Gombrich 1972, p. 459).

At times, I suggest a kind of play somewhat similar to what

Winnicott developed (the piggle game). The patient transmits what is on his or her mind and I paint in words what is on my mind as if letting the patient's unconscious meet with mine in a playful manner. This provides the space and means through which patients can live and experience, together with me, a transitional space in which both of us can find a relationship as well as an approach to the preconscious. "Summation or reverberation depends on there being a certain quantity of reflecting back to the individual on the part of the trusted therapist (or friend) who has taken the (indirect) communication. In these highly specialized conditions the individual can come together as a unit, not as a defence against anxiety but as an expression of I Am, I am alive, I am myself. From this position everything is creative" (Winnicott 1971, p. 56).

I listen without thinking, on several planes at the same time, while also trying to pin down the exact quality of the feelings expressed by the patient through the various feeling signs. For instance, I consider whether it is pessimistically sad, submissively sad, or ironically sad. I underline in myself what feels meaningful—without yet knowing why—until a gestalt is formed, which I then share with the patient.

The form in which I ask for associations often has a strong impact on their nature and flow. Thus, for instance, my asking for associations in a general way will affect the patient differently than if I specify the feeling state or scene conveyed by the patient, repeating it so that it can be felt in all its concreteness and freshness.

A question that frequently guides me is how to enable the patient to see the world afresh, how to be open with one's senses, feelings, and imagination and reach the depth that forms the substratum of our being. Thus, I treat each session like a new session, not like the continuation of the previous session (Bion 1967). What has been said previously is "forgotten," until a sudden link is created that brings the forgotten components back into mind, often in an immediate and striking way, leading to an emotionally meaningful insight either in the patient or in me.

Though I am aware of the patterns created, each moment in the
hour is still regarded as different from what was seen and experienced before. It is like not being able to enter the same river
twice; everything is flowing (Heraclitus). This attitude, particularly when it is internalized by the patient, often invites a willingness to be open to the present and the future, rather than the
premature application of one's knowledge and thinking about
the past. When working with such near-to-self-experiences and
sensations, there is often some surprise and a feeling of novelty
that furthers the patient's willingness to be engaged and to work
analytically.

When a feeling state is gradually identified during the hour,
I often "play it back" to the patient with its specific emotional
melody and resonance. Playing the music that I feel accompanies
the words often invites the patient to respond more musically
(Moses-Hrushovski 1992b). Sometimes I do this silently, in my
own mind. At other times I voice it so the patient can hear the
melodies and stresses, can sense and feel it so he or she attaches
more attention to it. In time, imprints created in this fashion,
become the tissues of emotional insights, in both the patient and
myself.

My working assumption is that whenever I encounter disturbance of functioning or feeling of the patient's self in the
present, I should expect to find a traumatic root in the past
(Modell 1984, Moses-Hrushovski 1986). Sensations felt in the
here and now are often related to affects disconnected from their
original source. When this happens I register them in my mind
and try to maintain two threads—one in the present and another
in the past—so that the contextual signs of the patient's current
sensations are allowed to reattach themselves to one of the
intermediate emotional stages. Abstracting the essence from the
present context and organizing the material according to the
modes of perception presented in the session often permit new
links to be formed.

"It is the empathic responsiveness, his active participation
in discovering what the patient is experiencing, that characterizes

the therapeutic dialogue" (Ornstein and Ornstein 1990, p. 333).
Greenson (1966) states:

> [The analyst] helps the patient work out the details of the
> character that the latter is creating. He becomes in a sense the
> stage director. Or he is like the conductor of a symphony. He
> does not write the music but he clarifies and interprets it. The
> interpretive work of the analyst as he listens to what the patient
> fantasizes is at its best related to the creative process in litera-
> ture, music and art. [p. 22]

I have learned that the more I share my responses to what is
brought up—in a way that the patient can feel and understand as
accurately as possible, both the essence of the emotional quality
and its degree of intensity—and the more spontaneous I can be,
the more responsive the patient becomes, and the more clearly
he or she brings up the attendant feelings and feeling states in
their complexity. "The analyst's spontaneity evokes a degree of
spontaneity in the patient which brings them together as individuals" (Klauber 1981, p. 197). Meaningful associations often
follow, which open up new landscapes and allow fruitful material to emerge from previously unknown or unthought-of areas.
I have sometimes found that the use of relevant metaphors
facilitates emotional understanding through imaginative participation.

The most difficult task is to mold all the material together so
that it makes a coherent whole. This demands that the analyst be
attuned to the seemingly inextricable web of sound, rhythm,
melody, tones, and colors; it means being alert to the uniqueness
of each element without losing sight of its function in the composition of the hour. Especially with deployed patients, I work in
accordance with Khan's (1974) view:

> Conflicted states are acted out (in the analytic framework),
> whereas dissociated states are enacted in life. The person is all
> the elements of his dissociated states and lives them as such. It

is for the analyst operating as an auxiliary ego to register these dissociations and help the patient to integrate them into a coherent totality of experience. [p. 244]

The analysis takes on an entirely different tone when I take the feelings and feeling states as basic units and allow the patient's experiences, thoughts, fantasies, and behavior to be organized around them, than when I primarily or exclusively follow the words and thoughts expressed. My aim is to enable the patient to reach, in a certain unit of time (within the session or a series of sessions), a coordination between the different parts of the self, between what one understands, feels, thinks, imagines, and does, to prevent the disconnection between the different parts of the self.

CATEGORIES OF FEELING SIGNS

The following categories of feeling signs are observed by me but not necessarily verbalized by the patient; they constitute important sources for productive analytic work.

Countertransference

Sandler (1976) proposes that in the transference the patient unconsciously attempts to induce and experience a role relationship with the analyst as a means of obtaining gratification for a spectrum of wishes arising from various sources. To the extent that the analyst is able to monitor his role responsiveness, he or she can use it as a sign for patient's unconscious needs or wishes.

The intense sense of entitlement, the demandingness that deployed patients tend to exert, often evokes reactions of anger and exhaustion in the analyst. Recognition of this type of countertransference can establish the presence of deployment in the patient, and the awareness of the countertransference may allow the therapeutic alliance to be reestablished. The feeling reaction of the analyst is primary data with regard to the unconscious communication of the patient. The crucial factor in treatment is the analyst's apprehension of these countertransference feelings, that is, containing them, analyzing them, and in some way utilizing them in treatment (Fromm 1989).

As container (Bion 1967), the analyst is not a passive recipient of the patient's projective identification. The analyst reflects upon and gives meaning to the projections he or she has introjected and then offers understanding to the patient in the form of interpretation. Patients can then reintroject the now-transformed aspects of themselves and modify their internal self-images with this new understanding. What is conveyed to the patient is both the transformed, original perception from the patient and an aspect of the analyst's self—the containing-analyzing function itself, which he or she wishes, however benignly and gently, to insinuate into patients so as to influence them (Hamilton 1990). "If a capacity for transference from its most primitive to its most developed form is a measure of the patient's analyzability, the capacity for countertransference is a measure of the analyst's ability to analyze" (Loewald 1986, p. 286).

Bodily Expressions and Sensations

Bodily expressions and sensations, such as postural tension, head or eye movements, hand movements, gestures, modulations, breathing rhythm, sighs, and headaches, may speak volumes. All differentiations through the senses, for example, variations in the pitch, volume, or rhythm of speech, are means of conveying messages (Tuckett 1982). They serve as springboards for reaching unrecognized feeling and self states. As Rogers says, gut feelings demand more than remaining passive. This means being active with one's senses. Siegel (1988) recommends that analysts stop ignoring their own somatic resonance with primitive patient productions and use the understanding of these somatic phenomena as a bridge-building device toward symbolic and

semantic expression for the patients. Anzieu (1985) wondered
how to bring up the subject of the smell that he experienced with
a certain patient without seeming aggressive or annoyed. His
training, Anzieu comments, had taught him nothing about olfac-
tory states.

Inflection of speech often reveals feeling states and attitudes
of which the patient is not aware. Some examples of feeling-signs
that may be sensed by listening to the vocal qualities of the
interchange (as opposed to only the content) are: (a) the patient
speaks and one senses that he or she is looking at what is being
said from the outside; (b) the patient speaks and one senses that he
is constantly trying to explain and justify himself instead of
saying what is on his mind in order to say, explore, understand,
and change; (c) the patient speaks and one feels the tension and
pressure behind what is being said; (d) the patient speaks, usually
after having organized his thinking (as can be inferred, e.g., from
his smooth tone and always stopping before starting to speak),
and is more in control than the patient who speaks before or
while thinking (at times hesitating). When these feeling-signs are
noticed and successfully reflected to the patient, an opportunity
is provided to work on the unconscious meanings, feelings, and
obstacles to free association.

I found that alerting the patient to pay attention to areas of
the body in which chronic muscular tensions are felt that blocked
awareness and expression of feelings is another avenue to emotional and verbal expression. Repeating to myself certain gestures observed in the patient—gesturing them or using them
imaginatively, as if entering into the patient's mood in a kines-
thetic way—facilitated a more empathic understanding of the
patient's feeling state.

The more I respond to what I see, hear, smell, sense kines-
thetically, the more it becomes part of the patient's associative
material. Using feeling-signs is especially productive in working
with deployed patients, who have a tendency to bring up ideational material or what has been turned into factual data, in a
compulsive way—trying to put aside feelings or deny them.

Rather than be carried away by ideational material, the use of feeling-signs enables many deployed patients to listen to their own sensations and tensions, thereby introducing more liveliness and significance into the session. Such listening and responding to feeling-signs does not imply a one-to-one relationship between sign and meaning; it is, rather, the complex relationship of specific signs to the meaning these signs have had in the session for that person in a particular situation.

Moods

Moods are complex self states that may establish a mnemonic environment that the individual reexperiences and re-creates from former infant-child parts. "Just as the dream allows for the unconscious experience of the child parts of the self in elaborating and negotiating with adult life, so does mood experience allow for previously evoked self states to reappear in the ongoing negotiations with reality" (Bollas 1987, p. 102). Here is one way of detecting moods and working with such qualities:

Mrs. S. repeatedly told me, session after session, about injustices done to her by others. The predominant mood was one of sadness and despair. The repetitive theme and unchanging tone of voice suggested a wish to put me to sleep. I felt that it was like a transitional phenomenon. When I told her what I felt, a memory came to her mind: As a child, before falling asleep she liked to tell her teddy bear all kinds of sad happenings she had experienced during the day. Once her little brother pulled the teddy bear away from her and tore it. She was furious with her brother. But she was even angrier at her mother, who not only failed to understand how painful it was for her, but did not even punish him. Mrs. S. remembered that she decided to continue acting as if her teddy bear still existed. Every night she still told sad stories to the teddy bear that was no longer there. This self-soothing was like an enactment of a masturbation fantasy, a device to put herself to sleep and later not only in night situations.

In this manner she consoled herself, defiantly ignoring the reality factor and soothing herself with a fantasy-revenge game.

In the analytic situation, I represented the mother who should have listened to her, and also the teddy bear who was a transitional object. Until this child-self state was discovered in the hour, Mrs. S. was unconsciously directed to complain and to wait until her mother would listen carefully to what she—Mrs. S.—felt and for the mother to experience regret for what she—the mother—had done or failed to do. From identifying the mood and self state of not really being present in the hour, we came to meet and make sense of Mrs. S.'s child part, which had been repeatedly enacted in the hours and in her life. Mrs. S. had behaved in a rigid and fixed manner to punish her mother for the injustice done to her, and to achieve an alliance with her that would at long last compensate Mrs. S. for all she had endured. Clearly, this enactment not only blocked fruitful analytic work, but also prevented Mrs. S. from enjoying her present life and being creative in it.

Identifications

Identifications felt by the analysand while talking about other people in his or her life can be considered relevant to the analysand's self experience. For instance, Mr. G. referred several times to his being like the prophet Jeremiah. What he found hard to articulate, primarily because of his shame, was his grandiose part: how special he felt he was, and how he had been chosen to reveal God's will. Mr. G.'s bitterness that his specialness and his important mission was not recognized by the world was expressed indirectly through identifying himself with Jeremiah.

Before and After Dividing Lines

A patient's frequent mention of meaningful dividing lines or dates is a chance for the analyst to sense the possible indication for charged psychic material and to open new channels. When Mr.

D. mentioned occurrences from the past, he would often categorize them according to whether they happened before or after he began masturbating. This division line indicated the break that he experienced after having learned to masturbate: since then he lost his tranquillity, worrying constantly lest he be caught and condemned. Another typical dividing line that indicated a traumatic state was a patient's way to categorize manifold experiences according to whether they happened before or after his moving to a different city or country. My reference to this fact became a starting point for analytic work and an opportunity to work through intense feelings, shameful incidents, and fantasies of which he had not been conscious.

Patterns of Deployment as Signs for Disavowed Psychic Pain, Unidentified Vulnerabilities, and Panic Reactions

Since deployments are not brought up verbally and since they are central factors in the weakening of the self, I view the recognition of their manifestations in the analytic hour as of paramount importance. Once the analyst is aware of the phenomenon of deployment and understands its major characteristics, it is easy to detect when they are being enacted in the treatment situation.

For instance, trying to "correct" past experience through real or fantasy programs, at the expense of living one's present life, may serve as a sign for the unrecognized self injuries and conflicts that lie behind the deployments. Mrs. N. expressed her wish to be a man in many ways. Although interpretations regarding her penis envy were given and worked through, this process did not change her tendency to be deeply involved in all kinds of consoling fantasies, for example, about how she would become a famous athlete. She would often have a Walkman plugged into her ears, her head in the clouds, while she listened to music and invented comforting scenes disconnected from reality. Her deployment into these "consolation trips," which afforded her a great deal of pleasure, was unconsciously aimed at dissociating herself from the psychic pain she secretly carried with her.

In dealing with this deployment by taking it as a sign for what it was designed to correct, the deployment became linked with a traumatic event that she had experienced as a little girl, when some boys ran after her, caught her, and pulled down her pants. Shocked and terribly insulted at their mocking gestures at the time, the incident continued to haunt her. Mrs. N. remembered her internal definite decision: never again to let herself be humiliated by assuming the role of a woman. In her efforts to restore her lost honor, and to calm her shame and worries that something in her was shaming and different, she enacted in many ways her fantasy that only as a man could she feel worthy. This deployment also served to protect her from other painful feelings such as envy of her brother, shame for her base, inferior mother, and guilt around oedipal feelings toward her father.

Such enactments in the analytic sessions and in life can be transformed back into the feeling, thinking, and fantasy that these deployed patients are driven to correct. I have found that corrective programs are the most productive avenues to revive the encapsulated situations that cause these patients to remain encased in a cocoon and to help them connect what has been dissociated with their experiencing selves. One step in this direction is pointing up the manifestations of what moves patients emotionally in the session, such as associations they feel have "poignant" or "touching" qualities: themes from life, movies, or literature that touch a chord within them as a correcting device for past self injuries, or for lack of care or lack of empathy on the part of their caretakers (Kohut 1984). Unidentified and unexpressed feelings, previously disavowed, are then revived in the context of significant situations that have unknowingly been exerting heavy pressures on them and are also usually apparent in the transference.

Another example of such corrective devices is seen in Mrs. R., who invested her psychic energy in fantasy plans to become a famous singer and to give a concert in the same place where she had been sexually abused, in order to erase the stain of the shame she had disavowed. She felt that only after returning to the place where she had been humiliated and giving a successful concert would she be able to begin real life. Gradually the direction of their consoling, but self-defeating programs tends to change, when care is taken to draw attention to the energy invested in such corrective programs. They then gain more understanding into and empathy with the self injury of the child parts that has been driving them to harden themselves to reality and sink into a consoling fantasy life.

The deployments of these patients, that is, the ways in which they organize themselves on the cognitive, conative, emotional, and behavioral levels, are thus given no less attention than the anxiety and shame that lie beneath the deployment. By shifting the weight from what the patient's power was invested in, to what this aimed at correcting, we enter the emotional and subjective inner world that deployed patients are trying to efface. "The function of the analyst is merely to ensure that the energy shall flow along one channel rather than another" (Strachey 1934, p. 149). Rather than depict additional categories of feeling signs that I find myself using intuitively while working with deployed patients, my main goal here is to portray the attitudes and approach I utilize.

COGNITIVE ATTITUDES

Free-floating responsiveness and free-floating attention are two major cognitive attitudes that all analysts see as essential (Sandler and Sandler 1978, 1987). Among the cognitive attitudes of the analyst that I believe have a strong impact on the outcome of therapy is the ability to oscillate between certain diacritical poles. Here, what Grolnick and colleagues (1978) consider in their epilogue is relevant:

> Poets, artists, philosophers have consciously or unconsciously known that I and Thou, matter and mind, affect and cognition, and symbol and referent are not optimally distributed, either

as warring or as fixed polarities. To the extent polarities interplay paradoxically within a homeostasis, they can satisfy, comfort and synthesize. When this occurs, we can better achieve a
mental equilibrium, a creative activity or, perhaps even a work
of art. [p. 537]

Areas in which it is important to be able to oscillate flexibly
between opposing attitudes include the following:

1. Our receptive functions and our active functions, in
order to reach unconscious meanings. "The integrative functions of the ego include self-regulated regression and permit a
combination of the most daring intellectual activity with the
experience of passive receptiveness" (Kris 1956b, p. 236). This
oscillation involves a quality of commitment, together with
abandonment and absorption, involving the whole personality
of the analyst as participant. A capacity to tolerate a passive role
in the manner of Freud's "evenly suspended attention" is
followed by an active synthesis utilizing cognitive processes.
    The analyst is like an artist, for whom seeing is insufficient:
"He must get into the thing and feel it inwardly and live its life
himself" (Fromm et al. 1960, p. 13). This process requires immersing oneself in the patient's inner life—the feelings, the tones,
the colors; in other words, living the patient's life imaginatively
and feelingly—as well as actively using perceptions and reverberations for interventions like inquiring, settling problems, interpreting, or reconstructing. Gardner (1983) asks: "Search or let
it dawn? Both. We both (analyst and analysand) do both. Sometimes more the one, sometimes more the other, but always
alternatively together. Both connect, disconnect and reconnect
one thing and another; things thought, seen, felt, smelled, heard
and otherwise perceived, each separately and with the other" (p.
35). There is also an oscillation between wanting to know and
understand exactly and the capacity to wait for it to come. What
is needed here is the capacity to distinguish what we know with
certainty from what we know to some extent and what we do not

and/or cannot know. What seems essential for receptiveness is the capacity to be open to the manifold clues for the unknown—while at the same time being capable and ready to be in a state of not knowing.

2. Feeling with the patient—being accurately attuned to a wide range of affects and feeling states, as they change in nature and intensity—as against drifting along aimlessly with the stream of consciousness, allowing one's thoughts to wander, are two different mind-sets not easily held concurrently by the analyst. Freud (1912) urges the analyst to avoid reflection and to catch the drift of the unconscious—to listen to everything with all of him- or herself, allowing meaning to emerge rather than to be imposed by preformed notions. "The intent of evenly hovering attention is not to produce blocked minds, but uncommitted ones—minds receptive to the organization of this particular content from this particular patient in this particular hour in ways true to its potentially unique offering" (Pine 1988, p. 577).

3. Total identification with patients, feeling/thinking/imagining oneself into them while simultaneously or alternatively retaining one's own separate stance, is another polarity that is important for a more accurate and complex emotional understanding of the patient and for avoiding the problem of the analyst's overidentification with him. The analyst thinks with the patient and then about the patient (Beres and Arlow 1974). Greenson (1966) proposes that

> the primary task of the psychoanalyst is to gain a detailed understanding of the patient's emotions, attitudes, and actions. The most difficult part of this job is to comprehend the unconscious processes which go on in his patient's mind. . . . While he listens to the patient precisely and carefully, he also has to sense what lies behind the various subjects the patient is expounding. While he listens to the melody, he must also listen to the hidden themes, the "left hand, the counterpart." [p. 11]

He continues to describe the needed skill: "This kind of listening requires that the analyst have the capacity to shift from participant to observer, from introspection to empathy, from intuition to problem solving, from a more involved to a more detached position. It is necessary for him to oscillate, make transitions and blendings of these different positions" (p. 11). Solan (1991) discusses the continuous movement between simultaneously experiencing the mutual satisfaction of surrendering while concomitantly safeguarding separateness in the analytic encounter.

4. Peripheral vision, which works best when we relax, and sharp, focused sight. "By far the greater part of our important decisions depends upon 'hunch'—in other words, upon the 'peripheral vision' of the mind. Thus the reliability of our decisions rests ultimately upon our ability to 'feel' the situation, upon the degree to which this 'peripheral vision' has been developed" (Watts 1975, p. 35).

5. The zigzag approach, moving from present to past and back to the present while relating as fully as possible to transference manifestations and linking them to relevant childhood experiences and current stressful events, is another kind of polarity. Overemphasis on one pole at the expense of the other interferes with the creation of meaningful reconstructions and holistic development, especially in work with deployed patients. Bollas proposes that the receptive and evocative functions refer to the subject's availability for the arrival of repressed memories and for new internal objects. This will not occur unless the patient unconsciously perceives the analyst as prepared to allow this evolution. If the analyst fundamentally understands silence to denote resistance, then this state will not be achieved, and many discoveries will be lost. But if the analyst values the there-and-then, if he or she is willing to suspend transference interpreting momentarily, then he or she will enable the patient's ego to evoke mental representations of unthought knowledge (Bollas 1991).

The importance of dialectic movement between the poles is stressed as essential for the analytic work, on both the part of the analyst and the patient, who tends to internalize these attitudes.

Each art-science has its characteristic poles and its character-istic tools for seeking the fluidity of polar play. Where rule fails, hunch helps; where hunch fails, rule helps. When free attention holds sway there is no quibble between intuition and knowledge, thinking and feeling, words and vision, inner and outer, past and present and other ways of sensing and making sense. And when things go best a quickening of these moves of the free attending mind meets and is met by synchronous quickening in our free-associating patient. [Gardner 1991, p. 866]

CLINICAL ATTITUDES

Rogers (1958) points out some of the basic attitudes that charac-terize a "helping relationship" through the following questions: How can I create a helping relationship? (a) Can I be in a way that will be perceived by the other person as dependable in some deep sense? (b) Can I be expressive enough as a person so that what I am is communicated unambiguously? (c) Can I let myself expe-rience positive attitudes toward the other person—warmth, car-ing, liking, interest, respect (while assuming the analytic attitude, I would add)? (d) Can I be strong enough as a person to maintain my separateness from the other? Am I strong enough in my own separateness that I will not be downcast by a patient's depression, frightened by that person's fear, engulfed by his or her depen-dency? Is my inner self hardy enough to realize that I will not be destroyed by the other's anger, enslaved by his or her love—that I am not fearful of losing myself? (e) Am I secure enough within myself to permit the other separateness? Can I give him or her the freedom to be? Can I meet this other individual in the process of becoming (and, I would add, myself as well)?

Elsewhere (Moses-Hrushovski 1992a) I have described some of the clinical attitudes of Frieda Fromm-Reichmann por-trayed in the Hannah Green novel *I Never Promised You a Rose Garden*. Green, a pseudonym, was one of her patients. This book illuminates the subtle interactions between the therapist's attitudes and patient reactions such as basic trust in the healthy parts during the process of working with the disturbed portions of personality. It shows the power of the analyst's belief in therapeutic helping-potential to build mutuality and her deep respect for the patient's autonomy no matter at what stage the patient is. Authenticity is another attitude that is reflected in Reichmann's work. Nina Coltart (1991) talks about her work with an elderly patient with whom she had often felt pushed by introjected and/or subjective frustration, despair, or fury into a display of affect that was in tune with her interpretation. She said that she stands behind this behavior as she believes that with some authority we can, within limits of scrupulous self-observation, do no harm to a patient by showing authentic affect. "I am talking about Being, not Doing, perhaps I should emphasize. I am not arguing for emotionally directed action, such as touching, caressing, hitting, walking out—but for truth in our emotional being with a patient" (p. 217).

FURTHER INFLUENTIAL ATTITUDES

Attitude toward Acting, Enacting, and Acting Out

Instead of capturing the emotional crises that arise in daily life or in the analytic relationship, and their reflections upon them, many deployed patients tend to act out their affective experiences, discharging the affect through inappropriate action rather than feeling them and talking about them in the sessions. Another tendency of deployed patients is to enact, namely, to actualize, persuading themselves that a wish is being gratified rather than only wished for (Boesky 1989). I feel that the climate changes when I change my attitude toward acting, enacting, and acting out. While the psychoanalytic literature has tended to emphasize the resistance aspects of acting out, recent articles

view acting out as a way of remembering and expressing conflicts in a developmentally earlier form of thinking (Busch 1989).
Though resistance is the cornerstone of analytic work, many
deployed patients when told in some way or other that they are
acting or acting out feel criticized, as if they are not meeting
analytic expectations to feel or remember. This transmits implied
judgment. As I came to view enactment as a valid mode of
communication, and began placing emphasis affirmatively on
what was being revealed, analysis took on a different key and
patients began to remember and express more memories than
before. To provide the security that deployed patients require to
work analytically, I try and do anything and everything—as long
as it is not anti-analytic, and as long as I know what I am doing
and am in control of my personal needs—in order to avoid the
traumatic climate that many deployed patients have suffered in
the past—that of not meeting the parents' expectations. For most
of my deployed patients have at least one narcissistic parent who
unconsciously tried to live parts of his or her dissociated self
through the child, and who could therefore never be really
satisfied with the actual child (Modell 1984). Consequently,
many of these patients have become "allergic" to the pressure of
expectations, and often experience a need to vomit out whatever
was pushed into them, which they cannot do because they do not
want to be rejected as repulsive.

Rangell (1968) illustrates how misleading the pejorative
attitude to acting out can be and distinguishes between acting
out, neurotic action, and normal action. In a vignette that
Boesky (1989) presents about a woman who embroiled him in
arguments, he joined his patient in an enactment. When he
realized what he was doing he utilized that realization to help
both the patient and himself toward a better understanding of
what was happening. Boesky says that this view of enactments
provides a valuable window through which to see the enor-
mously important moment-to-moment shifting affective interplay between patient and analyst, which is still insufficiently
understood.

Being Alert to the Imbalance in Power between Patient and Analyst

Another change of attitude is expressed in the following way: I realized the central role that mistakes and failures play in the pathology of narcissistic patients. Modell (1984) described certain forms of narcissism as a response to perceived failure of the parents to provide a good enough holding environment. Much of their psychic energy is invested in trying to avoid situations where they might fail, and their efforts are in the direction of trying to undo the stains of shame before they can begin to live with dignity. Therefore, especially with deployed patients, the analyst's attitude toward errors and failures are of great importance.

Fritz Redl was said to start each staff meeting by sharing one of his failures with his colleagues. This loosened constraints on his staff when discussing their own case material. One of the inherent difficulties in analytic work with deployed patients relates to the gap that deployed patients perceive between themselves as "needy" patients, who are expected to say whatever comes to their mind and to give up control, and the "perfect" analyst, who is in full control, carefully phrasing interpretations before speaking, careful not to err. This perceived imbalance of power, and the fear of losing control and being shamed, represents a constant threat to the self-esteem of deployed patients, and often interferes with the working alliance. The analyst's capacity to empathize with this difficulty, especially in deployed patients whose supervulnerability leads them to constantly guard against allowing themselves to be cast in an inferior position, can alleviate the patient's vulnerability by his alertness to the situation. Also, since with any patient it is important that the analyst remember the common basis of emotional difficulties that he or she shares with the patient and all others, while working on the pathological aspects of the patient, this attitudinal ingredient is even more important with the deployed patient.

As Stone (1961) stresses, the analyst has a choice between arbitrary authoritarianism and the engagement of rational cooperation based on understanding. Frieda Fromm-Reichmann (1950) says that an irrational authoritarian attitude is harmful not only because it interferes with the patient's tendencies toward growth and maturation, but also—and more importantly—because it constitutes a traumatic repetition of the authoritarianism of the parental patterns to which most mental patients have been harmfully subjected in the past. This is certainly true in the case of deployed patients who have at least one parent with irrational authoritarian tendencies, and for whom being treated is often perceived as offending and humiliating.

One of the factors that influences my attitude is based on what I believe could make the patient feel freer to participate more fully, as long as I assume the analytic stance. A trusting, appreciative attitude (which does not ignore hostility, or other negative feelings) tends to create an atmosphere of affirmation, which in turn produces a willingness to collaborate in the analytic work, whereas an attitude of suspiciousness, which stresses deficiencies and mistakes, reduces the patient's readiness to cooperate (Hrushovski 1970). Devoting less consideration to exact phrasing of interpretations and giving more thought to possible words that will accurately reflect the feelings and feeling states and the subtle meanings as I am speaking (rather than always before speaking) is another example for possibly liberating the patient. It also means allowing myself to be fallible, to sometimes risk making mistakes, to let myself regress in the service of the ego, rather than being directed by the standard of perfection. This is one way to enable the deployed patients to decrease their deployments against insult, by trying to appear as infallible, and this in turn leads to an increased readiness to participate in the analytic process in a fuller and less defensive manner. "It is essential that we thoroughly analyze our attitudes and intentions. It's only by the analyst's recognition of his mistakes and a change in his emotional orientation towards his patient that the patient is allowed to feel freer" (Rosenfeld 1987, p. 35).

188   Deployment

Attitude toward Recognizing and Naming Feelings: Whose Responsibility Is It?

The emotional atmosphere changes when the analyst who is working with deployed patients views the identification of feelings and feeling states as a shared responsibility rather than always waiting for the patient to articulate them. When I become more of an active partner in the process of deciphering feelings and feeling states—by showing interest in what is felt and questioning the patient about it, by communicating what has been conveyed to me, by "translating" what has been heard, enacted, sensed, or said—and when I invite patients in one of many ways to become a partner in reading feeling signs, collaboration is enhanced. Also, when I speak the language of feelings, patients do the same, because feelings touch feelings in a direct way. "Playing the music" that accompanies the words invites a more musical response. When the analyst's response feels unconventional, as something coming from within him or herself, as he or she actively tries to feel and think about what the patient has transmitted, the patient is indirectly encouraged to respond in kind, in an immediate way and on an emotional level. "This experiencing and sharing with the analyst as well as the verbal understanding is the agent of permanent psychic change" (Stewart 1990, p. 65). This is particularly important when working with deployed patients, who have a strong tendency to cast all feelings aside, and with whom every channel must be tried to bring back to life what has been frozen and seemed dead.

Modell (1990) proposes that prototypical deficiencies in a person's affective experience include the following:

1. Failures in the process of containment of his affects;
2. Failures in the process of recognizing and identifying his affects at the beginning of treatment in order to establish self-object transferences and make optimal therapeutic work possible.

3. States of psychic deadness and inauthenticity where the therapist is enlisted to provide a sense of aliveness; although he cannot fully restore what has been missing in development, there is also no doubt that this kind of affective interaction can for some individuals be ameliorative.

Viewing affective interaction as part of my responsibility has decreased the pressure that I unknowingly exerted by placing on the patients the whole responsibility for discovering and expounding on what they feel. Adler (1980) claims that "these patients often require an awareness of the person and personality of the analyst as someone appropriately interested, caring, warm and wanting to be helpful" (p. 553). Adler continues: "For the more primitive patients who have earlier and more serious developmental failures, this 'new beginning' [Balint 1968], with its opportunities for introjection and identification, is crucial" (p. 554). These patients may also require greater activity from the analyst through a demonstration that he or she is willing to clarify, explain, be helpful, and meet the patient's level of regression.

Attitude toward Aggression

Kernberg (1974, 1987) assigns a primary etiological role to intense aggression, as an outgrowth of the interplay between drive and deprivation. For him, unmanageable aggression—in the context of overwhelming dependency needs—generates the intrapsychic conflict as well as the associated primitive defenses anchored in splitting, which define pathological narcissism. For Kohut (1977), this aggression and the conflicts and defenses that it spawns are not primary etiological agents in the pathogenesis of narcissism. They are secondary "breakdown products" of empathic failures in mirroring failed idealizations.

One's attitude to aggression alters when it is conceived of as a drive rather than when it is viewed primarily as a result of the thwarting of patients' needs. The patients need to feel that they are being recognized and responded to as individuals, that their existence, individuality, and inner life are acknowledged as legitimate, unique, and valuable. Regarding the driving force behind deployments as a need to restore the dignity and inner serenity that have been lost in stressful situations, rather than as primarily based on aggressive drives, is another important attitudinal change that has facilitated my analytic work with deployed patients. Similarly, a different understanding is gained when the narcissistic rage and aggressive reactions of deployed patients are perceived primarily as a natural accompaniment to shame (Lewis 1987), or as the result of a narcissistic injury (Kohut 1971).

Understanding rage as a sign of concealed shame, and becoming interested in the details of the shaming events, encourages patients to move from vindictive anger and humiliated fury to opening themselves up to their previously disavowed humiliating experiences. This approach not only alleviates shame anxiety, but also promotes the capacity for analytic work (Levin 1971).

I have found it useful to distinguish between aggression that is assertive in the service of self expression, and aggression that is an orgy of revenge; between aggression as primarily a protest to be listened to even though it is dramatized, and aggression as a counterphobic reaction against unidentified panic; and sadistic aggression as compared with aggression as a defense against unconscious guilt: "Guilt is often unconscious and not so readily understood . . . many of the impasses in the treatment of the borderline patient can be conceptualized as evidence of a self punishing guilt that leads to attempts to destroy the treatment" (Adler 1989, p. 780).

Attitude toward Judgment

Schwaber (1990) believes that the analyst is in no better position to know the patients' truths or the correctness of their perceptions than the patients themselves. Like Schwaber, I focus on the psychic reality of patients while staying as close as possible to their experiences of the moment. But, unlike Schwaber, I place emphasis on using our judgment to evaluate the conscious or unconscious intentions of patients, especially of deployed patients whose behavior in the analytic situation and in life is often driven by unconscious trends and is understood only by taking the interaction of the various components into account. Using our power of judgment does not mean being judgmental or judging who is right. Assuming such an evaluative attitude does not mean we would be mistrusting or suspicious. Wilhelm Reich (1948) illustrates how everything the patient presents is in the service of a secret unrecognized resistance. "What makes such a chaotic analysis dangerous is that the analyst continues to believe for a long time that they are running very well simply because the patient brings material" (p. 24).

I find myself becoming immersed in what deployed patients transmit in trying to follow their vantage point, but concomitantly I use my judgment by allowing what has been felt, sensed, thought, and imagined to become translated into what to me seems most relevant at the specific moment. Likewise, I remain alert to unconscious intentions meant to distance both of us from some painful, psychic truth. From my work with deployed patients I find that as important as it is to contain the aggression of the patient and have an accurate understanding of the overall dynamics, it is not of less importance to discover anti-analytic trends (Moses-Hrushovski 1986) as soon as they occur in the session, and to place them in context. If analysts take the words and actions of deployed patients at face value, without using their own judgment as to the real meaning, deployed patients tend to get lost in their automatically enacted deployments. When deployments occur without the analyst's awareness of the anti-analytic trends, the patients tend to lose trust in the under-standing and judgment of their analysts.

The more lonely and forsaken they feel in the analytic situation, the more rigidly deployed patients sink into their private fantasy world and become more deeply lost in self-defeating strategies. They have climbed so high up the tree that they cannot easily return to earth. However, when these trends are recognized and firmly pointed out, they can serve as springboards for reaching erased self injuries and encapsulated stressful events in the process of analytic work. By being attentive to the dynamics behind deployments, which may be intended to counteract shame, we are more likely to discover the shame events that have been hermetically sealed off. This attentive judgment may then stop the vicious circle of shame—protected by deployments—that creates even more shame.

"The purpose of the analyst's alertness to distortion is not to correct his patient, but to allow him to understand the needs that are dictating the patient's construction" (Cooper 1987, p. 95). In this context, Schafer (1983) observes that analysts, too often acting with the assumption that the process goes its own way, legitimize far-reaching and unproductive therapeutic inactivity. Likewise, Stone (1961) concludes that excessively schematized principles of analytic attitude, which many follow (or construct!), have too often been invoked as substitutes for the travail of difficult and delicate judgment and decision.

Attitude toward Change

I find it useful to respond to obstacles that impede change, from the very beginning of treatment, whether these obstacles are connected with fear of change evolving from expectations that cannot be met; whether they are connected with a reluctance to give credit to the therapist, since this would mean defeat for the patient or having to face his or her envy and rivalry; or whether they are connected with the patient's need to be punished because of unconscious guilt feelings. Some of the major obstacles that need working through from the very beginning of the treatment, are discussed in the next section.

OBSTACLES DERIVING FROM THE FEAR OF HUMILIATION

Obstacles connected to humiliation are of such importance in treatment that neglecting to attend to them from the outset may easily cut off the possibility of a successful analysis in which patients feel "emotionally touched." "In the light of our increasing understanding of the narcissistic aspects of character and what has been termed narcissistic defenses, around the issues of shame, embarrassment, and self-esteem maintenance, one cannot stress enough the crucial impact of experiences of humiliation" (Baudry 1989, p. 672).

The mere fact that change is expected is offensive to many deployed patients. It reminds them of the paralyzing expectations of their parents—who were never pleased with their child as he is in the present—that they have felt so frequently. If change were to occur, this would imply that they were in the wrong, that it had been their problem, whereas—in the framework of their power conflicts—they are oriented to prove the opposite.

Following are some of these obstacles:

1. Some deployed patients display an arrogance (out of fear and/or as a result of having been insulted) that suggests that they may be narcissistically wounded rather than helped by any discovery not made by themselves, and may therefore display a negative reaction to therapy (McDougall 1989). Thus, out of defiance over being offended, a struggle against the treatment is enacted that prevents them from establishing and maintaining the needed working alliance if contextual signs are not used to work through the frequently hidden resistances.

2. A typical resistance, related to feelings of guilt, shame, and humiliation in deployed patients, is a desire to ascribe their disturbance to organic causes rather than emotional difficulties. Thus, Mrs. S. was not happy when she discovered the psychological dynamics behind the constraints that paralyzed her. She would have preferred to suffer from an organic, physically based

paralysis rather than a hysterical one in order not to feel the humiliation.

3. A frequent reluctance to maturing stems from the anxiety that one may no longer regress without public censure. After many struggles for his entitlement to be taken care of as a child who had not been able to grow up at his own pace—always being pushed to be understanding and mature—Bryan grew out of his protests against a too-early and abrupt "weaning." But what interfered with his real investment in his will to be an adult was the fear that once having arrived there he would be in constant danger of being humiliated and shamed if he regressed (for instance, by masturbating instead of having sexual intercourse). Thus it was safer, after all, to remain a child.

4. Another typical kind of resistance is to be wrapped up in revenge, following one's triumphing and punishing pattern to the end, never admitting being wrong even when they know they are—all this because of their vulnerability from having been considered silly, childish, evil, or crazy. Not letting the opponent "get away with it"—without taking his part of responsibility—has justified these patients' lifelong battle with significant adults.

5. Deployed patients navigate themselves automatically into manifold self-arrangements or games of honor in order to avoid humiliation. They assume tough poses such as (a) "They can beat me up, but I won't cry." (b) "Instead of crying I will laugh just to show them that I cannot be hurt!" (c) "I'll turn whatever was shameful into a source of pride!" (d) "I'll magically turn what disgusted me into pleasure." The function of these self-arrangements is to protect themselves from feeling humiliated. Since they are designed to win or gain moral superiority over the enemy, and to make that person change rather than to explore self-knowledge and express inner truth, these patients often become confused as to their real identity vis-à-vis deployments utilized for self-survival. Helping them to discriminate between false and real parts of identity also enhances their sense of self.

6. Many deployed patients protect themselves from feelings of humiliation by displaying a strong sense of entitlement (Moses and Moses-Hrushovski 1990), which prevents them from taking responsibility for the direction of their lives. Others are used as objects of addictive demands, for the purpose of self-soothing, or as objects to be mastered and attacked. When the analyst's attitudes relate to the above-mentioned obstacles, the latter can be utilized for eventual self-growth.

RESISTANCE TO CHANGE AS A RESULT OF A DISSOCIATION BETWEEN PRESENT AND PAST

A frequent obstacle to real change through analytic work is found in the attitude of deployed patients toward their past. One of the analytic goals in the treatment of these patients consists of trying to inhibit immediate action—when it is used to escape feelings—and facilitating the shift of emphasis from action to the feeling, thinking, imagining, wanting person in the present while keeping constant and open contact with the past and future. The problem, however, is that there is a massive dissociation between present and past in these patients in terms of their experiencing selves, and they do not have the ability to shift flexibly between their child and adult parts. When deployed patients do bring up memories, it is often more like reaching abstract points on the maps of their lives, or assuming memories whose experience eludes them, than revisiting the real landscapes of childhood regions. How can we enable deployed patients to feel themselves into the concrete scenes of their childhood, to link their numerous selves through emotional reality? "It is the child's emotional reality that is conserved, so that the eight-year-old self is holding his five-year-old self's emotional experience" (Bollas 1991, pp. 196–197). Tagore wrote that he spent much money traveling around the world to see rivers and mountains, but that he forgot to notice the drop of dew near his house in which all the universe that surrounds him is reflected. How to reach memories that allow one to feel what the child feels, thinks, imagines, is one question. Another is how to turn memories reported as stories-that-might-have-happened into concrete memories with the texture of inner experience.

Mrs. Z., who had previously been in a long, classical analysis, told her new therapist that a memory of sexual abuse at the age of 6 had helped her understand her apologetic position and feelings of guilt. But it was not until her daughter was 6 years old that she could sense the helplessness of the child vis-à-vis the "big man": that even though she had complied willingly with her abuser because of the sweets he offered her, she, the child, could not be blamed as though she had been an adult. How can one help such a woman to feel the child in herself, to see herself from the eyes of a child rather than as a 6-year-old adult, and to forgive herself without needing a daughter to be of the same age?!

Some of the approaches that help build affective contact between adults and their child parts are exploring the dynamics of specific resistances such as being constantly on guard against being looked down upon or treated as a child; evoking interest and curiosity about themselves as adults and as children by asking detailed questions (Boesky 1989); enabling patients to feel their child parts empathically in a variety of ways without either condemning the child within or overidentifying with it; and "making, breaking and remaking the contexts" as an outcome of patient–analyst dialogue (Schafer 1991).

Opening the coffins of long-buried feelings is a frightening process. Out of fear and anger at what is perceived as insensitivity toward their psychic pain, deployed patients tend to react with narcissistic rage (Kohut 1971, 1972, 1977). At such times they need an analyst who "holds" them firmly and gently, similar to a child who kicks and hurts the caretaker in a temper tantrum. These enacted dynamics evoke strong countertransference reactions. How to be firm, yet not aggressive? How to be neutral, yet not lose emotional touch with the patient as a result of his or her defensiveness? These are some of the problems each analyst tries to solve in order to build and maintain the atmosphere that facilitates change.

Some other factors that contribute to the dissociation between present and past relate to attitudes toward one's child and adult parts. Often it feels as if one can be either a child who tyrannizes the adult or the adult who suppresses the child. Many of the deployed patients felt that they had had to function as adults too early and too abruptly, whether because of illness or death of one family member or because of other traumatic events. In order not to be overwhelmed by longings to be taken care of like a child or be threatened by insults of being treated like a child, they hardened themselves into a rigid position of a child who acts in the role of an adult, which interferes with an ongoing dialogue of relationships among the various parts.

THE GOLDEN FANTASY—A SIGNIFICANT RESISTANCE TO CHANGE

Sidney Smith (1977) discusses a specific hidden fantasy that he found in the course of analysis with many patients: the wish to have all of their needs met in a relationship hallowed to perfection. The patient's position in respect to this fantasy is always passive. I have found a great similarity in the fantasy life of deployed patients. As Smith (1977) says, "To maintain the fantasy intact, to search endlessly for its fulfillment in every relationship becomes the *raison d'être*. It is as if they must deny 'the Fall' and in this way deny as well any real loss" (p. 311). Novick and Novick (1991) say that denial was maintained by an omnipotent fantasy in which everything painful was turned into a sign of special favor, uniqueness, and magical power. It is difficult for these patients to give up such "perfect fantasies," in which they have invested so many years of feelings and imagination. Acknowledging the difficulty is one step toward its eventual solution.

Often, patients such as those described by S. Smith as well as many deployed patients assume the role of the therapist in their treatment—not only out of a competitive sense of one-upmanship, but even more out of a need to fill the gaps in the internal representation of their own limited, ego-fragmented mothers (Searles 1973). With S. Smith (1977), I believe that analysts must first immerse themselves in the fantasies of their patients, in the hope that the patients' identification with their analysts will enable the analysts to serve as a bridge between the patients' fantasy and reality. The struggle in analysis is to keep alive the conflict—inside the patient—between that side of the self that wishes to indulge in fantasy and the side that wishes to force the infantile self into a position of renunciation. It is necessary then to relentlessly confront these patients with their efforts to project one side or the other of these self-representations onto the analyst.

OTHER FACTORS MAINTAINING THE STATUS QUO

Addiction and automatic behavior play a leading role in the defensive dynamics of deployed patients. Some of the questions in the back of my mind while working with deployed patients are the following: What psychic pain are they trying to numb through the strategies they are addicted to? What is the role of a self-image of powerlessness that does not change, in spite of evidence to the contrary? What is the role of automatism when patients constantly act—without any relation to what they feel or what is relevant, even despite changed feelings and increased understanding? What is the role of preserving their tension? Is it in order to be prepared against being shocked by sudden catastrophes once again? Does the tension provide a pleasurable sense of excitement?

I have found it crucial in my work with deployed patients to stop and look at such conserving factors whenever they occur in the session—be it in the transference or the extratransference situation. As Nemetz (1979) says,

> This allows the patient to evaluate previously unacknowledged and therefore unchanged danger situations, relationships, and traumatic experiences. These include shifts and changes in the importance of specific traumatic effects and relationships, an evaluation in the perception of key objects from the past and maturation in the various self images in keeping with the patient's changed status as an adult.[pp. 130–131]

SUMMARY

I have presented, in telescoped form, what I experience as the principal attitudes and conceptions that guide me in my work with deployed patients. The emphasis here is not on techniques or methods, but rather on attitudes. In trying to untwine these attitudinal elements from the fabric of my clinical work with such patients, I have come up with about a hundred different sets and attitudes. This makes me feel like a centipede walking on all hundred feet at once. It is the beginning of the long process of determining the even-larger number of elements that I have discerned as playing a role in my clinical work with deployed patients. The more I think and write about it, and the more I meet it in the literature, the more differentiated and enriched my analytic instrument becomes. Kohut's remarks about the possibility of developing the capacity of empathy within us (1977) is relevant also to other attitudes.

"When you come right down to it," Picasso is said to have remarked while visiting a Braque exhibition, "all you have is your self! It's like a sun in your belly with a thousand rays." This reflects my views on the analyst's inner laboratory and his attitudes.

REFERENCES

Abend, S. (1979). Unconscious fantasy and theories of cure. *Journal of the American Psychoanalytic Association* 27:579–596.

Adatto, C. P. (1957). On pouting. In *The World of Emotions*, ed. C. W. Socarides. New York: International Universities Press, 1977.

Adler, G. (1980). Transference, real relationship and alliance. *International Journal of Psycho-Analysis* 61:547–558.

_____ (1989). Uses and limitations of Kohut's self psychology in the treatment of borderline patients. *Journal of the American Psychoanalytic Association* 37:761–787.

Anzieu, A., and Anzieu, D. (1985). Between past and present: the interpretation of the container. *European Psychoanalytic Federation* 24:43–59.

Arlow, J. A., and Brenner, C. (1988). The future of psychoanalysis. *Psychoanalytic Quarterly* 57:1–14.

Balint, M. (1968). *The Basic Fault: Therapeutic Aspects of Regression*. London: Tavistock.

Balter, L., Lothane, Z., and Spencer, J. H. (1980). On the analyzing instrument. *Psychoanalytic Quarterly*, 49:474–504.

Baudry, F. (1989). Character, character type and character organization. *Journal of the American Psychoanalytic Association* 37:655–687.

_____ (1991). The relevance of the analyst's character and attitudes to his work. *Journal of the American Psychoanalytic Association* 39:917–939.

Beres, D., and Arlow, J. A. (1974). Fantasy identification in empathy. *Psychoanalytic Quarterly* 43:26–50.

Bion, W. R. (1967). *Second Thoughts*. London: Heinemann.

Boesky, D. (1982). Acting out: a reconsideration of the concept. *International Journal of Psycho-Analysis* 63:39–55.

_____ (1989). The questions and curiosity of the psychoanalyst. *Journal of the American Psychoanalytic Association* 37:579–605.

Bollas, C. (1987). *The Shadow of the Object: Psychoanalysis of the Unthought Known*. London: Free Association Books.

_____ (1991). *Forces of Destiny: Psychoanalysis and Human Idiom*. London: Free Association Books.

Boyer, J. B. (1989). Countertransference and technique in working with the regressed patient. *International Journal of Psycho-Analysis* 70:701–725.

Busch, F. (1989). The compulsion to repeat in action: a developmental perspective. *International Journal of Psycho-Analysis* 70:535–545.

Coltart, N. E. C. (1991). The analysis of an elderly patient. *International Journal of Psycho-Analysis* 72:209–221.

Compton A. (1987). Objects and attitudes. *Journal of the American Psychoanalytic Association* 35:609–629.

Cooper, A. M. (1987). Changes in psychoanalytic ideas: transference interpretation. *Journal of the American Psychoanalytic Association* 35:77–96.

Dorpat, T. L. (1991). Female homosexuality: an overview. In *The Homosexualities*, ed. C. W. Socarides, and V. D. Volkan. New York: International Universities Press.

Duncan, D. (1990). The feel of the session. *Psychoanalysis and Contemporary Thought* 13:3–23.

Eiserer, P. (1959). Personal communication.

Emde, R. N. (1990). Mobilizing fundamental modes of development: empathic availability and therapeutic action. *Journal of the American Psychoanalytic Association* 38:881–915.

Freud, S. (1912). Recommendations to physicians practicing psychoanalysis. *Standard Edition* 12.

―――― (1923). Recommendations to physicians practicing psychoanalysis. *Standard Edition* 12.

French, T., and Wheeler, D. (1963). Hope and repudiation of hope in psychoanalytic therapy. *International Journal of Psycho-Analysis* 44:304–316.

Fromm, E., et al. (1960). *Zen Buddhism and Psychoanalysis*. London: Candor Books.

Fromm, M. F. (1989). Impasse and transitional relatedness. In *The Facilitating Environment: Clinical Applications of Winnicott's Theory*, ed. G. Fromm, and B. L. Smith, pp. 179–204. New York: International Universities Press.

Fromm-Reichmann, F. (1950). *Principles of Intensive Psychotherapy*. Chicago: Phoenix Books.

Gardner, M. R. (1983). *Self Inquiry*. Boston: Little, Brown.

―――― (1991). The art of psychoanalysis: on oscillation and other matters. *Journal of the American Psychoanalytic Association* 39:851–871.

Gill, M. M. (1954). Psychoanalysis and exploratory psychotherapy. *Journal of the American Psychoanalytic Association* 2:171–197.

―――― (1982). *Analysis of Transference v. Theory and Technique*. New York: International Universities Press.

Goldberg, A. (1989). A shared view of the world. *International Journal of Psycho-Analysis* 70:16–20.

Gombrich, E. H. (1972). *The Story of Art*. London: Phaidon.

Green, H. (1964). *I Never Promised You a Rose Garden*. New York: Signet Books.

Greenacre, P. (1971). Play in relation to creative imagination. In *Emotional Growth*. New York: International Universities Press.

Greenson, R. R. (1960). Empathy and its vicissitudes. *International Journal of Psycho-Analysis* 41:418–424.

———— (1962). On enthusiasm. *Journal of the American Psychoanalytic Association* 10:3–21.

———— (1965). The problem of working through. In *Explorations in Psychoanalysis*, ed. R. R. Greenson, pp. 225–267. New York: International Universities Press.

———— (1966). That "impossible" profession. *Journal of the American Psychoanalytic Association* 14:9–27.

———— (1978). *Explorations in Psychoanalysis*. New York: International Universities Press.

Grolnick, S. A., Barkin, L., and Muensterberger, W. (1978). *Between Reality and Fantasy*. Northvale, NJ: Jason Aronson.

Guntrip, H. (1975). My experience of analysis with Fairbairn and Winnicott. *International Review of Psychoanalysis* 2:145–156.

Hamilton, N. G. (1990). The containing function and the analyst's projective identification. *International Journal of Psycho-Analysis* 71:445–453.

Hrushovski, R. (1970). The teacher's attitudes in establishing a climate of growth in the classroom. In *Counseling in Education*. Jerusalem: Hebrew University Press.

Hurwitz, M. R. (1986). The analyst, his theory and the psychoanalytic process. *Psychoanalytic Study of the Child* 41:439–467.

Isakower, O. (1963). *Minutes of faculty meeting of the New York Psychoanalytic Institute*. Unpublished.

Jaffe, D. (1986). Empathy, counteridentification, countertransference: a review. *Psychoanalytic Quarterly* 55:215–244.

Katz, R. L. (1967). *Empathy: Its Nature and Uses*. London: Free Press of Glencoe.

Kernberg, O. F. (1974). Further contributions to the treatment of narcissistic personalities. *International Journal of Psycho-Analysis* 55:215–240.

———— (1987). Projection of projective identification: developmental and clinical aspects. *Journal of the American Psychoanalytic Association* 35:795–821.

Khan. M. M. R. (1974). *The Privacy of the Self*. London: Hogarth.

Klauber, J. (1981). *Difficulties in the Analytic Encounter*. Northvale, NJ: Jason Aronson.

Kohut, H. (1971). *The Analysis of the Self.* New York: International Universities Press.

_____ (1972). Thoughts on narcissism and narcissistic rage. *Psychoanalytic Study of the Child* 27:360–400.

_____ (1977). *The Restoration of the Self.* New York: International Universities Press.

_____ (1984). *How Does Analysis Cure?* Chicago: University of Chicago Press.

Kris, E. (1952). *On Preconscious Mental Processes: Psychoanalytic Explorations in Art,* pp. 303–318. New York: International Universities Press.

_____ (1956). On some vicissitudes of insight in psychoanalysis. *International Journal of Psycho-Analysis* 37:445–455.

Levenson, E. (1988). Real frogs in imaginary gardens: facts and fantasies in psychoanalysis. *Psychoanalytic Inquiry* 8:552–568.

Levin, S. (1971). The psychoanalysis of shame. *International Journal of Psycho-Analysis* 52:355–362.

Lewis, H. B. (1987). *The Role of Shame in Symptom Formation.* Hillsdale, NJ: Lawrence Erlbaum.

Loewald, H. W. (1960). On the therapeutic action of psychoanalyst. *International Journal of Psycho-Analysis* 41:16–33.

_____ (1986). Transference and countertransference. *Journal of the American Psychoanalytic Association* 34:275–289.

Malcone, L. (1975). The analytic situation. *Journal of the Philadelphia Association for Psychoanalysis* 11:11–13.

May, R. (1969). *Love and Will.* New York: Laurel.

McDougall, J. (1982). *Theatres of the Mind.* London: Free Association Books. New York: Basic Books, 1985.

_____ (1989). *Theatres of the Body.* London: Free Association Books.

McLaughlin, J. T. (1991). Clinical aspects of enactment. *Journal of the American Psychoanalytic Association* 39:595–614.

Modell, A. H. (1984). Self preservation and the preservation of the self. *The Annual of Psychoanalysis* 12:69–86.

_____ (1990). *Other Times, Other Realities: Toward a Theory of Psychoanalytic Treatment.* Cambridge, MA: Harvard University Press.

Morrison, N. K. (1986). The role of shame in schizophrenia. In *Essential Papers on Narcissism,* ed. A. P. Morrison, pp. 51–57. New York: New York University Press.

Moses-Hrushovski, R. (1986). Interpretation of the present or the past. *Bulletin of the European Psychoanalytic Federation* 25:15–25.

_____ (1987). *In search of the self and its lost parts: location of attitudes and skills of an analyst at work.* Presented at the Mini-Conference at Austen Riggs Center, Stockbridge, MA.

_____ (1992a). The role of the therapist's attitudes in psychotherapy. *The Austen Riggs Center Review* 5:10–14.

_____ (1992b). Transference and countertransference. *International Journal of Psycho-Analysis* 73:561–576.

Moses-Hrushovski, R., and Moses, R. (1989). *"Deployment" in self-defeating persons: a specific configuration met in the treatment of self disorders.* Presented at Austen Riggs Center, Stockbridge, MA, June.

Moses, R., and Moses-Hrushovski, R. (1990). Reflections on the sense of entitlement. *Psychoanalytic Study of the Child* 45:61–77.

Nacht, S. (1964). Silence as an integrative factor. *International Journal of Psycho-Analysis* 45:299–302.

Nemetz, J. (1979). A panel report: conceptualizing the nature of the therapeutic action of psychoanalytic psychotherapy. *Journal of the American Psychoanalytic Association* 27:127–145.

Novick, J., and Novick, K. K. (1991). Some comments on masochism and the delusion of omnipotence from a developmental perspective. *Journal of the American Psychoanalytic Association* 59: 307–333.

Ogden, T. H. (1989). Playing, dreaming and interpreting experience: comments on potential space in the facilitating references. In *The Facilitating Environment: Clinical Applications of Winnicott's Theory*, ed. G. Fromm and B. Smith, pp. 255–278. New York: International Universities Press.

Ornstein, A. (1989). Contribution to the theory of psychoanalytic psychotherapy. Revised version of paper delivered in the Distinguished Lecturer Series, American Psychiatric Association, San Francisco, CA: May.

Ornstein, A., and Ornstein, P. H. (1990). The process of psychoanalytic psychotherapy: a self-psychological perspective. *Review of Psychiatry* 9: 323–340.

Parson, E. R., and Schachter, S. O. (1988). The difficult patient: psychotherapeutic strategies, conceptual and therapeutic dimensions. (Special issue). *Contemporary Psychotherapy* 18.

Pine, F. (1988). The four psychologies of psychoanalysis and their place in clinical work. *Journal of the American Psychoanalytic Association.* 36:571–597.

Rangell, L. (1967). Psychoanalysis, affect and the human core. *Psychoanalytic Quarterly* 36:172–262.

_____ (1968). Symposium: acting out and its role in the psychoanalytic process. *International Journal of Psycho-Analysis* 49:195–201.

_____ (1975). Psychoanalysis and the process of change. *International Journal of Psycho-Analysis* 56:87–98.

_____ (1981). From insight to change, *Journal of the American Psychoanalytic Association* 29:119–141.

Reich, W. (1948). *Character Analysis*. London: Vision Press, Peter Nevill.

Rogers, C. R. (1958). The characteristics of a helping relationship. *Personal and Guidance Journal* 37:6–16.

Rosenfeld, H. (1987). *Impasse and Interpretation: Therapeutic and Antitherapeutic Factors in the Psychoanalytic Treatment of Psychotic and Neurotic Patients*, ed. D. Tuckett. London: Tavistock Routledge; New York: The New Library of Psychoanalysis.

Roth, S. (1990). *Psychotherapy: The Art of Wooing Nature*. Northvale, NJ: Jason Aronson.

Rycroft, C. (1962). Beyond the reality principle. *International Journal of Psycho-Analysis* 43:388–394.

_____ (1968). *Imagination and Reality*. London: Hogarth.

Sandler, J. (1960). The background of safety. *International Journal of Psycho-Analysis* 41:352–356.

_____ (1976). Countertransference and role responsiveness. *International Journal of Psycho-Analysis* 3:43–48.

Sandler, J., and Sandler, A. M. (1978). On the development of object relationships and affects. *International Journal of Psycho-Analysis* 59:285–296.

_____ (1983). The "second censorship": the three box model and some technical implications. *International Journal of Psycho-Analysis* 64:413–425.

_____ (1987). The past unconscious, the present conscious and the vicissitudes of guilt. *International Journal of Psycho-Analysis* 68:331–341.

Schacht, L. (1988). Winnicott's position in regard to the self with special reference to childhood. *International Review of Psycho-Analysis* 15:515–531.

Schafer, R. (1983). *The Analytic Attitude*. London: Hogarth.

_____ . The search for common ground. *International Journal of Psycho-Analysis* 71:49–52.

Scharfman, M. (1979). Panel report: conceptualizing the nature of therapeutic action of psychoanalysis. *Journal of the American Psychoanalytic Association* 27:627–643.

206   Deployment

Schwaber, E. A. (1990). Interpretation and therapeutic action of psychoanalysis. *International Journal of Psycho-Analysis* 71:229–240.

Searles, H. F. (1973). Concerning therapeutic symbiosis. In *The Annual of Psychoanalysis, vol. 1*. New York: Quadrangle.

—— (1977). Dual- and multiple-identity processes in borderline functioning. In *Borderline Disorder: The Concept, The Symptom, The Patient*, ed. P. Hartocollis. New York: International Universities Press.

Siegel, E. (1988). *Female Homosexuality: Choice without Volition*. Hillsdale. NJ: Analytic Press.

Smith, H. F. (1990). Cues: the perceptual edge of the transference. *International Journal of Psycho-Analysis* 71:219–229.

Smith, S. (1977). The golden fantasy. *International Journal of Psycho-Analysis* 58:311–324.

Solan, R. (1991). "Jointness" as integration of merging and separateness in object relations and narcissism. *Psychoanalytic Study of the Child* 46:337–352.

Stewart, H. (1990). Interpretation and other agents for psychic change. *International Journal of Psycho-Analysis* 17:61–69.

Stone, L. (1961). *The Psychoanalytic Situation*. New York: International Universities Press.

—— (1981). Notes on the noninterpretive elements in the psychoanalytic situation and the process. *Journal of the American Psychoanalytic Association* 29:89–119.

Strachey, J. (1934). The nature of the therapeutic action of psychoanalysis. *International Journal of Psycho-Analysis* 15:127–159. (Reprinted in *International Journal of Psycho-Analysis* [1969] 50:275–292.)

Thomson, P. (1980). On the receptive function of the analyst. *International Review of Psychoanalysis*. 7:183–204.

Tuckett, D. (1982). *Words and the psychoanalytic interaction*. Presented in London, October 1982.

—— (1989). A brief view of Herbert Rosenfeld's contribution to the theory of psychoanalytic technique. *International Journal of Psycho-Analysis* 70:619–625.

Viederman, M. (1991). The real person of the analyst and his role in the psychoanalytic cure. *Journal of the American Psychoanalytic Association* 39:451–491.

Wallerstein, R., Hartley, D., and Rosenberg, S. (1989). *Scales of psychological capacities: a new approach to the assessment of structural change*. Presented at Austen Riggs Center, Stockbridge, MA, June.

Watts, A. (1975). *The Way of Zen*. Harmondsworth: Penguin Books.

Weigert, E. (1954). The importance of flexibility in psychoanalytic technique. *Journal of the American Psychoanalytic Association* 7:702–710.

Winnicott, D. W. (1965). Ego distortion in terms of true and false self. In *The Maturational Process and the Facilitating Environment*, pp. 140–152. London: Hogarth.

_____ (1971). *Playing and Reality*. London: Tavistock.

8

DEPLOYMENT IN COMPARISON WITH OTHER DEFENSE SYSTEMS AND CLINICAL PICTURES

THE PHENOMENOLOGY OF
DEFENSIVE STRUCTURE

To begin, I will map deployment with respect to other defense mechanisms, clinical pictures, and forms of self organizations such as character or casts of mind. There are strong elements of masochism in deployed patients that are primarily employed as defenses against feelings of impotence and humiliation. Novick and Novick (1991) note that all their masochistic patients exhibited a pervasive delusion of omnipotence. By the time they came for treatment, their unfused primitive hatred and overstimulated, excited libidinal impulses had interacted with a fragile defense system and a deficient superego. In this respect, deployment is a form of intrapsychic adaptation to such unpleasant affects as anxiety, shame, and guilt aimed at warding off threats of annihilation and feelings of disintegration resulting from these affects. The pathological equilibrium they thus create and re-create interferes with their capacity to tolerate feelings that threaten the integrity of the self, especially feelings of shame, guilt, depres-

211

sion, and envy. The treatment of masochistic character problems has long been considered one of the more difficult analytic challenges. Their fixity and self-defeating nature, in life and in treatment, as well as the countertransference they engender, are major constituents of this difficulty. Thus, difficulties similar to those described by Novick and Novick are experienced in clinical work with deployed patients.

Anne-Marie Sandler (1977) describes a structure of defense that I too have found in many deployed patients. Her patient, Mrs. B., reacted to pressure with an overwhelming feeling of confusion and panic. She would freeze or immediately rush to comforting daydreams or relatively stereotyped patterns of behavior rather than face her reasons for feeling pressured—as if she had to desperately and impulsively reach out for safety. Mrs. B.'s reactions exhibited a specific quality of defensiveness, relating to earlier phases, somewhat similar to the ways in which an 8-month-old baby reacts to stranger anxiety—the fear of strange things and people. Sandler concludes that an understanding of these patients' functioning may provide a further dimension to the understanding of "complicated narcissism." The reactions of deployed patients to pressures are very similar to what she describes.

Disaffected or alexithymic patients described by McDougall (1989) reflect another kind of defense structure typical of deployed patients. These patients need to escape their feelings and do so by tending to somatize their feelings under stressful conditions or by numbing, for example, using sexuality as a drug. McDougall suggests that their chance of overcoming the problem of addiction depends on their readiness to discover why they flee to the soothing substance at the slightest signal of stress. The defensive pattern described by McDougall is similar in some respects to that of deployed patients whose self organization is based on putting feelings aside in order not to be paralyzed by contradictory or overwhelming feelings.

In his paper "Grievance" (1993) Michael Feldman talks about patients who are again very similar in their phenomenology to deployed patients, though in a different way. According to Feldman, grievance represents a relentless attack on the object, where it is difficult to identify what if anything would release the object from the implacable grip. Patients in a state of grievance have a strong sense of entitlement, Feldman continues to say. It seems like a moral obligation to them to achieve a state that is just and right. The patients sense themselves to be innocent victims who are considerate and generous, whereas the people who are the cause of their grievance are felt to be unquestionably guilty of neglect, malice, or cruelty. Feldman views grievance as based on an underlying delusional set of beliefs that the patients cannot bear to relinquish.

Many deployed patients show similar characteristics. There is a preoccupation with grave errors committed by their significant others. Deployed patients invest much energy in demonstrating the wrong inflicted on them. But while their stubborn hold on these beliefs at times has a psychotic quality, their grievance seems to be primarily related to their strong corrective needs: they want to find words for the experienced unfairness and are deployed into a corrective program to discover jointly with the analyst the unique configuration of injustice they had experienced in their past; and they want to obtain acknowledgment, affirmation, and correction for injustices inflicted on them—all this before they would be willing or able to relinquish their grievance and take responsibility (Moses-Hrushovski 1992, 1993).

Wilhelm Reich (1933) suggests that character is essentially a narcissistic protection against both the threatening outer world and the instinctual impulses that are crying out for expression. While being deployed into grievance may seem like a character trait, seeing it as such omits the specific nature of the phenomenon.

Robbins's (1988) descriptions of the defensive phenomena of "primitive personalities," who seem unwilling or incapable of thinking in a conflict-perceiving and conflict-solving mode, remind me in many ways of the functioning and defensiveness of deployed patients. Like all fundamentalists, they often think in extremes of black or white. It is just as difficult for them to simultaneously hold conflicting thoughts in mind as it is to allow themselves to consciously experience emotional ambivalence toward an object. Robbins sees many gifted, creative, charismatic individuals as belonging to this group of patients. They are usually accomplished in their occupations, and often appear to be socially adaptive; but, in contrast to the more mature neurotically organized personalities, they belong to the various narcissistic diagnostic categories that react to object-related desires and needs as intrinsically threatening and dangerous. In Robbins's view, conventional analytic therapy of individuals with such personalities is limited by the theoretical assumptions that analysts have developed through their work with neurotic patients. In trying to aid these patients, he endeavors to help them recognize and sustain their emotional predispositions, to become aware of the need to integrate extreme and contradictory cognitive-affective states with regard to the same object or mental content, and thereby develop the capacity to sustain ambivalence and conflict and to perceive connections and consequences from hitherto unconnected thoughts and behavior. In his experience, the foregoing often enables these individuals to cope with their conflict in an adaptive manner so that they do not then require further treatment.

Weinshel's (1989) description of unconsolable patients fits the dynamics and the defensive structure of deployed patients in many ways. These patients describe a definite feeling of stubbornness and of resolute determination to not give up their misery. They seem to suffer more and for a longer time than other narcissistic patients, and to produce more archaic material that at times suggests a psychotic substratum. Moreover, these patients are frequently unable to tolerate the pain and pressure of their disconsolation and need to withdraw, to ruminate or brood alone. Often, in desperation, they may resort to such compulsive forms of action as drinking and drug-taking or compulsive, repetitive masturbation that may be free of any accompanying fantasies. It is not always clear what factors are capable of precipitating such reactions; even more enigmatic is the process whereby the inconsolability gradually diminishes, and then disappears altogether. Weinshel suggests that better understanding may provide us with a more detailed knowledge of a number of atypical clinical pictures that often frustrate our attempts at diagnosis and classification. At times, inconsolability appears to have the structure and genesis of a symptom; at other times, that of a mood or a mourning process. In some cases, the defensive elements are more conspicuous; in others, the inconsolability seems to be the nodal point of a complex character structure.

In deployment, as in the defensive modes and clinical pictures described above, there is a focus on the maladaptive defenses against being affectively overwhelmed and disintegrated. But in deployment a paramount role is assigned to the feeling of shame. Just as anxiety is the central motive behind what has been described as the ego's defense mechanisms, I view shame as a central motivating force behind deployment. Shame is one of the main affects defended against in deployment; guilt, envy, and depression are often inextricably intertwined with shame.

PSYCHODYNAMIC ASPECTS OF THE STRUCTURE OF DEFENSE

Within the past twenty years a variety of trends have emerged in the psychoanalytic understanding of the concept of defense mechanisms. S. H. Cooper (1989) has compared several of the more recent trends in terms of their contribution to the theory of these mechanisms. These include Schafer's (1968) and Kris's (1984) theories of the complex motivational properties involved, Brenner's (1982) functional theory, Kernberg's (1976) object representational theory, Modell's (1984) two-person theory, and Kohut's (1984) self psychology. Cooper focuses on several threads that have become central to defense theory: mechanisms of defense being one aspect of the broad array of ego functions, the role that object representations play in the theory of defense, and the relation between the external world and intrapsychic processes. The following discussion proceeds along Cooper's lines, and includes what I deem to be characteristics of deployed patients in comparison with conceptions of patients exhibiting other defense mechanisms.

One of the major differences among defense–mechanism theorists involves the variety of referents: impulse, drives, drive derivatives, object loss, environmental failure, and the enfeebled self. "What is really at issue and a matter of varying opinion among us," says Wallerstein (1981), "is the place of vicissitudes of drive and defense of infantile sexuality and the anxieties which it gives rise to within the personality, the individual, the self" (p. 382). The psychoanalytic literature on this subject reflects a bifurcation in which one group of theorists places more emphasis on defenses against instinctual drives and drive derivatives, and a second focuses more on the self as the reference point for defense.

A comparison of two definitions of defense mechanisms, that of Wallerstein (1985) and that of Laplanche and Pontalis (1973), may reflect the different emphases relevant to the defense structure of deployed patients. According to Wallerstein, the defense mechanism is a construct that denotes a way in which the mind functions, which is invoked to explain how behavior, affect, and ideas serve to avert or modulate unwanted impulse discharge. To Laplanche and Pontalis, mechanisms of defense, as a group of operations, are aimed at reducing if not eliminating any change perceived as threatening to the integrity and stability of the biopsychological individual—including behavioral operations related to attack or flight. While Wallerstein's definition is pertinent to deployment, the stress that Laplanche and Pontalis place on the elements of change and self organization is very relevant.

Different levels of analytic observation and theoretical discourse are utilized by the different theorists. Self psychology views defense as an attempt to mitigate an awareness of painful affects associated with the exposure of structural deficits. The self psychologist's primary focus is therefore on the state of the self, its structural and functional weaknesses, deficiencies, defensive and compensatory structures, on the one hand, and their cohesiveness, vigor, and vitality, on the other (Ornstein 1991). The self psychologist does not view behavior as primarily motivated by instinctual libidinal and aggressive drives and by defenses against them, but rather as fitting a person's need to organize his or her psychological experiences into a psychological structure, the self, that provides for a coherent sense of selfhood (Wolf 1988).

While the various referents of defense mechanism—impulse, drive and drive derivatives, object loss, environmental failure, and enfeebled self—can all be observed in deployed patients, I believe that there are different points of emphasis and a different view of the interplay of forces. Thus, rather than focusing on the analysands' unconscious wishes and on the defenses instituted against them, there is more emphasis by Kohut (1984) on the patient's person, on the patient in a given situation, on the patient's defending himself and fighting for his dignity. My view of deployment is similar to that of the self psychologist, in that its focus is on the self, but it differs from self psychology in some ways such as the following:

1. The self psychologist focuses on defenses as involving experiential deficiencies rather than mechanisms of defense per se, and believes that some form of idealization and other narcissistic defenses are not resistances to be analyzed. From the point of view of deployment, however, all defensive phenomena—including the idealization of the analyst—are parts of corrective structures to be analyzed and opened up to reach psychic wounds.

2. Unlike Kohut's notion of the vertical split-off parts of the psyche, which overlap to some extent with Winnicott's (1965) description of the defensively motivated "false self" and often involves compliance with an empathically faulty object

(Cooper 1989), deployment refers to different states of self-presence and self-participation. Thus there is no reference to the "false" self versus the "real" self, as two distinct diagnostic entities, but rather a view of distinct states of the self as they vary or change in the analytic sessions and in life. This places the focus on the exploration and interaction of specific factors that weaken, restrict, and falsify the self or lead to its complete loss.

3. Whereas Kohutians tend to emphasize the role of the thwarted emotional needs to be recognized, my deploymental view gives much more space to aggressive and sexual vicissitudes as they unfold in the course of the treatment, and to motives that cause the analysand to be so insistent on having certain needs gratified—motives such as not having to feel envy. There are also specific encapsulated situations in which the patient unwittingly remains frozen so as to have the right to demand legitimization and be saved from feeling the unconscious burden of shame and guilt.

SHOULD WE VIEW DEPLOYMENT AS ENACTMENTS? AS CHARACTER TRAITS? AS CHARACTER RESISTANCES?

The ambiguity concerning the definition of *character* has been amply demonstrated by the frequently confusing use of the term by various authors. Rosen (1961) writes that the term *character* is meant to convey the sense of an overall expressive style that determines in frequently predictable ways how an individual will react to situations or cope with tasks. Character is then an aspect of ongoing individual functioning that implies neither health nor pathology. Weinshel (1971) distinguishes certain moods he refers to as casts of mind or temperament that might be included under character, specifically because of a "more enduring tendency and of their syntonicity with the sense of self" (p. 314). Perhaps most similar to my view of deployment is Jacobson's

(1964) description of moods as a "generalized modification of all discharge patterns lending to our thoughts, actions and feelings a characteristic color" (p. 133). Thus, while deployments are similar in some ways to the views and formulations of other authors, they are also different in certain respects.

Deployments are universal enactments mobilized by normal, psychotic, and neurotic persons. A deployment becomes pathological when a person invests excessive energy in overly restrictive ways of perceiving, feeling, and acting. In my view of deployment, patients playact their conflicts in the way they behave in the analytic situation as well as in their lives. Along with Sandler and colleagues (1980), I distinguish between the behavior of those who act out and that of habitual "enactors" whose life-styles are characterized by the living out of their impulses, wishes, and feelings. Sandler (1992) notes that little attention has been paid to ego restrictions and their consequences in adult life.

> We need to distinguish between resistance which results from heightened defensiveness when a specific conflict is reactivated, particularly when this occurs in the transference, and the inability of the patient to change because of the unalterable psychological bedrock in the patient's psyche: a specific psychobiological bedrock which involves to a very large degree the structures created by a specific individual's development within the specific reciprocal relation between the person and his environment. [p. 192]

The resistances inherent in the mental structure of deployed patients are present from the beginning of the treatment, and differ from those that develop as a consequence of the analytic process and transference, namely, as a defense against the emergence of anxiety-evoking material. Deployments do resemble the character resistances met in neurotic or narcissistic patients in some way. But they are not only character resistances; they are also a way of life that seems like an enactment of a mission these patients need to carry out, a mission to demonstrate injustice and unfairness until responsibility will be taken by those who deny it and until a correction for the self injuries will be achieved.

DEPLOYMENT AS A DEFENSIVE STRUCTURE OF THE SELF

Brenner (1982) suggests that the ego can make defensive use of such phenomena as ego attitudes, perceptions, alterations of attention, fantasy formation, and identification. Similarly, deployment, viewed as a defense of the self, serves multiple functions (Waelder 1930), including defensive functions, corrective self-consoling functions, and communicative functions. Brenner argues that defense is an aspect definable only in terms of its consequences, namely, the reduction of anxiety or depressive affect associated with drive derivatives or a superego function. In the deploymental view the role of the numerous affects and feeling states is emphasized. When we refer to defense, we traditionally think of anxiety as a stimulus. The role of other painful affects such as anger, shame, envy, or depression in motivating character defenses has often been underplayed (Baudry 1984). Another aspect of the deploymental perspective is its teleological orientation, in that much of the behavior is viewed in terms of the consequences it has for the survival of the patient's self.

Deployment is not only a battle against feelings, oppression, and perceived injustice. It is also a struggle for values like openness, flexibility, and respect.

Defensive Functions of Deployment

Deployed patients show a wide use of the mechanisms of splitting, disavowal, self-erasure or effacement, denial, and somatization—all in order to avoid states of disintegration and such unbearable feelings as envy, guilt, shame, and humiliation. Whereas classical psychoanalytic theory and technique emphasize the role of the repression of aggressive and sexual impulses toward early incestuous objects within the context of the transference relationship, the deploymental view deals more with the patients' strategies of the self, such as taking refuge in refusing to be blamed and shamed. In a similar way, it is not so much that their anger is repressed; rather they prefer being angry to being vulnerable and weak. They are motivated to not forget unforgivable behavior in principle because it has caused them unfair suffering, which often is viewed as the seeds of a catastrophe to come. What matters most to them is to maintain control, to fight for their mission, to protect themselves from disintegration, to achieve power to prove their righteousness, and to win their battle for justice; or at the very least not to be defeated once again.

Many theorists stress the importance of the analysand's having at least some spark of motivation for emotional introspection and insight and a will to recover in order to benefit from psychoanalytic treatment. This kind of motivation is lacking or is in a very minor key in many deployed patients. Their motivation is of a very different kind. It is not a willingness to express their tensions and psychic pain in order to obtain relief, or to understand the dynamics and obstacles to change and growth. Rather, it is a strong determination to obtain in analysis and in life the rights they feel entitled to, together with a strong determination to change others rather than themselves. It is a defensive motivation but more than that—it is often also a political stance, a *weltanschauung*.

The Reparative-Corrective Functions

One major form of the reparative-corrective function is consoling oneself. It is dissociated from the person's experiencing self and disconnected from the fears and the shame anxiety against which it is designed to protect. What is meant by the corrective-reparative function in deployed patients is very different from the reparative drive that Melanie Klein considered as the restoring of internal objects that have been damaged (Klein and Riviera 1937). This is also different from what Kohut (1984) defined as the need for narcissistic wounds to be recognized, mirrored, and thus repaired. The corrective wish of deployed patients is to correct the gross imbalance of power between them and their important others, and to correct the unfair and humiliating treatment meted out to them in the past. Much psychic energy is invested in widely elaborated reparative correcting and consoling programs with fantasies of creating a world for themselves within which they would never be vulnerable to a recurrence of their formative disappointments. Among the consoling programs enacted by deployed patients is a preoccupation in fantasy with their love objects in order not to have to deal with the disappointments and self injuries of real life.

To try to correct forcefully and magically the feelings of having been humiliated and hurt unconsciously involves an element of power, whether it is through programs of revenge in reality or in fantasy or through exerting pressure on the other to undo the wounds inflicted. This often becomes a battle to be emotionally understood, to be legitimized, and to be given the needed corrective emotional experience. The deployment into reparative-corrective trends is thus consciously a battle to achieve justice and unconsciously a defense against humiliation. These corrective programs, perceived as a source of comfort and as enabling survival of the self, are in fact self-defeating since psychic energy is invested largely in the attempt to correct past injuries rather than in their expression or exploration, in understanding and mourning them. This means living more in the past than living in the present with an eye toward the future.

Communicative Functions

The major form of communication of deployed patients is to act and to enact. One typical way of not being weakened by conflictual feelings is to quickly organize onself into action. One reason is that they have so frequently felt that their feelings and emotional needs are disrespected and not understood, they tend to act on them. In the analytic process, the analyst is asked to become a witness to the performance so that he should feel and understand what has been enacted (Boesky 1982). One form of enactment is a particular kind of dramatization, where the patients themselves become the feeling that they could not express verbally. An example of the different functions of such an enactment can be seen in the patient's turning into a zombie. It is an unconscious mechanism that leads to an affective response being elicited from the other, to be reflected back into the patient who otherwise feels empty and dead (Modell 1987). What is embodied through being a zombie is a protest against the climate that the patients had experienced as oppressive, a climate that had caused them to suppress their real feelings, thoughts, and fantasies. Being a zombie also has its defensive function—it seems to legitimize the disavowal of responsibility for their behavior and feelings, thus freeing them from feelings of guilt. A consoling function derives from the self-drugging aspect of the behavior, as if the patients could thereby sleep off their unbearable tensions and at the same time punish both the others and themselves through actively enacting inactivity.

COMPARISON WITH MELANIE KLEIN AND OTTO KERNBERG

Theorists such as Kernberg and Klein place the concept of internal objects at the center of their contribution to defense theory. Klein emphasizes the infant's unconscious fantasies as always being active and alive in the deepest layers of the mind. Thus, Klein's portrayal of the inner world describes how the aggressive impulses and fantasies arising in earliest relations of the infant to the mother's breast (e.g., sucking the breast dry and emptying it) lead to further fantasies of entering the mother and robbing her of the content of her body (Klein and Riviera 1937).

In the deploymental view, the emphasis is placed more on the self experience of the patient interacting with persons and details of his life history as they had been experienced and reacted to, in accordance with the perceptions and fantasies of the infant, child, and adolescent parts of the patient and as they are revived in the transference situations.

Kernberg (1975, 1983) extended Klein's work by delineating the relation between drive and object representations more clearly. To Kernberg and Klein's way of thinking, internalized objects are always influenced by the infant's instinctually based fantasies and projections. For Kernberg (1983), impulse and defense are expressed through an affectively imbued internalized object relationship.

The deploymental viewpoint focuses less on the internalizations of objects and more on the subject's experiences, on the etiological effect of the objects' responses to the former's instinctual vicissitudes and to the individual's ways of responding. It then leads to a different kind of understanding and a different atmosphere in the analytic situation.

Another basic difference between the Kleinian approach and that of looking at deployment relates to the "positions." The Kleinian model of desirable psychic change is bound up with hypotheses of the paranoid-schizoid and depressive positions, the anxieties of which require constant working through (de Bianchedi 1989). Whereas Kleinians use the term *position* in the developmental sense, I view deployment as a system of positions in the sense of roles, poses, and attitudes into which the patient rigidly organizes himself as part of his response to stress. In contrast to Klein's two basic positions—the paranoid-schizoid and the depressive positions—deployment is seen as the patient's self-programming into a variety of positions designed to protect him from feeling oppressed, humiliated, or weakened by subjective perceptions that endanger self-esteem and the survival of the sense of self, and which often cause him to become stuck in nonadaptive behavior patterns.

Paranoid-schizoid object relationships as described by Klein are mainly based on projective identification. In viewing deployment, emphasis is placed less on the mechanism of projective identification, even though this can be seen to be widely used by deployed patients, and more on the patient's specific tensions, on his need to control and to pass on his pressures in a speedy and automatic way, and on the different patterns that he uses to deal with his tensions. Projective identification is thus primarily regarded in the deploymental view as one of the patient's methods of communication. The leading anxiety in the paranoid-schizoid position, according to Klein, has to do with the survival of the self. It is either the operation of the death instinct inward—self destructiveness—or the fear of persecutors destroying the self and the ideal object (Segal 1979). In contrast, the patient's deployment, while it is also regarded primarily as protecting the self's survival, is viewed as an organization into certain positions that are capable of being transformed back into the self's feelings, feeling states, thoughts, and fantasies (as felt and inferred from the specific context of an analytic session). These positions are not seen as based on the death instinct. The destructive and aggressive drives—in my view—are reactions resulting from frustrations such as abuse, humiliation, shame, and helplessness, but not from the death instinct. The complicated question of whether aggression is a drive per se or arises reactively in response to frustration will not be discussed here.

Examples of positions into which deployed patients frequently organize themselves are the following: being a victim; being in the consoling role, which prevents them from being their complex and real selves; being the "older sibling," which may be a position of superiority and a defense against envy, inferiority or impotence; sitting on the fence, which unknowingly prevents them from investing themselves in their present, in that they view each state as a temporary one; being the sleeping beauty who waits to be awakened by the prince; being Peter Pan as a protest against having to grow up too soon, as a defense against death fears, or as a message of one's not wanting to belong to the adult world. These positions, when enacted blindly, arrest growth and change. When their protective functions vis-à-vis their specific hurts are identified and when the ways the patients organize themselves in relation to pressures are worked through, the direction of their psychic investment can change from a self-defeating into a self-developing one.

These and other positions are constantly enacted in the analytic situation. In the depressive position according to the Kleinian view, the anxiety concerns injury to the object through one's own aggression and through (fantasized) loss of the object. The relation to the object is ambivalent and when it is introjected, this results in a depressive superego. The degree to which the depression has been worked through and to which internal good objects have been securely established within the ego determines the degree of maturity and stability of the individual, according to Klein. In the depressive position, the ego is more integrated and the objects are persons and not parts of persons. In the deployed patients it would be difficult to determine to which of the two positions they belong, since they tend to move from one to the other, depending on the strength of their sense of self, on the degree of pressure exerted on them, and on the situation in which they find themselves. When Betty Joseph (1983) describes the motivations of those patients who are not interested in understanding their dynamics—very similar to what we see in deployed patients—her emphasis is on the patient's functioning at the paranoid-schizoid level, on his splitting off parts of his self, on his complex system of fantasies, anxieties, and defenses. The deploymental approach would stress more the factor of shame and countershame strategies that restrict the person's feelings and functioning, as well as the role of multiple positions to be transformed back into feelings, feeling states, thoughts, and fantasies as part of the analytic process.

SUMMARY

A major focus of treatment from the deploymental view is the emphasis on the various aspects of affects, intentionality, and their influence on behavior. Sandler (1989) states that we need to modify the very rigid position of seeing unconscious wishes as powered only by instinctual energy or by desexualized and neutralized forms of energy. Whereas defenses are usually conceptualized in relation to drives, deployment is related primarily to a variety of feelings and feeling states that are unconsciously designed by the person to be erased in times of stress or disconnected from his or her experiencing self, as well as the positions taken toward these.

One of the cardinal goals in the treatment of patients according to the deploymental view is the identification of feelings and feeling states through a variety of lenses, entering the person's feelings and feeling states in one's imagination, and then communicating what has been decoded in the session, giving the experiences words; it is giving feelings space and differentiating among them so they can exist and be reconnected to thoughts, fantasies, and needs from which they had been dissociated. Rather than stressing predominant aggression, envy, delusional beliefs, and denial, concomitant with primitive forms of projection and omnipotence, as Kleinians would, the emphasis according to the deploymental view is on the specific situations in which the patient froze, and on her or his specific ways of perceiving and fantasizing the instigating events that led to aggression, sexualization, or other self-defenses as they are relived in the transference situations. This then leads to a clarification of specific events of deprivation, humiliation, or abuse that had been encapsulated and thus never given full verbal and affective expression. All this, in addition to the analysis of defenses and unconscious fantasies, allows the patient to open up a road to reach the part of the inner emotional and subjective life against which the self had deployed such an imposing array of forces.

Much of the psychic energy of deployed patients is invested in trying to change the power imbalance between themselves and others by doing everything possible—often through insistence on their entitlement—to not feel humiliated, shamed, or abused once again. When the specific deployment is seen in the light of such a power struggle, which they relentlessly repeat, as a sort of correction for being wronged, it can serve as a signpost to reach the specific situation in which the patient remained frozen. It is then an opportunity to create contact and a dialogue with the child parts that had been dissociated. To discover states of shame and facilitate their direct expression (rather than a mobilization of countershame strategies) necessitates special attention, according to the deploymental view.

The deploymental view addresses the sense of self in many ways. But whereas self psychology emphasizes narcissistic hurts and defensiveness utilized to ward them off, the deploymental view's emphasis involves an ongoing exploration of (a) what the person was exposed to in traumatic situations that caused discontinuity in self-experience; (b) the specific ways the events were perceived, fantasized, experienced, and reacted to in accordance with the child-parts mentality; and (c) the specific ways the patients organized themselves in these situations, which continue into their present.

Modes enacted in the interpersonal context, intended to minimize anxiety, shame, and narcissistic insult, are regarded as an ongoing, self-perpetuating, and self-equilibrating system behind the repetition compulsion (Levenson 1988). Priority is thus given to sets, attitudes, and positions that are not brought up verbally in the treatment situation. Making them explicit, transforming these attitudes, modes, and positions into discrete feelings and feeling states, and telescoping the affective experiences from different times often lead to the removal of barriers to inner change and to meaningful—previously unthought of—territories that allow for new analytic explorations.

To achieve these analytic goals, the therapist's or analyst's attitudes that contribute to the therapeutic ambiance are viewed as of paramount importance. The deploymental view gives much attention to what transpires between the patient and therapist/ analyst and the atmosphere created, which is influenced to a large extent by the therapist/analyst's attitudes (Moses-Hrushovski 1992, Rowe and Mac Isaac 1989).

REFERENCES

Baudry, F. (1984). Character: a concept in search of an identity. *Journal of the American Psychoanalytic Association* 32:955–979.

Boesky, D. (1982). Acting out: a reconsideration of the concept. *International Journal of Psycho-Analysis* 63:39–55.

Brenner, C. (1982). *The Mind in Conflict*. New York: International Universities Press.

Cooper, S. H. (1989). Recent contributions to the theory of defense mechanisms: a comparative view. *Journal of the American Psychoanalytic Association* 37:865–893.

de Bianchedi, E. T. (1991). Psychic change: the "becoming" of an inquiry. *International Journal of Psycho-Analysis*. 72:6–15.

Feldman, M. (1993). *Grievance*. Presented in Jerusalem on April 23, 1993.

Jacobson, E. (1971). *Depression*. New York: International Universities Press.

Joseph, B. (1983). On understanding and not understanding: some technical issues. *International Journal of Psycho-Analysis* 64:291–298.

Kernberg, O. F. (1976). *Object Relations Theory and Clinical Psychoanalysis*. New York: Jason Aronson.

_____ (1983). Object relations and character analysis. *Journal of the American Psychoanalytic Association* 31:247–271.

Klein, M., and Riviera, J. (1937). *Love, Hate and Reparation*. London: Hogarth, 1962.

Kohut, H. (1984). *How Does Analysis Cure?* Chicago: University of Chicago Press.

Kris, A. O. (1984). The conflicts of ambivalence. *Psychoanalytic Study of the Child* 38:439–458. New Haven, CT: Yale University Press.

Laplanche, J., and Pontalis, J. B. (1973). *The Language of Psychoanalysis*. New York: W. W. Norton.

Levenson, E. (1988). Real frogs in imaginary gardens: facts and fantasies in psychoanalysis. *Psychoanalytic Inquiry* 8:552–568.

McDougall, J. (1989). *Theatres of the Body: A Psychoanalytic Approach to Psychosomatic Illness*. London: Free Association Books.

Modell, A. H. (1984). Self preservation and the preservation of the self. In *The Annual of Psychoanalysis*, vol. XII, pp. 69–86. Chicago: Chicago Institute for Psychoanalysis.

_____ (1987). *Psychoanalysis in a New Context*. New York: International Universities Press.

Moses-Hrushovski, R. (1992). Transference and countertransference. *International Journal of Psycho-Analysis* 73:561–576.

_____ (1993). Discussion on grievance. Presented in Jerusalem, April 23.

Novick, J., and Novick, K. K. (1991). Some comments on masochism and the delusion of omnipotence from a development perspective. *Journal of the American Psychoanalytic Association* 39:307–333.

Ornstein, P. H. (1991). *Sexuality and aggression in pathogenesis and in the clinical situation: a self psychological perspective*. Presented to the Israel Psychoanalytic Society in Jerusalem, November.

Reich, R. W. (1933). *Character Analysis*. New York: Orgone Institute Press.

Robbins, M. (1988). The adaptive significance of destructiveness in primitive personalities. *Journal of the American Psychoanalytic Association* 36:627–653.

Rosen, V. (1961). The relevance of "style" to certain aspects of defense and the synthetic function of the ego. *International Journal of Psycho-Analysis* 42:447–457.

Rowe, C. E., and Mac Isaac, D. S. (1989). *Empathic Attunement*. New Jersey: Jason Aronson.

Sandler, A. M. (1977). Beyond eight-month anxiety. *International Journal of Psycho-Analysis* 58:195–209.

Sandler, J. (1989). The id or the child within. In *Dimensions of Psychoanalysis*, pp. 219–239. London: Karnac Books.

Sandler, J., Kennedy, H., and Tyson, R. L. (1980). *The Technique of Child Psychoanalysis in Discussions with A. Freud*. Cambridge, MA: Harvard University Press.

Schafer, R. (1968). The mechanisms of defense. *International Journal of Psycho-Analysis* 49:49–62.

Segal, H. (1979). *Klein*. Brighton, Sussex, England: The Harvester Press.

Waelder, R. (1930). The principle of multiple function. In *Psychoanalysis, Observation, Theory, Application*, ed. S. A. Guttman, pp. 68–83. New York: International Universities Press, 1976.

Wallerstein, R. S. (1981). The bipolar self: discussion of alternative perspectives. *Journal of the American Psychoanalytic Association* 29:377–395.

———— (1985). Defenses, defense mechanisms and the structure of the mind. In
Defense and Resistance: Historical Perspectives and Current Concepts, ed. H. P.
Blum, pp. 201–225. New York: International Universities Press.

Weinshel, E. M. (1971). Some psychoanalytic considerations in moods. *International Journal of Psycho-Analysis* 51:313–320.

———— (1989). On inconsolability. In *The Psychoanalytic Core: Essays in Honor of
Leo Rangell, M. D.*, ed. H. P. Blum, E. M. Weinshel, and F. R. Rodman,
pp. 45–71. Madison, CT: International Universities Press.

Winnicott, D. W. (1965). Ego distortion in terms of true and false self. In *The
Maturational Processes and the Facilitating Environment*, pp. 140–152. London: Hogarth.

Wolf, E. S. (1988). Case discussion and position statement. *Psychoanalytic Inquiry*
8:546–552.

9

THE DEPLOYMENTAL ASPECT IN ALL OF US

Deployments are universal enactments designed to ward off unbearable tensions—tension that may be felt due to being "overloaded," tension related to fears of being awkward or inadequate or of losing control, and tension related to feelings such as envy, depression, and particularly shame, guilt, and humiliation. We all have moments when we feel that our self is not being actualized, when it is dissociated from the situation in which we are unwittingly stuck. We then wait for others to act before we do, so that we will only have to react and not to make the space and take the time to discover what we feel and think, and to choose what to do. In other words, our self is in certain circumstances hiding, playing a role or taking up a pose. This can occur when we witness abuse and watch without reacting as we would like to; or when, under pressure, we act like soldiers and carry out duties that are contrary to what our conscience tells us; or when we state extreme positions or ideas in the heat of an argument that later we realize we did not actually mean; or when a trifling issue in our life takes on the proportions of a life-or-death matter in order to preserve our honor.

All of us react in one or more of the foregoing ways when we experience the self to be threatened. In pathological deployment, however, the loss of self is more conspicuous, almost chronic, to the point where growth and development are blocked. Deployment becomes pathological when excessive psychic energy is invested in overly restrictive ways of perceiving, feeling, and acting. At such times, the narrowing of the perceptual focus and the setting up of rigid one-track reactions to pressures dominate people to a point where they are unable to open themselves up to their emotional world and senses, unable to broadly, complexly, and freely experience their present in relation to their past and future, unable to act out of choice. By examining deployment in its most extreme forms, we can learn about the more subtle aspects of deployment in each of us.

POWER

Power is central to deployment. Deployed individuals undergo a strong self-hardening when their muscles are used, so to speak, to allow them to distance themselves from their subtle feelings and sensations, so that they will not be embarrassed, guilt ridden, or hurt. This hardening occurs also when people assume a tough pose to keep from being weakened by inner contradictions, confusion, and doubts, or to keep the other "off their back" in order to safeguard their identity.

One major aspect of power relates to the *mobilization of psychic energy* for conscious and unconscious priorities. For instance, all psychic energy may be invested in wanting to succeed. In this context, the questions in the back of our minds are: What are efforts being invested in and why? Under what circumstances are people investing excessive psychic energy in trends aimed primarily at correcting injustices or other unidentified difficulties, insults, and wounds, trends that are self-restrictive or self-defeating!? What major "fall" or rupture is still unconsciously directing their lives? In which instances do they deliberately and obstinately wait for others to do something that will relieve their plight instead of investing themselves in attaining their life goals? Why are people predisposed to give up in despair before giving their utmost to solve a problem, whether in work or in love? What specific "unfairness" that cannot be forgiven is still directing their lives to the point where they cannot fully achieve their life goals? When is the person stuck unwittingly in motives of revenge, in wishes to humiliate others and win at the expense of living in accordance with what really matters to him or her? Such questions may serve as feeling-signs (see Chapter 7) for locating the specific situations that keep the power of individuals fixated on the hidden, wounded self and prevent them from opening up to new, complex states.

In this same area we find *power ploys* that constitute unconscious obstacles to change and growth. These ploys are often triggered unconsciously in the course of an analysis. Working them through can have a significant impact on the working alliance between analyst and patient. Furthermore, identifying these ploys when they are brought into action with the analyst in the analytic situation can help us reconstruct important child-adult conflicts from the past and discover encapsulated situations in which the patient is unconsciously fixated.

This search takes place along the path from the vindictive anger expressed in aggressive acts to the vulnerabilities that entitlement or other self-arrangements are designed to erase—vulnerabilities regarding the analyst and others that deployed patients are frequently so reluctant to admit or even feel. These range from the emotional needs, the satisfaction of which patients regard as essential to their self-survival, to whatever pain these needs are to mitigate, such as feelings of depression, envy, or jealousy that the aggression has been designed to ward off.

Power positions are assumed by everyone, every day. Our own power positions and those of others have a considerable impact on our feelings, states of self, and our functioning. However, whereas we might sometimes be preoccupied with questions of prestige and status, or might vacillate between power and powerlessness, deployed patients tend to adopt more extreme power positions more often. At one pole are those who run their lives almost like automatons; they are extremely task-oriented, rarely stopping to feel or think about what they are experiencing at the moment, or about what is really important for them either in analysis or in life. They are workaholics who revel in their work because it offers them an escape in times of stress and/or fulfills their compulsion to prove their worth. Such individuals adopt a pose of power aimed at producing such tremendous awe in themselves and in those around them that the real and complex person that lies behind the tough armor becomes secondary to the pose—or lost.

Such people are often driven by rigid inner rules unconsciously adopted from past stressful situations to protect them from insult, shame, inner chaos, or other psychic pain—rules that must remain disconnected from their functions. They refrain from admitting to feelings that might overwhelm them, distract them, weaken them, or expose their weaknesses. For example, they refuse to be shamed or blamed and they do everything in their power to turn the tables on the shamer by engaging in battle to win, while avoiding being in touch with, or communicating what they feel and think. They are also driven not to give in, not to end up being a "sucker" or being treated as one. If they invest their power in trying to appear perfect, they can, they hope, avoid facing their underlying feelings of imperfection and shame. What often motivates them to seek treatment is more the wish to be understood and to obtain power than the wish to deal with their underlying feelings of distress and understand themselves. (The case of Mr. L. in Chapter 10 illustrates such a dynamic.)

At the opposite pole are those who emphasize their weakness and helplessness by appearing to give up easily whatever it is they want, thereby dramatizing the feeling that their needs do not count anyway, that they are treated like furniture that can be moved around at anyone's will, as if they were not persons in their own right, as if they had no feelings of their own. Their defensive certainty establishes them in the eyes of the beholder as individuals who live in a closed system. They construe all relevant experience in terms of powerlessness. As a result—like a self-fulfilling prophecy—they usually manage to find confirmation that their conviction of powerlessness is indeed correct. What follows is often a vicious cycle of powerlessness, defensive certainty, inner passivity, and more powerlessness. (An example of this dynamic can be seen in the case of Mrs. Z. in Chapter 10.) The more such patients become fixed in their passive position, the less they know what they feel, think, or wish. They thereby give credence to the feeling that everything is determined by others, that only a minimal degree of choice is available to them, and that personal willpower has no impact on either themselves or others. The less they rely on their will, on their understanding, and on their resources, the more they make themselves dependent on others, and consequently lose even more of their sense of self.

Although these two extremes of power dynamics are most prominent in deployed patients, power dynamics play an important role in the treatment of other patients as well. Sometimes there is no significant change in patients' power positions even after they have gained insight into the major dynamic aspects of their central problems. In such cases, a change may be effected when special attention is paid to the complex power dynamics that lie behind the self-defeating behavior itself, to the style of the person, or to his or her positions and attitudes, which often are enacted automatically and held on to.

TENSION STATES AND THE DEPLOYMENTAL APPROACH

States of tension are unavoidable in an era where so much is demanded of us. There are so many goals to achieve. So many of us are pressured so much of the time. There is a constant pattern of making efforts, of avoiding mistakes, of being on time—of achieving excellence in order to survive in a technocratic society. At the same time, we are expected to be autonomous: to be ourselves, to feel, think, and act while taking our authority responsibly and using our imagination to create our unique life situations. To find one's own way among the manifold and contradictory pressures, needs, possibilities, limitations, and wishes—and to do this without becoming lost in fantasy or in self-defeating behavior—can create immense tension and fear of failure in anyone. Being "caught as if by a muscle that is tensed," not able to move about freely, "under pressure," "overloaded," feeling "exhausted"—these are some of the feelings that accompany this feeling of tension. But this is even more true of deployed individuals, who have experienced sexual abuse, physical abuse, or emotional abuse and who are therefore driven constantly and rigidly to watch out and prepare for dangers that lie ahead in order to keep from being overwhelmed again. Deployed persons may be aware of their immense tension, which is often somatized, but usually they have no understanding of its nature or sources. Their tension is often accompanied by an unidentified panic reaction: a fear of losing control, of suddenly fainting, of becoming nauseated or having to vomit—all involving feelings of impending anxiety, insult, shame, and humiliation.

One of the psychoanalytic goals in the deploymental perspective is to try and decipher the specific pressures that are unbearable in specific contexts, the specific situations in which intolerable pressures are felt, the ways in which these individuals deal with the pressures and how they organize themselves in times of stress, and the childhood situations or other past circumstances—for instance, those in which they felt unfairly treated—that determine how deployed individuals act in their present lives.

Not only the difficulty involved in tolerating and containing tensions is relevant in the deploymental approach, not only the need to explore their sources and find more adequate channels of self expression, self regulation, and self organization, or to see what prevents us from finding these. It is also important to be aware of the tendencies that lead so many of us toward preserving states of tension, or even re-creating it deliberately in order to be prepared. In deployed patients their unconscious motivation to maintain a state of combat readiness for a perceived impending danger—the danger that their self might be crushed—is one of the tenacious ways of preserving tension. Indeed, people are often surprised to realize that a state they have found so difficult to bear, and which had frequently paralyzed them, has been of their own making. They are even more surprised to find that their need to manufacture tension may be reduced once they become aware of what they have been doing and why, or once they are free to let go and find more constructive ways to express and release their tension.

FIXITY AND RIGIDITY VERSUS OPENNESS AND FLEXIBILITY

When we stop to examine our patterns of behavior we all can find some that are fixed and rigid out of the power of habit or because of unrecognized deeper motives. There are those who can never be on time no matter how busy or free they are; as there are those who are always on time even when circumstances are such that it would be more adaptive not to be on time. Both illustrate fixity. There are circumstances when we tend to feel free, emotionally attuned, taking things easy without having to make an effort, and there are circumstances when we tend to be more self-inhibited, not really ourselves. Examples of issues relevant to the deploymental approach are the following: exploring sources of blockage in one's ability to be free and emotionally present, to feel and express whatever is being experienced, fantasied, or thought; investigating where one is stuck. What makes it difficult to put a stop to one's automatic behavior and liberate oneself from one's compulsions? What kind of psychic pain is being numbed by this seemingly addictive behavior? Which of the roles that we assume during times of stress interfere with our being ourselves and adapting flexibly?

Rather than concentrate on the real versus the false self from the outset of treatment, in the deploymental approach analysts are constantly on the lookout for what it is that may be interfering with their patients' capacity to be their real selves, to be emotionally present and self-participating in therapeutic sessions and in life, for what it is that causes them to rigidly repeat self-defeating patterns rather than be open and flexible. Factors that weaken, restrict, or falsify the self and thereby cause deployed persons to become inextricably stuck in rigid ways of perceiving, experiencing, and responding, factors that underlie their inability to alter this behavior even when external circumstances and inner developments have changed, become the starting points for analytic work. It is by identifying and examining the self-defeating trends in which deployed patients invest so much of their psychic energy from the very beginning of treatment, and by always keeping these trends in the back of our mind, that we can uncover the well-concealed but clearly existing counteranalytic and counterintegrative tendencies that impede change.

I shall now discuss in brief some of the major factors that impede inner development and change and that are taken as springboards in the analytic work with deployed patients.

SHAME

Shame is the main cork or plug that seems to hinder the free flow of associations, feelings, and fantasies in deployed persons. Shame, which comprises a family of feelings ranging from embarrassment to severe feelings of humiliation, results in the painful experiencing of oneself as a failure, as impotent, inadequate, defeated, deficient—and exposed as such—as feeling wrong in the very essence of oneself. Since shame inherently leads to attempts at avoidance—a turning away of the face, a breaking of contact—it is not surprising that it so often remains hidden and must be actively sought out (Stone 1992). One cannot overestimate the amount of psychic energy that is unknowingly invested in different ways in order to avoid facing shame, embarrassment, guilt, or a combination of them.

A pervasive feeling of shame often results in a constant attempt to deploy control and power to correct the self injury brought about by shaming. Shame can also cause people to rush into action in the attempt to rid themselves of what they are ashamed of, often by humiliating and disrespecting the other in reality or in fantasy. Repeated utilization of countershame strategies prevents such individuals from being themselves and from building their inner structures in a differentiated way that would enable them to contain and regulate their tensions. As unpleasant as the feeling of shame is, it is sometimes used unconsciously to protect oneself from even more unbearable feelings, such as jealousy or envy.

DISSOCIATION AND DIFFICULTIES OF COMMUNICATION

Dissociation exists along a broad continuum with coexistent, alternative ego states of which we all are at least partially aware (Davies and Frawley 1992). Arlow (1992) describes a condition not foreign to the ordinary range of psychological experience, when someone feels as if there were two selves functioning at the same time. One self appears to be standing off at a distance in a detached, relatively objective manner, observing another representation of the self in action. The common belief "It can't happen to me," as in times of war (Moses 1986), is another example of the adaptive use of dissociation. Cases of abusive trauma often represent an excessive use of dissociation. "The abandonment and isolation wrought by these traumas so freezes and paralyzes the ego that the grieving processes of mourning, essential for maturation, are either bypassed or are too pitiable in power to deal with the horror endured" (Roth 1992, p. 113). In pointing out the high cost of dissociation, Putnam (1992) lists the following: discontinuity of the sense of self; detachment from the physical self; and the inability to transfer basic conceptual information across dissociative states, which results in a failure to learn from experience.

The quick tendency of deployed persons to dissociate whenever they are upset makes meaningful communication with others difficult, if not impossible. One reason for refraining from sharing personal matters and feelings often lies in the person's recurring disappointment at not being understood properly and in the fear of being offended, blamed, embarrassed, or shamed. The use of this mechanism—of deliberate noncommunication—that is found in all of us but is excessively used by deployed patients is doubly unfortunate; in addition to preventing oneself from using such channels for tension release and reaching further differentiation for self strengthening and self expression, it also increases one's feelings of loneliness and isolation from others.

CORRECTIVE TRENDS

The wish to have our lot corrected or bettered exists in all of us and is often based on mixtures of reality and fantasies. But when the distress of the past determines a person's life more than the complex needs, capacities and possibilities of the present, when a person is driven to activate programs aimed at correcting self injuries from the past at the expense of one's emotional living in the present, then the corrective motivation is considered pathological, that is, harmful.

Such a striving for correction can take place on individual, group, and national levels. It is also pathological when excessive amounts of energy are invested in remembering and reminding oneself of catastrophes and in taking steps to ensure that they will never occur again, instead of negotiating between conflicting aspects and risking compromise in the effort to reach constructive solutions—and thereby intrapsychic, interpersonal, group, or national peace.

Any deployment becomes pathological when too much weight is placed on one aspect that drives one's life. This occurs when corrective programs are triggered automatically and as a sacred rule, without attempting to recognize what it is that is designed to be corrected; when some needs are over- or under-emphasized to avoid emotional and cognitive contact with what is oppressing and distressing one unconsciously; and when certain needs are related to out of proportion. In all these cases alertness to the corrective motivation is essential in order to move forward.

It is then one of the goals of analysis to explore the reasons for the overemphases that restrict one's life and do not allow appropriate space for the complexity and diversity in one's self-actualization and development to be opened up for the direct emotional and verbal expression of insults, shame, and other psychic pain that has been disavowed. The analytic aim, then, is to revive the stressful situations in which the imbalance or "break" began and is still unfinished business, in which the tendency to split, dissociate, or be rigidly restrictive in other ways continues in the present. Otherwise, the person who has become partially frozen—an observer from the outside rather than an experiencing and coexistently observing person—will not be reached and changed.

A dominant corrective need of the deployed patients is to go back and reexperience in the transference and in extratransferential relationships the ways in which they feel they had been wronged. What is of particular relevance here is the deep need to reexperience the injury each time anew and to become more specific about the unfairness that is strongly felt. These patients need to feel now that they were right then, that not all that they perceived and felt was based on fantasy and that what had happened in the past did warrant their feeling of being injured. They need to correct the feeling of having been mocked and not taken seriously. The repair lies, in the first place, in fixing on what was wrong with the parents, or with others. Only then is the patient ready to examine what was inappropriate in their view of events as a child. Only then are they willing to see the relative role of their behavior and fantasies and make the relevant distinctions.

A strong corrective need of many deployed persons is the need to be consoled. Pressured to grow up too quickly and too abruptly, often because of a traumatic event in the family, many realize in the course of analysis that it would have been easier for them if they had been listened to and comforted then—even though the objective situation was overwhelming and dreadful. Had this happened—they now understand—they would not have had to become deployed into such self-hardening and self-defeating patterns of behavior. But they did not have an opportunity to obtain consolation then, because meaningful others were too wrapped up in their own miseries or perceived the patient's complaints as personal attacks on them. Instead, not only did the adults fail to avoid the calamity that precipitated the incident, prepare the children for it adequately, or soothe the children when they needed it most, but they added insult to injury by blaming, shaming, or rebuking the children, thus adding to the psychic pain they already felt over being traumatized or having failed. Such patients' aim in analysis is to have their feelings of helplessness, humiliation, and loneliness and their sense of being wronged corrected by the analyst.

Deployed patients expect their analysts to become a source of solace. The analyst is needed to allay their anxiety, relieve depressive affects, and provide the soothing climate they lacked in their childhood. This need to be soothed may turn into clamoring demands for gratification, redress, or restitution. In extreme cases, this may bring the analytic work to a halt (Peltz 1992). Sometimes this preoccupation with compensation is similar to a repetitive masturbation fantasy that is reenacted in the analysis in order to console themselves for hard times long forgotten, a masturbation fantasy to which they often become addicted.

But just as the soothing transference may serve as a resistance, it may also be used in a very productive way. Whatever is identified in the analytic process as clues to a corrective process can facilitate the discovery of particular stressful situations that have been encapsulated or erased, situations in which patients remain unconsciously frozen and stuck. In her theory of the development of human beings, Schacht (1992) includes the idea that "it is normal and healthy for the individual to be able to defend the self against specific environmental failure by a freezing of the failure situation" (p. 63). She continues: "Along with this goes an unconscious assumption (which can become a conscious hope) that an opportunity will occur at a later date for a renewed experience in which the failure situation will be able to be unfrozen and reexperienced with the individual in a regressed state, in an environment that makes adequate adaptation" (p. 63).

CLINICAL VIGNETTES

Corrective wishes predominate in deployed patients as ways of dealing with shame and humiliation. The following vignettes illustrate the special dynamics of the corrective motivation in deployed persons and how such motivation may be used to recover situations and states that seem to have been erased.

Mr. M.'s wounds from the Second World War still had a strong impact on his living patterns. When he came for treatment, he said that he wished either to be dead or to be needed by the whole world—all out of a forlornness and shame he was unable to tolerate. The ambition to be perfect and infallible, which permeated all his actions, was found to be related to feelings of humiliation to which he now began to give words. Mr. M. was a captive of his past in that he continually attempted to correct his wounds. He had a strong drive not to be a "sucker" again, not to have to give in; he needed to correct the many situations in which he had had to helplessly accommodate to others and to what they decided for him. His uttermost satisfaction, he said, would be to see the faces of those who had humiliated him and to stand before them as a proud Israeli professor who survived their humiliations and no longer needed to hide his identity or his religion. This would be his revenge! To correct his humiliation became his *raison d'être*. All his other satisfactions were minor. In the analytic process, while he explored the dynamic of this kind of deployment—such as putting efforts into going back to Poland, where he had been beaten forty years ago, and presenting a lecture there as a distinguished professor of chemistry—he started to open up his psychic wounds rather than to act on his corrective wishes.

Another patient, Mr. S., exhibited the wish to correct through action the feelings of loneliness and envy that he experienced in his present life, but he could not or would not connect it to experiences in his past. Mr. S., a father of three, insisted that he wanted a fourth child, even though his wife objected and the couple had neither the time nor the means to raise another child. While exploring his grief and bitterness around this issue and living it out in the transference situation, he began to talk about how, as a child, he had felt lonely with his two older siblings, who were like a couple. It then became clear that, unconsciously, he wanted a fourth child to provide his third child with the sibling he himself had never had, to retroactively correct his loneliness, envy, and the feeling of being an outsider, which he could not tolerate or admit to. After having explored these feelings in the analytic process, it turned out that Mr. S. did not really want another child. What he wanted was to correct his past wounds, which had been sealed over. My intuition that his wish to have a child was not based on real present desires enabled me to help him open up this area for further analytic work. Once his psychic pain from the past was expressed and the "corrective program" into which he had been deployed became clear, Mr. S. was happy that he no longer felt the need to act on his wish.

As another example of correction through fantasy life, a person may wish to be "reborn," or to unconsciously enact this fantasy in a different body, different family, or different country, or by belonging to a person with whom emotional or physical contact would correct unconscious and deep self injuries. This was often one unconscious motive in the homosexual choice— when a man who was ashamed of his body tried to correct it by being transformed into an athlete in the trance of his masturbation fantasies or through having sexual relations with a strong man, or when a woman fell in love with another woman, who represented the opposite of what she experienced transactionally with her mother. Their real present life was in the shadow of these fantasies until the corrective programs came to be transformed back into the painful experiences that had been designed to be erased and a renewed search for their identity could take place.

Another example is provided by Mrs. K., who caused confusion at a Tavistock conference when she joined a group to which she had not been assigned. This was an unconscious correction of her deep feeling of rejection as an illegitimate daughter. Coming to a group she did not belong to formally, and finding even so that she could both feel and be accepted emotionally by the group and the consultant, served in her fantasy as a correction.

When the corrective value of feelings, wishes, or needs is deciphered and understood, it not only highlights the meanings they held for the patient but also changes the whole direction of the analytic work. Thus, for instance, when I took an interest in what Mr. N. was saying excitedly about an old neighbor and his admiration for her, I learned that this woman had come to visit his family when he was an adolescent in a new country, without any friends, books, or toys. Not only did the woman befriend the immigrant family, but she brought Mr. N. books and toys, without asking whether he needed anything. He liked her presents so much that he kept them to this day—and liked them even more because he would never have admitted that he needed anything, then or now. Had I not perceived that there was primarily a corrective element in this relationship, Mr. N. would have proceeded to discuss present events that were often superficial, as he tended to do in the analytic session, or make efforts to cherish the relationship that in the present he actually did not enjoy rather than explore and discover what it had meant to correct. Exploring what I felt to be corrective not only threw a new light on his confused and complex relationship to this neighbor, it also opened up themes that he had left in the dark, such as his feelings of despair, shame, and embarrassment at being a new immigrant and having nobody who would listen to or empathize with him.

Another example of how specific frustrations from the past can be reached through using corrective behavior and wishes as a springboard to recover suppressed or repressed emotional experiences and encapsulated situations is provided by Mr. R. Mr. R. saw the down side of each and every situation and sulked most of the time. With exploration, it turned out that one of the motives behind this behavior was Mr. R.'s wish to correct his relationship with his father, who always tended to see the bright side of life. Mr. R. wanted his father to know what he really felt, and to stop living a life of constant denial.

Upon investigating Mr. R.'s strong desire for a special relationship with one of his nephews, it became apparent that this craving was unconsciously designed to correct and repair his relationship with his father, whom Mr. R. had perceived as unfriendly and distant and on whom he seemingly had given up long ago. Now the need for correction through establishing an intense relationship with his nephew became the focus of our analytic work. Deciphering this unconscious intent enabled Mr. R. to open up his old wounds of rejection and to mourn his losses.

In this chapter I have focused on self-defeating trends in life that are part of the deploymental aspect in each of us, and how the deploymental approach might build analytically on these patterns when they become pathological in deployed patients.

REFERENCES

Arlow, J. A. (1992). Altered ego states. *Israel Journal of Psychiatry and Related Science* 29(2):65–77.

Davies, J. M., and Frawley, M. G. (1992). Dissociative processes and transference–countertransference paradigms in the psychoanalytically oriented treatment of childhood sexual abuse. *Psychoanalytic Dialogues* 2(1):37–47.

Moses, R. (1986). Denial in non-psychotic adults—some adaptive and non-adaptive aspects. *Samiksa* 40(3):77–93.

Moses-Hrushovski R. (1986). Past and present in interpretation: a discussion. *Bulletin of the European Federation of Psychoanalysis* 25:15–25.

——— (1992). Transference and countertransference: from deployment against feelings of loss through psychotic regressions to a better capacity to feel and to mourn. *International Journal of Psycho-Analysis* 73:561–576.

Peltz, M. L. (1992). The wish to be soothed as a resistance. *The Psychoanalytic Quarterly* 61:370–400.

Putnam, F. W. (1992). Discussion: are alter personalities fragments or figments? *Psychoanalytic Inquiry* 12:95–112.

Roth, S. (1992). Discussion: a psychoanalyst's perspective on multiple personality disorder. *Psychoanalytic Inquiry* 12:112–123.

Schacht, L. (1992). The setting in child and adolescent analysis. *Bulletin of the European Psychoanalytic Federation* 38:63–80.

Stone, A. M. (1992). The role of shame in posttraumatic stress disorders. *American Journal of Orthopsychiatry* 62:131–137.

10

THERAPY OF DEPLOYED PATIENTS

I often had the feeling that explaining phenomena of deployment and the impact of the corrective tendency on them, and clarifying the complexities involved, would be a major challenge. Now, as I near the end of the writing of this book, the feeling persists. At times the uniqueness and complexity of these phenomena crystallize in me so clearly that I am certain it must be possible to formulate it in a simpler way. At other times I feel that it is still obscure, that I have not portrayed it clearly enough in all its subtle differentiations and intersections, and that it awaits a better understanding and a clearer conceptualization.

Therefore, I would like to bring together some of the developmental changes by describing two of my deployed patients and and my thoughts on the deployments involved. This will shed further light on the unique phenomena of deployment.

In the following clinical material I shall describe the steps of development as they were experienced by each of two patients and by me in the analytic process. I will focus on how the deploymental aspects inextricably interacted with my working concepts and attitudes.

MR. L.

Mr. L., a high-ranking business manager in a large company, is a heavily deployed person representative of the powerful, totally task-oriented person who has little space for feelings. Mr. L. is greatly respected for his brilliance, his skills, and his efficiency. Those who work under him fear him. He becomes furious when somebody makes a mistake or works below the high standards he demands. This work situation is quite similar to how he acts toward and is experienced by his wife and two children at home. Because Mr. L. suffers from headaches and high blood pressure, his physician recommended that he enter into psychotherapeutic treatment. He did so and was under treatment for many years with two different psychotherapists, a man and a woman, but according to what he felt, he had not been helped.

Mr. L.'s father had been a frustrated plumber who worked hard trying to provide conditions that he hoped would prevent his children from feeling inferior and ashamed. But he was never satisfied with his children's achievement. He beat Mr. L. harshly when he did not bring home the best grades. Mr. L.'s mother was a very intelligent woman who felt unfulfilled because she had given up her career as a nurse to care for her husband and children. What disturbed Mr. L. most was that both his parents, especially his father, lived vicariously through him. He was greatly pressured by them and he was upset that they never admitted this. Because he was the genius of the family, they unconsciously expected him to fulfill all their frustrated ambitions. The more Mr. L. was admired as a child of great intellect, the more humiliated he felt whenever he had to admit that he did not know something. To avoid error and hide his failures became a matter of life and death for him. Often he considered his talent to be a curse that made it necessary for him to always be on guard to keep from being trapped. He also often had the feeling that while he was appreciated for his talents, he was not really loved. His pose was to never show his sadness or other feelings that he considered as weakness, to pretend to be indifferent toward physical and emotional pain, and to do everything possible not to let others put pressure on him. He was constantly driven to achieve and to prove his special worth. What this constant race was intended to correct he did not know. But he did know that he was an angry man, even though he presumably did not show his anger; instead, he acted on it—to get even—and, above all, to always remain in control.

The following material is from the fourth year of Mr. L.'s analysis with me. It illustrates the deployment into excitement, omnipotence, and tension through which Mr. L. unconsciously tried to deal with his feelings of humiliation, envy, and inner deadness.

Mr. L. often mentioned the fact that he "worked like crazy" from early morning until late at night. He would have liked to spend more time at home with his wife and his two small children, but there was in him a force stronger than himself to be a success. Behind his compulsive working we discovered also his need to escape from his wife, with whom he was experiencing much tension during this period. The tension was partly related to his "being allergic" to her demands for order, and somewhat moreso to the lack of sexual satisfaction.

While we explored the motives behind his spending his life running in a frenzy, his compulsive need to be creative came up. As became clear in the analytic process, the overemphasis on having to invent ever new projects was overdetermined. Thus, for instance, it helped him not to be preoccupied with fears of dying, which he had secretly suffered from; it also became connected with a fantasy wish, felt strongly since childhood, of wanting to do the impossible—perhaps to bear a child of his own. This served to correct the disavowed envious feelings he had had when his mother was pregnant and he had felt extremely lonely and betrayed. This fantasy wish related also to his need to prove through such a drastic achievement that he was not just a silly child who could not distinguish between fantasy and reality, as he was some-

times ridiculed for being, and that he had special, unusual powers.
We understood that feelings of omnipotence had protected him
from being depressed since his early childhood.

In a subsequent session Mr. L. commented that this was the
first time in all the years he had been seeing me that he almost
came late to the hour. Until then he had always taken into
consideration the possibility of traffic jams or other delays that
might make him late; but this time it seemed he could not. And
yet he had arrived exactly on time. It seemed that while his
superiors permitted themselves to be late, he did everything
possible to prevent such a failure from happening to either
himself or to his subordinates. I pointed out how much energy he
was investing in trying to avoid being late. To myself, I wondered what stream of association might come up in the session
that might serve as further signs for the catastrophes he unconsciously had to avoid or correct. One of the themes that had come
up in many previous cycles related to Mr. L.'s fear of making an
error and feeling shamed for having lost control—as had happened when he occasionally wet his bed at night until he was 8.
Another cycle related to primal scene experiences and fantasies.
He remembered violent scenes when his father was quarrelling
with his mother and he could not fall asleep; for years he had
shared his parents' bedroom but he had only vague memories of
it. Later Mr. L. had been geared to listening to what went on
behind the closed door of his parents' bedroom, imagining himself in the role of a savior, always on guard to prevent a catastrophe that might occur if he were not on hand to prevent it.
Until recently, Mr. L. would not look at couples or see them play
with each other in T.V. shows. He would immediately walk
away, fantasizing all kinds of battles and disasters that would
develop from their play.

In spite of coming closer to some of the sources behind Mr.
L.'s deployment, he proceeded to prove to me the objective need
for his insistence on his own as well as others' always being on
time even when it was not called for. He expressed his deep
worry about people's low standards, his anger at those who live

comfortably while not doing what they should. He wanted no excuses! He wanted high quality! From similar repetitive accusations, I could sense his rage when his brother took life easy, frequently did not show up on time when he had to fulfill some job, and refrained from taking responsibility on the pretext of being sick. I did not comment on that theme but focused on his tension, his excited tone and speed when I found myself almost out of breath trying to follow his words, meanings, and feelings. This brought up a detailed quarrel situation with his brother and the unfairness he had felt when his mother sided with his brother.

As had happened often, there was a strong feeling that he was dealing with a matter of life or death, and I said so to Mr. L. "Yes," he reacted. The image he had in his mind was of an operation when he, the chief physician, pushed aside the hand of a careless student who almost disrupted the medical procedure. I could sense how real this fantasy felt, as if he lived coexistently in different worlds; and I could feel my suffocated tears when sensing the constant enormous pressure Mr. L. felt. Life for him was like a war in which one had to function and act! There was no time for feelings. There was no space for compromises.

At times we played a game similar to Winnicott's squiggle game in which Mr. L. talked about his associations and I would "draw" my reactions, usually closely corresponding to the world of his associations, images, or other clues until we met at an unexpected but meaningful point. The introduction of playfulness enabled Mr. L. to feel more at ease and often facilitated the participation of preconscious processes and the creation of a sense of "we-ness." Using our imagination alongside thoughts, feelings, and understanding enabled us to capture experiences that seemed frozen or erased. Surprisingly, one of these sessions led Mr. L. to bring up the miscarriage he knew his mother had suffered when he was 3 years old. He recalled vague memories of the tensions around it, of his worries and preoccupation as to why it had happened, and of the unconscious guilt he had felt, fantasizing that it was his fault. This may explain his extremely strong deployment into self-control as well as the role that he had adopted in life, of being on guard, of striving for high standards to unconsciously correct the catastrophe that had happened. He, who felt that he had such immense power, should have been able to prevent it. And still worse, perhaps he did cause it, perhaps his power had a destructive quality.

In another session, Mr. L. brought up the tensions between him and his wife and the friction between him and his 11-year-old son, when the latter refused to go with the family to visit Mr. L.'s mother. The mother lived in another city, and Mr. L.'s son did not want to go because of the crazy way in which his father drove. This was the first mention in his analysis that Mr. L. drove extremely fast, and that other family members, too, were frightened to ride with him. He did not care that they were afraid, but their lack of trust offended him! For Mr. L. this way of driving was a sport—not a problem. He had never had an accident, he said, though he used to drive at speeds up to 100 m.p.h. (where the speed limit was 55 m.p.h.). Driving fast made him feel as if he were competing with himself. It was not something he had meant to bring up in analysis, just as he had not brought up his smoking as a problem. It felt like playing with fire, like being on the verge of death, and it gave him the thrill of coming through safely. It seemed that in this way he dealt with his fears of death.

I was quite surprised. How could it be that somebody who appeared so overresponsible and who was so furious at those who did not care, could behave so carelessly! I felt both worried and somewhat irritated that Mr. L. had never before brought up this symptom, one that caused his family to suffer and that could cost him his life and that of others. I felt conflicted between my analytic neutral stance to understand and help him to understand his unconscious motivations, and my responsibility as a human being and a therapist to stop his perilous acting out. In a way I felt that if I waited patiently for the analytic process to take place I would be like a bystander who colluded with the patient in a dangerous situation. I felt also that in addition to conflicts about my professional ego ideals there were more personal countertransference reactions.

A passage from Kohut's book, *How Does Analysis Cure?* (1984) came to mind. For reasons of which I was not aware, I reread it. I found a passage in which Kohut's patient reported, with a trace of challenging arrogance, that he had once been stopped when speeding on the expressway. In an unrepentant, angry tone of voice, he talked about similar incidents that had occurred over the years before and during the analysis. Kohut listened to the outpouring in complete silence, but when the patient stopped after about five minutes, he told him that he was going to give him the deepest interpretation he had so far received in his analysis. Kohut could see his surprise at this announcement: it was totally different from anything Kohut had ever said to him before. After several seconds of silence, he said very firmly and with total seriousness: "You are a complete idiot." There was another second or so of silence, after which the patient burst into warm and friendly laughter and relaxed visibly on the couch. Kohut then expressed his concern about certain aspects of the patient's behavior, especially about his potentially destructive and self-destructive outbursts of reckless driving, but also about other forms of tantrum-like behavior, including aggressive behavior at his place of work when dealing with unresponsive sales people. Kohut added that he of course needed to understand what in the patient's past—in particular what it was in his childhood—that made him so vulnerable in certain situations and led him to respond as he did. But first things first: if the patient killed or injured himself in an accident he would certainly never be able to analyze his motivations.

I think that it was Kohut's capacity to respond so freely and with resonant emotionality that appealed to me. It seemed to me that Kohut's decision to leave his neutral stance momentarily in order to act—as would a caring parent when this was felt to be needed—liberated me to some extent to be free to think anew and to express both my concern and anger. But I still felt a mixture of helplessness, anger, and a wish to bring change about quickly.

My first problem was to avoid becoming the sort of moral censor who reproaches patients for being dangerous, delinquent, and inconsiderate, for this might lead to a sadomasochistic bond between us. How to figure out the role I had been driven into because of yet unknown factors—to not act on it, but to use it for a deeper understanding—was not a simple task. One of the ways I dealt with this countertransference reaction was to write down my feelings and thoughts in a free, associative way. My associations led me to wonder whether it might not be the fear of death that was causing Mr. L. to behave as he did. Then I found myself pondering: He abuses others! He, who at this stage was very considerate and empathic, did not even feel sorry for ignoring his family's fears when he drove! He even seemed to be enjoying it! There was no sign of remorse for the fear and pain he was causing! And when they screamed out their fear, he became furious that they did not trust him, which probably echoed his own fears that he hoped to silence through his exciting "sport."

Wandering with my thoughts, I came to the idea that Mr. L. had perhaps been abused himself. The abused turns into the abuser. What did he find too unbearable to remember or admit, to express, or to mourn? What were the specific self injuries that his behavior was designed unconsciously to correct? These were some of the questions I had in my mind.

After a process of further self-exploration, I felt calmer. It was as if whatever had been blocking my capacity for empathy had now been removed.

It was some time before Mr. L.'s speedy driving ceased to be ego-syntonic and he began to realize the dangers involved and the tension that he had been causing his family. Although it was difficult for Mr. L. to give up the excitement involved in his demonic driving, as driving more slowly seemed to exhaust him, he did make an effort to slow down.

Focusing on what the driving experience meant to him, and what it corrected, opened up many other daring activities through the excitement of which he sought to console himself. These activities included gambling in casinos, being totally excited to see whether he would win or lose, and masturbating compulsively, stimulated by exciting dangerous fantasies. We

could now see how Mr. L. lived in excitement to defend himself
from the depression and envy which he knew that he felt; but he
had not yet gotten in touch with live memories of having experienced these feelings.

He now remembered that there had been a period of delin-
quency during his adolescence when he would play hooky from
school, steal bicycles and, for a short period, even take drugs. He
figured out that this had occurred when he was 15, when his
mother had gone abroad with his brother and left him alone with
his father, who, as usual, was emotionally unavailable although
Mr. L. needed him desperately. Here, too, it turned out that these
excitements helped Mr. L. to deal with his envy and depression
when his loneliness became too much for him to bear.

Mr. L. began talking more about his fantasy preoccupation
while he was driving, for example, racing another driver, over-
taking him, and not letting the other driver regain his position in
front of him. From his associations we learned that his compet-
itiveness was primarily related to his strong need to prove his
masculinity and to be in a superior position vis-à-vis both his
younger and older brothers. This brought up incidents of envy
that Mr. L. had not been aware of previously and that he found
extremely difficult to admit.

What came as a surprise to both of us as he proceeded to talk
about his fantasy games on the road, was an association of rape
that suddenly came to his mind: If he were ahead of the driver, he
would not be raped! Mr. L. repeated what he had told me
previously, that he often had the sensation of seeing a shadow
behind him but that when he turned around there was nobody
there. This now reminded him of the shocking experience of a
rape. Some months previously Mr. L. had briefly referred to the
most humiliating experience he had ever had—being raped by an
older person—but at the time he felt too ashamed to talk about it
in more detail. He had never told anybody else about the rape.
Now, Mr. L. said with a flavor of a discovery, when he overtakes
another driver, he kind of "corrects" this humiliating experience; now, when he drives fast, he is the stronger and the quicker

one! He will never again have to suffer from an abusive man. It must be, he said, again with more conviction, that this was a way to "avoid the rape retroactively," as it were. This, then, was one of the unconscious motivations behind his deployment into playful excitement, I thought: to correct the pain and the stain of shame that was persecuting him.

I asked him to talk more about the rape experience. Mr. L. described in detail how it had happened, when he was 11 years old, and how he had felt.

Mr. L.'s greatest humiliation was the fact that he had agreed to cooperate in the act even though the rapist did not use force on him. "It was actually his fault," said a voice of guilt, which he tried to silence. "It was more the authoritative tone of the rapist that caused me to follow," he continued, as if it would have been inconceivable to refuse. This was the tone of his father. Nothing was ever open for discussion with him. There was no point in arguing, or even thinking about what he, Mr. L., wanted.

The rapist was 17 years old, 6 years older than Mr. L. Mr. L. tried to empathize with himself in order to "forgive" himself for cooperating with the rapist by concretizing the difference in age, size, and power. Yet he had felt terribly manipulated and deceived because the rapist had seduced him by promising to show him something special. Mr. L. continued to explore what it had been that tempted him: maybe he had been curious. But what he remembered of the experience was only his pain and shame. And, even more difficult for him, he now remembered, was that he could not talk about it with anybody. His whole family—his parents, his brother, and his relatives—had been there in the village where it happened, celebrating his father's birthday. But he did not feel safe enough with any one of them to tell them what he had experienced and how he was suffering. Other memories of suffering from sexual and power abuse came up in the following sessions, as did Mr. L.'s shame mixed with guilt regarding his own emotional abuse of his younger brother.

Gradually he gained a greater capability to contain his guilt and shame and give space to his inner conflicts, thereby making it

was most difficult for him to share with me. What depressed him particularly was that he was always hypocritical in that he appeared innocent and pure on the outside while he was really filthy and cruel inside!

When we explored what these fantasies were intended to correct, we found several sources. One was to change the state of utter helplessness that Mr. L. had experienced during his adolescence when his father had had an affair with a younger woman, which caused a family crisis. It turned out that undressing women in his fantasy and humiliating them was one of his biggest consolations at that time. But at the time his guilt made him program himself into an ascetic way of life. As he was able to express shame and guilt about his fantasies and acts, verbally and emotionally, as he felt, saw, and understood the previously disconnected chains-of-experiences, acted on by his deployments, Mr. L. began to soften further.

He could now allow more space for his feelings. Among the changes that could be noted on the deploymental line were that, from being automatically set in the direction of immediate action, whether by stepping out of a situation, by ignoring the others, or by assault, he could now move in the direction of being more emotionally present and of gaining more control over his impulses through a continual weighing among his various needs, goals, and feelings. Although he still found it difficult to find the right way to react when he was in touch with the complexities of a situation, this no longer paralyzed him. Moreover, he could free himself from the trance of doing and acting to rid himself of the shame, guilt, and fears that he had refused to admit. And he could enjoy being leisurely and relating to friends on the emotional level.

A further change in the direction of the "defreezing" process in Mr. L.'s psyche, which is a crucial step in the analytic work with deployed patients, is illustrated in the following case material.

"Something happened and I did not understand it," said Mr. L. at the beginning of a session. A detailed account of the events that related to disturbances he was suffering during the night followed. Fleetingly, he commented that I, too, looked tired. When I asked him to say more about this and how he felt about it, he noted that he had a headache. He had seen somebody leave my office when he came to his session ten minutes early, but that had no effect on him. He did, however, think that I did not have enough time to rest between patients. This was like ending his statement with a period or perhaps even an exclamation mark, letting me know that there was nothing more to discuss on the subject. Being deployed into such a resolution was one of the feeling signs for the overwhelming feelings that Mr. L. would try to suppress, and a sign for an inner confusion that needed to be opened and explored. There was the flavor of enactment in the air, as if he were part of a drama that he now reproduced in a series of sessions all of which began with his saying that something happened that he did not understand. I listened to him with free-floating attention, listening also for the "headache" that had frequently been a possible sign for specific disavowed psychic pain for us.

Regarding the night disturbances, Mr. L.'s son woke up in the middle of the night and his wife went to sit by the child trying to calm him. As if in dispute with me, Mr. L. insisted that he was neither angry nor envious even though his anger was felt to be related to his jealousy and was transmitted nonverbally. Mr. L. then went into the child's room "only to ask my wife if they were there." He repeated to me that he was not angry. He had hardly fallen asleep when he heard loud noises from a neighbor's apartment. He was angry that others would be able to determine whether he slept, while he was helpless to do anything about it. Then he quickly fell asleep. When he hurried to work next morning he saw a sour look on his wife's face. She was distant and cold. This really made him furious. She complained that he made her feel guilty, that she felt torn between Mr. L. and their son and was therefore unable to fall asleep herself. Mr. L. felt wronged. "Not only was I disturbed because she spoiled our little son and because of other noises in the night; not only did I refrain from complaining about it, but now she blamed me for disturbing them," he said bitterly. Then, as is typical of deployed patients who unconsciously turn to the other in times of stress, he was silent as if waiting for me to calm him, waiting for me to feel what he could not or would not say, and to do what he was expecting me to do—to soothe him—while he remained passive, disconnected, and withdrawn.

I felt blocked by a mixture of empathy with his psychic pain, with his cognitive dissonance, and need to be consoled on the one hand, and a feeling that I was being manipulated on the other. He reminded me of children who come into their parents' room under the pretext of wanting water when they feel both needy and the desire to control the parents due to their fear, loneliness, and the insult of being left out. I reflected out loud on the quality of playing-innocent-yet-feeling-guilty that caught my attention in this session, thereby inviting Mr. L. to associate to it.

I often feel the impact of sharing with deployed patients a feeling that has been transmitted to me or a typical childhood situation that comes to mind as a result of their associations and the manner in which these are talked about or enacted. When their feelings and mine touch, a deeper reverberation is possible in both of us than when the major discourse is based on thoughts. This also relates to the strong need of deployed patients, who are often used to living in an emotional void, to feel that they are being given something on a more personal—yet not an intimate—level. They can then perceive this not as a general, seemingly impersonal interpretation, but rather as one directed at them personally.

A response from me, evoked by his associations, which was perceived as my giving something from myself, often enabled Mr. L. to proceed to work productively in his analysis. He would often indicate what part of what I had said struck a chord in him, and also that he appreciated this personal response instead of a learned interpretation. This time, however, he was silent for longer than usual. When I asked what was on his mind and what he felt, he expressed anger at me. I related to his feeling misunderstood by me and to his disappointment that he was not only deprived of the comfort he needed from me but also felt accused of being manipulative! This repeated the original trauma, he said, when he was good about not disturbing his mother and tried hard to sleep in spite of the many noises. Not only were his efforts overlooked and his action not appreciated, but he ended up being reproached and condemned. Acknowledging the nature of the feeling state that he conveyed and recognizing my part in the injustice he was experiencing in the session through my tone without many words, seemed to be one step of relating to the experience of the psychic pain that had led to his deployment against being wronged. In the following sessions the child–adult battles that Mr. L. had been caught up in were reconstructed, and the process of working through the primal scene experiences and fantasies, which came up vividly, continued.

Mr. L. referred to the headache that had disappeared in the meantime. I said that we could both feel what his headache had partly transmitted to us in this session. As if he were still in the night situation, Mr. L. pondered another night experience that came to mind. His mother had never read stories while putting his younger brother to sleep. Had she read to him? He knew that she sang lullabies to his brother, but could not recall whether she sang to him. Perhaps he was envious when he saw them so close. Now when he hears songs on the radio, he often has tears in his eyes. He was hiding them when he sang lullabies to his own children. It felt as if something in him that had been frozen was now melting. From the more abstract points of envy and rage against the world, he now approached more concretely the landscape of the psychic pain of loneliness, longing, and hatred that emerged whenever he felt envy. We were now traveling together in this landscape, and would grapple with feelings that had previously been frozen through his deployment.

Mr. L. related an incident that had occurred at work. He had forgotten to come to an important meeting. First, he was upset, trying to find excuses. After a short while, he felt that it was not so shameful to admit that he had forgotten and to simply say that he was sorry. Admitting a mistake also meant giving up the "sacred battle against errors" that had been an ideology for him. Now that he was no longer a robot but belonged to the human race he lost his justification to be angry all the time. But he thereby gained much more tolerance toward himself and others, which helped him be more calm and relaxed.

Mr. L. had invested much energy in self-hardening to buttress himself against being hurt. He now began to realize the price he had paid for the safety that this deployment provided. He was sure that if he had been in touch with his feelings of fear, humiliation, envy, and depression in the past, he would not have been able to function. But now he no longer felt it necessary to be encapsulated obstinately in his previous attitudes and positions. By gradually giving them up, he was able to experience a richer, more relaxed, and peaceful quality of living, to enjoy both work and love, to be with others, and to be more creative in many ways.

MRS. Z.

A different type of deployment is illustrated by Mrs. Z.: deployment into powerlessness. A bright lawyer in her late thirties, Mrs. Z. came for treatment because she suffered from periods of depression that interfered with her ability to function. This was a short time after she had made a suicide attempt. What made her in the present feel particularly ashamed and desperate was her failure to pass the examinations that were necessary for advancement in her profession. She had been in psychoanalysis for several years, but did not feel that it had helped. She also agreed with the previous analyst that she was not in real contact with her feelings. What frequently came up in her sessions was a paralyzing envy of well-organized women who were successful in their professional fields, an envy that was completely disconnected from her past experiences with her sister and her mother. In her previous analysis as well as in the beginning of her analysis with me, Mrs. Z. was not able to recall any experience of jealousy or envy from her childhood. On the contrary, she remembered that it was she and not her sister who had been the favorite of both parents.

When Mrs. Z. talked about her difficulties in establishing stable social contacts we focused on her tendency to cut herself off at the first hint of any danger of being emotionally hurt, which also occurred at times in our sessions. Dwelling on this pattern of hers, she discovered that it was not only protecting her from feeling hurt. It also provided her with a deep satisfaction to leave the world and live her fantasy life. She added that she had had a similar experience when, up to the age of 10 she sought relief by sucking her fingers. This relief was a source of pleasure and consolation; yet, as became clear in the process of her treatment, it was also a source of much shame, which affected her life in that she constantly needed to be in a mode of concealing something.

Mrs. Z. often felt very lonely, unable to communicate what was meaningful to her. At such times she would think that nobody wanted to listen to her anyway, so why try? And she acted on this belief. Whenever Mrs. Z. was faced with differences of opinion or a conflict of interest with anyone, she would never say what her position was. She tended to disconnect herself emotionally, fearing that she would lose control if she allowed herself to be flooded with aggression when asserting herself. This increased her feelings of helplessness. Another part of her being deployed into helplessness related to her difficulties in organizing herself, especially in times of stress. When I referred to the protest against order that she seemed to feel, she would insist that it was not a protest or an unwillingness to plan and keep order. It was her inability to do so! She could never trust herself to be on time. This was the case also in her analysis, as she would often come late. It took her a long time to experience and realize that not being organized was indeed a protest; that she was rebelling thus against me in the transference as if I were her controlling mother. It also served her as a correction! In contrast to her mother's having been so well organized, Mrs. Z. was "spontaneous!" Her reluctance to become organized was one obstacle to change also in the analytic process. It felt as if she were reaching a meaningful corner, gaining some understanding, and then had to mess it all up again.

A further obstacle to change lay in Mrs. Z.'s retaining a stranglehold on her self-image as somebody who "cannot" be organized, as somebody who had to either yield or to oppose, but who could not say what she felt and thought. In discussions with friends she felt that she could not say to the end what she meant. She would remember her thoughts when they were different from those of another, but only for a moment, after which she promptly forgot them, fusing with the other, abandoning herself as if she had no personality of her own. Later on this pattern became connected with sexual abuse she had suffered in her early adolescence and about which she had told nobody. It also became related to earlier separation-individuation issues. Distinguishing the parts of deployments condensed into her self-image (which she unwittingly had used to protect her self-esteem) from aspects of her identity became part of the working-through process.

A session from the third year of Mrs. Z.'s analysis may provide clues to the life situations in which she organized herself into specific self-defeating power positions that—unknowingly to her—were still operative. In this session Mrs. Z. described an incident when she had suddenly burst into tears because she was ashamed. Usually she did not express her anger, but this time she could not control herself and screamed at one of her colleagues, who had irritated her by not doing her own job, yet criticized Mrs. Z. Recognizing the feeling of being ashamed and admitting it was a new development. When I asked her what came to her mind as she focused on the tears that had reappeared as she related the incident, she replied that it was another traumatic incident when she had also exploded. Mrs. Z. had shouted at her mother—who was hospitalized in a psychiatric institution from time to time —that she was a liar, that she was not really sick, that whenever her father came home her mother would laugh and be happy, but when she was alone with Mrs. Z. she acted depressed and cried. Mrs. Z. had often been puzzled and angry about this, wondering whether her mother was healthy or sick, but had never talked about it with anybody. There were other issues that she was not free to ask about, she said. One was a hint that her mother had had a baby some years before she was born, and that this baby had died a few days later. It had been taboo to talk about that, Mrs. Z. said. The less she knew about it, the more it caused her to become preoccupied with her fantasy life. I continued to listen to her free-floatingly, while being attentive also to what in particular bothered her. I sensed that the confusion and cognitive dissonance regarding her mother's "mysterious states," which she had never opened up before, was one factor that kept her in a position of somebody who cannot or must not know, a position we analyzed on other occasions.

Mrs. Z. continued to relate that she had felt so guilty after finally saying to her mother what she had been feeling for such a long time, that she ran to the bathroom and cried. She remembered exactly how she had looked into the mirror and spoken to herself: "Look how miserable you are!" she said. "There is nobody with whom you can talk about your experiences!" After having described this to me in some detail, she realized for the first time that this actually was still her pose, that in many ways she tended to demonstrate to others how miserable she is. It became clear through the analytic process that what had contributed to her deployment into the "role of the poor miserable one" and to her self-defeating trends of behavior were her anger, her confusion in situations she did not understand, her guilt over ambivalent feelings toward her sick mother, and especially her shame about having a mentally ill mother. This serves as an example of the deploymental perspective: how thoughts, conflicts, and feelings are condensed in the position enacted in the present. This traumatic situation in which she remained frozen, threw light on her way of organizing herself automatically since then, as if she were the helpless child in that stressful situation also in the here and now.

The following material, from the sessions that followed this insight, includes some further explorations of feeling states from the psychic layers that contributed to Mrs. Z.'s deploying herself into the position of being a "helpless failure." Once Mrs. Z. came to her morning session a little late. She felt nauseated. Perhaps it was because she did not have time to eat. Actually, she rarely ate in the morning even though she would later often feel hungry and restless. Her not eating breakfast was presented like a fact, a given, as if there was nothing she could do about it—a mode typical of deployed patients. I continued to listen without saying a word, wondering what her words and nonverbal transmissions would convey. In the past Mrs. Z. had brought up her conflict with her mother who, too eager to feed her, was perceived in her fantasy as a dangerous person against whom she must be on guard—a feature that had also been experienced in the transference situation when she was guarded against my "feeding" her forcefully. Her strong though fleeting identification with a child from a movie she saw who was afraid of being poisoned by her mother opened her up to similar fears she had had in her childhood. This time, however, her associations led to another source. Mrs. Z. talked about the friction between two friends with whom she had difficulty being with on the previous day. After giving more details and getting to the essence of what especially irritated her, I suggested that she open these states up to whatever would come. Gradually she remembered a fight between her parents. "My mother is impossible when she gets offended," Mrs. Z. said. She remembered when the mother had stopped cooking for a while in protest and had turned into a different, more withdrawn person. Since this event Mrs. Z. had felt that her parents were on the verge of divorce. When she was younger, she sometimes feared that they would separate, and worried about whom she would live with. At other times she thought that it might be better if they divorced because it would at least relieve the tension they had all been living with—the fear that a divorce might be in the offing, and that she would have the problem of having to choose one of the parents. Here, then, was another layer behind Mrs. Z.'s helplessness and loneliness, which was strongest when guilt about her being the possible reason for the divorce came up.

In the next session Mrs. Z. was sorry that she came late. She could find no reason for this. She felt now that there was change in many areas, but arriving late almost everywhere was still endemic. She also tortured herself for having forgotten to attend a lecture she had looked forward to. It had been canceled and was later rescheduled. "I am an automaton! When there are changes, I do not function. I can't rely on myself. There is nothing I can do!" she exclaimed, moaning and complaining as if she had internalized a shaming and blaming person. Astonished at what I felt to be an inordinate amount of shame and disproportionate amount of distress and despair, I became interested in Mrs. Z.'s bodily associations, her tensions, sensations, and images. She had heard a kind of noise in herself, a voice—no, a sound. I asked if she could listen to the sound and hear what it said. She replied that she automatically tended to remove whatever was not clear to her, or was disturbing. I recalled the feeling states that had been transmitted at the beginning of the session—the "How did I forget?" "There is nothing I can do!" "I am torturing my- self!"—and I suggested taking them as melodies to reverberate to (rather than as subjects to think about). I have found in my work with patients like Mrs. Z. that it is often productive to formulate the feeling parts and then wait for associations to come, rather than—or in addition—to ask in a general way what might come up or to express interest in what she is thinking.

Not being on time brought to Mrs. Z.'s mind the memory of having let her daughter wait when she was in kindergarten. "It was so cruel!" she said. Nevertheless it happened often, she continued sadly, demonstrating how awful it was that she had not been on time! Her eyes filled with tears as she described how her daughter had stood there, waiting; her daughter had cried and felt helpless and abandoned.

As she pondered this experience, Mrs. Z. suddenly remembered that she had done the same thing to her younger sister. She knew how awful it felt to have to wait. Her mother had done the same to her. She recalled her own feeling of being abandoned, especially after a fight with her mother. It was one of those frequent fights when her mother had forced her to eat because she was so thin. Once her mother even beat her when she refused to eat. Since then she had decided not to let her mother force her anymore. Mrs. Z. then described how she did this passively. She would not say what she felt or thought. She would not expose her feeling of pain, "not give her the pleasure of seeing that I suffered." I commented that she had been enacting the same pattern here, in the analytic situation, in the many sessions when she came in closed mouthed as if she were in danger of being force-fed by me. "It was much stronger in my previous treatment," Mrs. Z. responded.

There was so much pressure on the part of her mother, Mrs. Z. continued, that she found no other way but to close up. In her childhood she had often been constipated. To be passive, to keep it all in, and to sustain the pose of one who was wronged became a typical mode of deployment for her.

In the following sessions, several sequences of experiences that centered around being forced were opened up verbally and emotionally, while the position of having-nothing-to-open-her-mouth-for, that she had been holding on to so tightly, softened. Reflecting on this process, Mrs. Z. commented that there still were some insults that felt like swords stuck into her belly. These did not allow her to be reconciled yet; they were stronger than her and beyond reach. She had no control over this, she said. One path of associations led to her being abused by her mother, for instance when she had forced her to eat her vomit, and later on by bigger boys from her neighborhood, and her reaction of abusing younger kids and thereby regaining control. Another path led to aggressive acts and fantasies related to sibling rivalry and the ensuing shame and guilt.

Even before her sister was born, Mrs. Z. had been looking

forward to having somebody who would be a friend, but who would also obey her and do what she wanted, so that she could control her and the previous balance of power would be resumed. To her great disappointment, it turned out that her sister, five years younger, had a strong will and was very powerful even as an infant. Mrs. Z. mentioned a specific incident, when her sister did not allow an older boy to harass her while she herself did not have the courage to stand up to him, thereby failing to protect both herself and her little sister. This recollection brought back memories of other experiences that had contributed to her helplessness and her feelings of envy. She felt ashamed of her weakness and cowardice. She was even ashamed to talk about the dizziness that she experienced at times, including in the analytic session, as if this were an indication of weakness and loss of control for which others would mock her. As a child, her solution had been to seek somebody whom she could control, frighten, or humiliate—as if she could in this way pass the weakness on to somebody else and thereby feel stronger. I saw her sadistic behavior of letting the younger one wait as a way to punish the powerful little sister whom she envied, as well as a way of repairing her own wounds of helplessness. Now she would not be the passive victim who had to wait, but the stronger one who made others wait for her.

This opened up yet another path. Mrs. Z. now remembered how painful it had been when her boyfriend, now her husband, used to torture her by frequently keeping her waiting. When they had a date he would come late or just not show up. She had felt terrible. She had wanted to stop seeing him but could not. Each time she returned despite her distress and humiliation. This was typical of their relationship, Mrs. Z. added; he was seductive when he felt like it, but then withdrew, keeping her in the position of having to wait for him. It was so unfair! But this was what she deserved, she continued, as the guilt she felt about the several incidents where she had abused her little sister came to mind. The self-punishment related to disavowed guilt added understanding to the dynamics of Mrs. Z.'s continuing self-defeating behavior and feeling of helplessness.

We now noticed another factor behind her being deployed into utter helplessness whenever feelings of failure threatened her. Mrs. Z. repeatedly mentioned her despair in the sessions, raising her hands helplessly as if saying, "If it is hopeless, let it be . . . " losing control, being an automaton, unable to stop patterns of behavior like coming late. From these and other subtle signs, a typical childhood situation came into my fantasy mind: the scene of a child who postpones going to the toilet and then cannot hold back anymore once he or she begins to wet.

I often register such associations in my mind without telling them to the patient, and then "forget" them until they are rekindled by the patient's associations so that a new understanding or a new path is opened up. This time I shared what was in my fantasy mind. Mrs. Z. responded immediately. My association brought back a meaningful emotional experience about which she had felt so terribly ashamed that even talking about it in therapy was difficult: When she was about 7 years old, Mrs. Z. had been sent to a neighbor at whose house she liked to sleep overnight. The neighbor suggested that she bring a rubber pad with her, but Mrs. Z. assured her that she had stopped wetting her bed now for some time. She remembered exactly what happened in the night: she dreamt that she was sitting on the toilet, and when she woke up she was all wet—not having distinguished between dream and reality. This was a stain that kept her shame alive to this day. She also remembered that ever since the first grade—but, also much later, whenever she was asked to read before an audience—a fear of suddenly losing control and being laughed at had been persecuting her.

After this session Mrs. Z. reported that she had an experience that was extremely rewarding. She had dared open her mouth and say what she thought at a professional meeting, without entering into a panic. This was a meaningful change, Mrs. Z. said. Everything that she wanted to say had come out clearly, fluently, and in a well-organized manner. She would not have believed that this could ever happen.

In the following sessions, states came up that threw light on one of Mrs. Z.'s motives for not taking enough care of her bodily needs, for instance when she was hungry. It became clear that she was unconsciously oriented toward turning the wheel back to before her mother had suffered her major crisis, hoping in her unconscious fantasy that her mother would then correct the rupture that had taken place at that time—when Mrs. Z.'s mother had become mentally ill and was hospitalized—so that Mrs. Z. would at last cease to suffer from the abandonment.

The last session I will describe is one in which Mrs. Z. told me she would like to make peace with her husband but still felt a need for revenge. "What comes up today when you think about retaliating?" I asked. Whatever she did was not appreciated, she said. Everything was taken for granted. She became furious when she talked about it in the session. She never had a chance to be consoled. In her childhood whenever she felt sad, this was ignored or canceled by comparison with the great suffering of her mother. While expressing several sources of her grievance she realized that perhaps she was demonstrating her right to be sad, perhaps overdoing it. Often she also felt as if she had to apologize for enjoying something in her life, as if she had to justify her existence by doing or being something special.

Mrs. Z. then spelled out another thought behind her refusal to give up her familiar patterns: she had invested so much energy in building up a whole system, a way of life to justify her failures, that to give it up now would mean an additional defeat and failure, would serve as proof that she had been wrong, that she indeed had to change!

She realized that she had invested an enormous amount of energy in all kinds of games to master her "shame trauma." Thus, for instance, she would postpone doing what she had to do, and then do it at the last possible moment. At times this was sexually stimulating. This reminded Mrs. Z. of her attempts at suicide. She had always hoped that somebody would come to save her, that she could in this way convince herself that she was loved despite her failures.

She now felt more able to face her various "falls"—failures and disappointments—rather than having to justify them in devious ways. She was ready to give up her demands to be compensated for those times when she had been wronged, not having been empathized with and supported. Even if there was still much to be done, she said, the direction she now chose was different. Rather than investing in self-consolation and justification of whatever she had built up for the sake of self-survival—a multitude of self-defeating strategies, positions, and patterns of behavior—she now invested much more in feeling, in being, and in owning and accepting the different parts of herself in an attempt to take hold of her own life in a way of her own choosing.

After working through these psychosexual and deploymental conflicts, Mrs. Z. began to feel a significant change in the aspects of power dynamics. She could now see her own part in what had happened between her mother and herself; she no longer viewed herself as the victim of her mother's mental illness. Once the emphasis shifted to herself and her relationships, Mrs. Z. gave up her constant passive fight against injustice and came to have more empathy both for herself and for others. It was so good to feel that so much depended on her, and that there was always something she could do about things, even in situations where she had previously felt paralyzed, for example, when she felt hurt and offended by her husband. This also changed the nature of her relationship with her mother, for she realized that it was not only her mother who persecuted her, but that she, Mrs. Z., participated by only accepting her mother under certain conditions. "I can't really expect my mother to change much." Now she could accept her mother as she was. Her relationship with her husband also changed when she realized that she had been living parts of her previously disavowed shame through him. Whereas before she had tended to perceive him as abusive, and had reacted masochistically through blaming and nagging him (as she had been wont to react to her mother's abuse), she now felt less compelled to see him in this way. She had more strength to be self-assertive, more communicative, and open. The panic, anxiety, and fear of being shamed that she had experienced in so many life situations were now greatly reduced. The more she could establish living contact with the child parts of her fears, shame, envy, and jealousy, the less was she driven to live them out in the present. The power that Mrs. Z. had unconsciously used to hold on to her powerlessness had been transformed into resourcefulness and inner strength.

REFERENCE

Kohut, H. (1984). *How Does Analysis Cure?* Chicago: University of Chicago Press.

11

FROM DEPLOYMENT TO SELF-DEVELOPMENT

Allowing insights to emerge and broadening them into unconscious conflict and trauma is an analytic goal that is common to all patients and analysts. In the cases of Mr. L. and Mrs. Z. I have tried to illustrate the deploymental perspective that concentrates on: (a) the interaction between the broad range of conscious and unconscious feelings, feeling states, and fantasies in each session, as seen through a variety of lenses; (b) the specific obstacles to change, that is, motives and goals of deployment, as deciphered from contextual signs in which the patient invests much energy; (c) the psychic pain from specific encapsulated situations, which is unconsciously designed to be alleviated through specific correction programs and consolation strategies; (d) the self-image that often remains fixed rather than adapting to changing feelings, needs, perceptions, and circumstances; and (e) the ways in which the individual organizes him- or herself in times of stress, which perpetuates the self-defeating behavior.

What Moran (1991) says about chaos theory and psychoanalysis also applies to the deploymental perspective:

The multiple variables, such as the patients' affects, verbal associations, attitudes toward their feelings, sensations of physical posture on the couch and power investments, must all be considered not only incrementally, but also in relation to each other. Only then can we understand the nature of the psychoanalytic process at any moment and whatever interferes with it. The summation of the components of a single non-linear system and its characteristics is less than or qualitatively different from what one sees when the system is viewed as a whole. [p. 212]

Integrating what was discussed at the 37th International Psychoanalytic Association Congress in Buenos Aires in 1991 about the goals and aims of psychoanalytic therapy, Sandler (1992) mentions the distinction between process goals, which relate to changes that the analyst aims to bring about during the course of the analysis, and outcome goals, which refer to desirable improvements in the patient's condition. As Levy and Inderbitzin (1992) say, "Interpretation is a goal-directed activity. . . . Its purpose is to alter the dynamic balance between impulse and defense through exposure to the rational aspects of the conscious ego in order to promote greater conscious (ego) mastery of conflict" (p. 996).

I shall specify what I perceive to be the essential steps of change as I and the deployed patients sense them on our "we-go" (Emde 1990) of the analytic process. In a way, these steps toward change reflect the many levels of process goals that I had in my subliminal mind. As Betty Joseph (1992) says, "Although we try to focus on what our patients bring into the session and their own individual way of operating, at the same time we do keep at the back of our minds our own theoretical perspective which includes some idea of the kind of psychic change we are hoping for in the long run" (p. 238). And Blum (1991) points out that no analyst can approach the analytic situation without some theoretical notions and convictions, but that, at the same time, every analysis is a potentially new learning experience for both analyst and patient.

I view the essence of the deploymental aspect as an ongoing process of mutual exploration and working through, not only of the motivations and fantasies that drive us unconsciously—as they unfold in the analytic process—but also of the conscious and unconscious goals and values that direct our lives and make us run. Having such general directions in my mind does not prevent me from following the patient's lead and pace. On the contrary, I think that this inner map allows me to regress more easily in the service of the ego, without fearing that I will become lost in chaotic worlds. Being aware of my goals and values—one of which is to respect the separateness of each person and his or her choices—helps me not to impose them on the patient. This attitude is based also on the empathic stance: oscillating continuously between identifying totally with the patient and then disengaging and forming my own stance.

I shall analyze what is specific to deployed patients, from what they themselves experienced as basic steps of change, along multiple dimensions of the self similar to those described by Stern (1985):

> There is the sense of a self that is a single, distinct, integrated body; there is the agent of actions, the experiencer of feelings, the maker of intentions, the architect of plans, the transposer of experience into language, the communicator and sharer of personal knowledge. Most often these senses of self reside out of awareness, like breathing, but they can be brought to and held in consciousness. [pp. 5–6]

The changes I am about to summarize do not come instead of developments along the psychosexual and the separation-individuation lines, but rather complement them.

In the content analysis that follows, I describe the steps of development as movements from one pole to the other. They will be seen as global changes in the direction of softening deployments, as well as distinct operational steps in specific areas. These are based on experiential criteria, not on definite goals that have been achieved, but rather on general directions, with progressions and regressions. I present in schematic form the changes that patients undergo when they move from a deployed position to one of becoming more in touch with their feelings and integrating them into their selves.

CHANGES IN POSITIONS TOWARD TENSIONS AND PRESSURES

From: Being uptight and tense, hardly listening to the analyst's interpretations, not being able or willing to "take in"; being unable to take more pressures, afraid to open one's mouth lest one throw up, which was experienced as one of the constant threats against loosening up both inside and outside the analytic situation; being contracted into "one big piece" of tension, often expressed through restlessness or tics; investing power in keeping one's mouth and other body orifices closed out of fear of pain, often as a consequence of abuse, insult, and rejections; using one's muscles to avoid contact with feelings and sensations.

To: Realizing that much of the present tension relates to loads of unidentified pressures from the past; becoming liberated from being so stuck that nothing goes in and nothing comes out; overcoming one's basic resistance to collaborate, to take risks and let oneself be led by inner waves in the process of exploring one's grievance, until a new balance is created, based on the realization of one's disturbance and on interaction among feelings and various sectors of the self; becoming more free to find constructive channels of expressing one's tensions and feelings.

From: Collapsing quickly whenever one is not treated as one feels is needed or expected, thereby enacting

To: Differentiating between when one acts out of one's vulnerabilities and when one acts more integratively from one's helplessness; reacting like a child who wants to throw himself on the floor in a temper tantrum whenever he is under stress, as a result of having lost trust in others as well as in one's own self.

the complex self; being more contained and relying on one's own resources even when severely disappointed and upset.

From: Being protected by omnipotence and omniscience in order not to feel one's inner pressures, tensions, and helplessness; exerting pressure on the other, a desire to prove, explain, influence, and convince; thinking that there is only one way to be, one way to see things, one way to act; and sometimes using reality to reinforce one's delusional view of the world.

To: Loosening one's omnipotent narcissistic structure once the defensiveness that caused it has been explored and understood; exhibiting more tolerance toward different ways of being, feeling and thinking; being able to mourn what had to be given up; coming out of oneself and being more fully there.

CHANGES IN POSITIONS TOWARD FAILURE, SHAME AND HUMILIATION

From: Seeing in one's mind catastrophes that constantly threaten to occur; being totally oriented toward being prepared, to not be shocked again; investing much energy into proving one's worth, and being restricted in one's feelings, thoughts, and acts out of a fear of being shamed and trapped; adopting concealment as a way of life as well as

To: Becoming less directed by failure vis-à-vis success, less self-conscious and restricted; acquiring a more relaxed position in which one can conceive of mistakes as an integral part of life, while coming to better know how to minimize their detrimental impact and the unconscious motivations that perpetuate them (Simon 1993).

other countershame strategies in order to survive.

From: Having difficulties in developing dependable structures for tension regulation and self-soothing; being oriented to expect the other to comfort one in times of stress or when failing; being either extremely self-conscious and restrained or demonstrating one's failures, as if defending oneself, thereby, saying "It's I who told you so."

To: Becoming more tolerant of frustration, more able to contain psychic pain, more ready to express and explore one's subjective realities and shame events through sharing and building an empathic contact with what had previously been disavowed in oneself.

From: Being regularly shame-prone, constantly seeing flaws and defects in others and/or in oneself; doing everything possible to keep from making an error; focusing all one's energy on preventing others from abusing, humiliating, or shaming one anymore; reacting to perceived insults by instantly offending the perceived offenders.

To: Shifting one's weight to the lonely, angry, and fearful child within, who was once buried and suppressed but is now more able to express his or her pain of shame and disappointment, thus opening the heart that had been locked and one's mind and one's senses, enjoying a more balanced and richer life.

CHANGES IN POSITIONS TOWARD POWER

From: Living in an emotionally disconnected manner and being directed by anger at the world; being engaged in a continuous cold war that one

To: Softening the deployments, thereby permitting more access to the drives, affects, opinions, and intentions that are crucial in

hardly knows the source of; being geared to gaining points of power and superiority, where all that matters is whether one wins or loses; being geared into restraint out of the fear of the damage that might result from one's destructive power.

From: Using power to turn subjective life into objective reality, by insisting that whatever is perceived is in fact real; battling against admitting anything that might weaken or humiliate one.

From: Using one's power to try and make the other feel and do what one needs, never giving in, even when it would be appropriate, in order to keep from being a "sucker" once again; or giving up too quickly, before one is in touch with one's complex self, especially when interacting with a dominant personality.

shaping one's behavior; meeting and reconciling oneself with adversarial parts in oneself and outside while reconstructing the child-parts' internal and external conflicts that had been condensed into a state of war.

To: Reaching again the fragile and vulnerable child part that is helplessly and secretly crying behind one's deployments, the child who has been waiting to be understood without having to express verbally his or her feelings.

To: Appreciating the subjective mental world of oneself and others more, and being more ready to explore what the overemphasis on one's entitlement has meant; becoming more self-assertive while willing to respect boundaries and rights based on an increased differentiation between one's self and others.

CHANGES IN POSITIONS TOWARD SELF-DIMENSIONS AND THE SENSE OF IDENTITY

From: Being deployed, where one places one's whole weight

To: Ceasing to act automatically in a way disconnected

on fortifying the self; by acting compulsively in order not to feel and be with unbearable inner conflicts; by acting in restricted ways of ego functioning to avoid anxiety, insult, or shame; by drugging one's feelings through consoling devices like smoking excessively or work addictions; by hardening oneself through freezing one's feelings as a reaction to panic, or by using disregard and contempt for the other as a weapon against feelings such as shame, depression, or envy.

both from the external situation and one's inner motivation, while transforming and tolerating whatever has been hardened back into the feelings and emotional experiences that the fantasies and consoling acts were designed to correct; allowing one's behavior to be linked to its complex emotional sources and basing one's actions on differentiation, coordination, and integration (rather than on dissociation).

From: Being deployed, remaining in the bunker long after the war is over; being obstinately locked in one's attitude, unwilling to cooperate and listen to the diverse voices in oneself and in others.

To: Reexamining and transforming the positions, poses, roles, and mind sets that were adopted as "life belts" in stressful situations and that unwittingly became second nature.

From: Disavowing responsibility often related to feeling overloaded with tasks, and to the pain and shame of not being able to perform them according to one's—or the important other's—high standards; living in a sphere of being beyond despair, as if the

To: Gaining more self-confidence, pleasure, and hope while applying oneself in the direction of problem solving and self-realization, after giving up goals impossible to achieve; using one's original reservoir of reactions to meet problems in more

catastrophe had already happened and there is no sense in investing or planning because it is too late to alter or repair the situation.

adaptive ways rather than in self-defeating consolations; accepting a growing sense of personal responsibility for one's feelings, intentions, actions, wishes, and fantasies as part of an ongoing definition of one's complex identity.

From: Basing one's identity primarily on the need to correct one's self injuries from the past, for instance, by becoming the opposite of those who wronged one or whom one was ashamed of, and thus forming a "negative identity"—similar but not identical to Erik Erikson (1959)—that is determined by the other rather than by what one is and what one feels.

To: Opening up an ongoing process of exploration as to what part of one's identity is based on anger, shame, fear, or vulnerability as opposed to one's real and complex self; continuously translating what has been disavowed and corrected back into its relevance for the self.

From: Serving as a living memorial (cf. Volkan 1993) to what one's parents lost (or failed to achieve) in their life, thus living the lives of the latter, whether through being pressured into trying to fulfill these expectations, or through adopting the role for reasons of self-esteem.

To: Finding one's own identity and life goals while exploring such corrective aims as the wish to please or repair the parent, for instance, out of feelings of guilt, and be willing to check ever again whether what one is identified with is fixed and closed or whether it is open to assessments of changing feelings, needs, circumstances, and choice.

From: Having serious difficulties related to the sense of personal authority; not feeling entitled to express one's feelings, interests, and passions out of the "guilt of the survivor" or other sources of fear, guilt, or shame.

To: Feeling one's right to exist fully, to be oneself, to feel one's power, vitality, and creativity and be capable of regarding these functions also in others as possibly contributing to one's own self-actualizing experience.

CHANGES IN POSITIONS TOWARD COMMUNICATION

From: Being dominated by a strong need to control, pushing away or distancing whatever may touch one emotionally, or may confuse or hurt oneself; always thinking before speaking, to avoid the risk of being trapped or shamed; finding it difficult to talk about one's pain and distress and therefore expending much energy on skipping and belittling pain while bursting into rage at others or engaging in other externalizing processes.

To: Talking while thinking and feeling, without having to edit everything first; trusting one's gut feelings more; increasingly internalizing analytic attitudes, goals, and functions by saying more of whatever comes to one's mind as it comes; feeling less ashamed about, and more affinity with, one's child mental parts; evolving an internal map of feelings that can be experienced, shared, and explored while understanding what it was that drove one to dread so much the loss of control.

From: Never talking about what one experiences as weakness or failure; somatizing feelings and ideas asso-

To: Ceasing to act in accordance with the limiting standards of total success or total failure, viewing this construc-

ciated with conflictual affects to erase them from consciousness as soon as they crop up; immediately dispersing one's strong feelings by engaging in action of one kind or other; always feeling a sense of pressure brought about by having to prove oneself.

tion as one of the techniques needed for survival that can now be given up; allowing oneself to let go, to regress more in the service of the ego, and to use one's intuition in order to be freer to engage in creative ways of elaborating new meanings, as well as in other areas.

From: Withdrawing from real emotional participation in social situations, feeling detached; distant and tending to ignore the emotional needs and expressions both of oneself and the others; dreading the loss of one's separateness, one's power and equilibrium through coming close to the other; never exposing one's feelings and neediness, almost not admitting these to oneself; being stuck in a not-admitted state of deep and ongoing hurt from which many mental operations are mobilized to avoid feeling the hurt.

To: Being able to soften toward oneself and others; allowing oneself to accept and go with one's longing to be close, or cared for and helped when in need and expressing such a need; being less afraid of being blamed by others for self-indulgence (or other "vices"); being more trusting toward those formerly perceived as adversaries and considering the possibility that they may become empathic and caring partners in a mutually satisfying relationship.

CHANGES IN POSITIONS TOWARD FLEXIBILITY AND FIXITY

From: Being extreme and obstinate, like a fundamentalist;

To: Working through one's rigid self-restricting positions, unconsciously clinging to missions more pertinent to atonement or to correcting past injuries that have caused one to become frozen than to considerations of the present and the future; acting as an observer from the outside rather than an emotional participant.

unfreezing them and transforming them back into the feelings, feeling-states, perceptions, and fantasies that were condensed in them; allowing the coexistence of the participating and observing self; reaching and opening up to charged emotional states, as they are experienced in the interaction between oneself and one's analyst, as well as with significant others, thereby enabling one to come alive with new free-flowing energies.

From: Being driven by a strong sense of entitlement, demanding that first others correct and compensate one for perceived past and present injustices; being stuck in such positions as postponing acting in the service of one's needs and self-development; being self-righteously unwilling to give up the insults to which one was subjected, or to be extremely task oriented when no space remains for both what is to be solved and for the feelings involved.

To: Becoming more autonomous, differentiated, and interdependent by working through the felt and perceived grievance that rendered one totally dependent on others; shifting the emphasis from the-other-who-has-to-change back to oneself-in-relation-to-the-other; moving from accounts of the past to the problems waiting to be solved in one's present life; being open to the new and utilizing one's own resources to solve problems.

From: Overemphasizing such axes as the dimension of time,

To: Allowing the kaleidoscope of one's associations to move thereby allowing life to be determined more by either what is seen as having been lost in the past or by what has to be achieved in the future than by what is felt to be needed—and is possible—in the present.

continuously from present to past to present, to reach the mind-in-conflict, and thereby opening up what the disproportionate perception and action was designed to defend against; allowing more space to the present-in-the-direction-of-the-future, thereby facilitating choices more appropriate to present life goals.

From: Orienting oneself to a life as the conscience dictates it should be, with an overemphasis on duties and what should have been done; refraining from whatever the superego deems is enjoyable, whether it is related to unconscious guilt, shame, or other factors, which may become ossified as a result of automaticity and life habits.

To: Allowing life to develop as it will, always questioning the rigid sources of one's archaic superego forces when they interfere; revealing new self-integrated ways of relating, feeling, and reacting; enabling the development of mutuality, compassion, intimacy, and a nuanced and multifaceted sense of love.

CHANGES IN POSITIONS TOWARD OBJECT RELATIONS

From: A difficulty in bridging the gap between the child-in-the-patient and the mother-in-the-analyst; peremptorily needing much recognition; having to dramatize feelings that are perceived as not recognized; "becoming" the

To: Regarding the analyst as a new object; entering into a joint effort by immersing oneself in a deeply empathic interaction; building affective bonds with the analyst and others; being able to reexperience the past through the scary, shameful child part with which one is reluctant to have emotional and verbal contact whether out of difficulty in feeling, in exploring, or in talking about one's disappointments, insults, and frustrations of the present and past, or because of the battling stance in which one is caught up.

resulting special therapeutic atmosphere of shared meanings that permit the past to become a potential source of affirmative continuity; treating the child who one once was respectfully and feelingly, and establishing an ongoing dialogue and relationship with this child, which also serves as the basis of being more accepting of the other.

From: Relating to the analyst and the important others on the basis of one's perception of whether they are perceived as an ally or an enemy; constantly checking to see whether that person is on "my" side or on that of the other, without being in touch with previous rivalry situations and specific constellations of injustice and insults in which the need for exclusive attention and support had become a question of life or death.

To: Experiencing change through several different channels, thereby facilitating alterations in internalized self and object representations as well as in their affective constituents; relaxing one's fear and suspicion of the other and experiencing more pleasure in a relatedness based on the increased ability to experience and reflect upon the thoughts and feelings in oneself and in others, on a fuller receptivity, and on the capacity to acquire a fuller range of responses to one's own and others' perceived aggression and sexuality.

From: Having disturbed affects and object relational structures; living in an omni-

To: The day-by-day internalization of an analyst—or important other—who is not

potent fantasy world of narcissistic illusions due to deny-
ing, repressing, or splitting off
feelings and impulses as a result of trauma or disturbed
development.

omniscient, with whom one
sometimes needs a long time
together under conditions of
relative calm before coming to
the conclusion that one has
progressed to the point where
one is able to come to grips
with what it is appropriate to
change, and eventually discovering spontaneity (Speziak-
Bagliacca 1991).

From: Having to frighten the
other so one will not be too
intimidated; "refusing to be
happy," not yet ready to rec-
oncile oneself with inner or
outer demands; conveying the
feeling that "it is too late,"
tending to hold off fulfilling
one's life goals until those at
least partially responsible for
one's agonies and defeats acknowledge their responsibility, and change.

To: Creating an intersubjec-
tive construction with the
analyst by working through
those situations that caused
one to become locked into
lifelong power conflicts;
being able to reverberate to
the feeling and being states of
oneself and the others that
constitute the matrix of one's
internal world.

From: Delaying the carrying
on of one's life until the other
is far away or dead, as if there
were space only for one
person at a time.

To: Moving toward more
real, whole-object relationships, with a greater sense of
responsibility for one's own
impulses, feelings, and "active
ego"; accepting the fact that
analysis provides one with the
tools to recognize the possibility of change, but that any
change must be carried out by
oneself (Rangell 1992).

According to Stoller (1991) "Emphases change, stiff joints loosen, anger and its revenge turn to chuckles and tears and the domination of the past gets less oppressive" (p. 1101). These beautiful words describe in a different form the changes I have listed above. In delineating the dialectic tensions between the goals of deployment and those of self-development, I do not view the latter as ideal states to be achieved but rather as directions in which my analysands and I move together during the analytic process.

REFERENCES

Blum, H. (1991). Introduction to the pre-published papers for the 37th IPA congress. *International Journal of Psycho-Analysis* 72:1–2.

—— (1992). Psychic change: the analytic relationship(s) and agents of change. *International Journal of Psycho-Analysis* 73:255–265.

Cohen, D. J., and Mayes, L. C. (1993). *The social matrix of love and aggression: enactments, representations and self-understanding in the first years of life.* Presented in Jerusalem, January.

Cooper, A. M. (1987). Changes in psychoanalytic ideas: transference interpretations. *Journal of the American Psychoanalytic Association* 35:77–97.

de Bianchedi, E. T. (1991). Psychic change: the "becoming" of an inquiry. *International Journal of Psycho-Analysis* 72:6–15.

Emde, R. N. (1990). Mobilizing fundamental modes of development: empathic availability and therapeutic action. *Journal of the American Psychoanalytic Association* 38:881–915.

Erikson, E. (1959). *Identity and the Life Cycle.* New York: International Universities Press.

Gould, L. J. (1991). Contemporary perspective on personal and organizational authority: the self in a system of work relationships. In *The Psychodynamics of Organization*, ed. L. Hirschhorn. Philadelphia: Temple University Press.

Grinberg, L. (1990). *The Goals of Psychoanalysis: Identification, Identity and Supervision.* London: Karnac Books.

Joseph, B. (1992). Psychic change: some perspectives. *International Journal of Psycho-Analysis* 73:237–243.

Kernberg, O. (1970). Factors in the psychoanalytic treatment of narcissistic personalities. *Journal of the American Psychoanalytic Association* 1:22–38.

Levy, S. T., and Inderbitzin, B. (1992). Interpretation and therapeutic intent. *Journal of the American Psychoanalytic Association* 40:989–1013.

Loewald, H. (1978). *Psychoanalysis and the History of the Individual.* New Haven, CT: Yale University Press.

McDougall, J. (1989). *The Theatres of the Body.* London: Free Association Books.

Moran, M. G. (1991). Chaos theory and psychoanalysis: the fluid nature of the mind. *International Review of Psychoanalysis* 18:211–221.

Ogden, T. (1991). Analyzing the transference matrix. *International Journal of Psycho-Analysis* 72:593–606.

Pulver, S. E. (1992). Psychic change: insight or relationship. *International Journal of Psycho-Analysis* 73:199–208.

Rangell, L. (1991). From insight to change. *Journal of the American Psychoanalytic Association* 29:129–141.

_____ (1992). The psychoanalytic theory of change. *International Journal of Psycho-Analysis* 73:415–429.

Sandler, J. (1992). Reflections on developments in the theory of psychoanalytic technique. *International Journal of Psycho-Analysis* 73:189–198.

Shor, J. (1992). *Work, Love, Play: Self Repair in the Psychoanalytic Dialogue.* New York: Brunner/Mazel.

Simon, B. (1993). "Incest—see under oedipus complex": the history of an error in psychoanalysis. *Journal of the American Psychoanalytic Association* 40:955–989.

Speziak-Bagliacca, R. (1991). The capacity to contain: notes on its function in psychic change. *International Journal of Psycho-Analysis* 72:27–33.

Stern, D. N. (1985). *The Interpersonal World of the Infant.* New York: Basic Books.

Stoller, R. J. (1991). Eros and polis: what is this thing called love? *Journal of the American Psychoanalytic Association* 39:1065–1102.

Volkan, V. D. (1993). A non-Jewish analyst looks at the Holocaust. In *Persistent Shadows of the Holocaust*, ed. R. Moses. Madison, CT: International Universities Press.

Index